A PERSON-CENTERED
FOUNDATION FOR COUNSELING
AND PSYCHOTHERAPY

Second Edition

A PERSON-CENTERED FOUNDATION FOR COUNSELING AND PSYCHOTHERAPY

By

ANGELO V. BOY

Professor of Education
University of New Hampshire
Durham, New Hampshire

and

GERALD J. PINE

Professor of Education
Boston College
Chestnut Hill, Massachusetts

Charles C Thomas
PUBLISHER • LTD.
SPRINGFIELD • ILLINOIS • U.S.A.

Published and Distributed Throughout the World by

CHARLES C THOMAS • PUBLISHER, LTD.
2600 South First Street
Springfield, Illinois 62794-9265

© *1999 by* CHARLES C THOMAS • PUBLISHER, LTD.

ISBN 0-398-06964-6 (cloth)
ISBN 0-398-06966-2 (paper)

Library of Congress Catalog Card Number: 99-20307

With THOMAS BOOKS *careful attention is given to all details of manufacturing
and design. It is the Publisher's desire to present books that are satisfactory as to their
physical qualities and artistic possibilities and appropriate for their particular use.*
THOMAS BOOKS *will be true to those laws of quality that assure a good name
and good will.*

Printed in the United States of America
CR-R-3

Library of Congress Cataloging in Publication Data

Boy, Angelo V.
    A person-centered foundation for counseling and psychotherapy /
by Angelo V. Boy and Gerald J. Pine. -- 2nd ed.
        p.   cm.
    Includes bibliographical references and index.
    ISBN 0-398-06964-6 (cloth). -- ISBN 0-398-06966-2 (pbk.)
    1. Client-centered psychotherapy. I. Pine, Gerald J. II. Title.
RC481.B694
616.89'14--dc21   99-20307
                                                                         CIP

We dedicate this book to our grandchildren:
Erik, Katelyn, Kyle, Jocelyn, Rye and Samantha

Contributors

Beate Hofmeister
Lucy Weeks

PREFACE

When the first edition of this book was published in 1990, we hoped that it would broaden and expand the concept of person-centered theory to embrace new possibilities for helping people in the form of an integrated and synergistic person-centered eclecticism. Since the publication of the 1990 book, we have been delighted and excited about the accelerating exploration, creative extension, and further development of person-centered theory throughout the world. Person-centered theory and practice are flourishing outside the United States in the Netherlands, Switzerland, Sweden, Great Britain, Spain, France, Hungary, Italy, Belgium, Germany, Ireland, Denmark, Norway, Austria, Japan, Australia, Brazil, Argentina, Chile, Uruguay, Peru, Colombia, Venezuela, Mexico, South Africa, Poland, Portugal, Greece, Czechoslovakia, and Russia. The recent 1998 international conference, the Person Centered Approach Forum, held in South Africa, has demonstrated the continuing worldwide interest in and commitment to the person-centered approach just as the first international conference at the University of Leuven in Belgium did in 1988. During the nineties rich theoretical contributions have been made in more than a dozen important books published or about to be published in Britain and Europe by key person-centered theorists and practitioners including Barrett-Lennard (1999); Cohen (1997); Hutterer, Pawlowsky, Semid, and Stipsits (1996); Lietaer, Rombauts, and VanBalen (1990); Mearns (1994, 1997); Mearns and Thorne (1999); Merry (1995); O'Leary (1999); Prouty (1994); Rennie (1999); Thorne (1992); and Thorne and Lambers (1999). It is clear that the theoretical center and momentum for the person-centered approach has shifted from the United States to Europe.

While we are excited about the theoretical developments in Europe, we are disappointed that the person-centered approach does not enjoy the same level of therapeutic popularity in the United States. We agree with Kahn (1996) that this lack of popularity may be due to the democratic attitudes inherent in the person-centered approach with its values against elitism and materialism, its emphasis on equalizing the counseling relationship, and its commitment to broad social change. Person-centered practitioners seek to expand the boundaries of person-centeredness to include teaching, parenting, marriage, race relations, organizational behavior, pastoral work, medicine, community development, and international relations. We are elated with this evolvement. Our expectation is that person-centeredness will be applied in even more interpersonal areas in the decades ahead. Indeed, as we approach the dawn of a new millennium, the preservation of the human qualities of the person, in an increasingly depersonalized and technological world, requires a sustained commitment to the empathic attitudes and behaviors that are the core of person-centeredness .

Within this framework of expansion, we hope that this second edition of *A Person-Centered Foundation for Counseling and Psychotherapy* will renew interest in the person-centered approach in the United States, make a significant contribution in extending person-centered theory and practice, and promote fruitful dialogue and conversation and further development of person-centered theory. The focus of the book is on counseling and psychotherapy. While the person-centered movement is committed to issues and relationships that go beyond individual and group counseling, we want to reaffirm our commitment to counseling as a fundamental process for influencing attitudinal and behavioral change among troubled persons. While beneficial person-centered general concepts are being implemented in other areas of living, we want to be sure that the psychological needs of individuals are also being met through a humanly sensitive counseling process. These needs must receive the attention of those professionals who provide counseling services. While person-centeredness nurtures the generic development of humans within society as a whole, counseling must also maintain its special sense of responsibility to troubled individuals within that society.

Our concept of person-centered counseling is synergistic. We join established concepts of person-centered counseling with other concepts in the hope that each enriches and expands the other and makes the other more effective. We desire that person-centered counseling possess a freshness and vigor that makes it applicable to a widening range of client needs. We desire that it continues to be viable in a rapidly changing world.

In the concept of person-centered counseling contained in this book, we want to clarify the following:
- Our rationale for an eclectic application of person-centered counseling.
- The rationale and process for reflecting clients' feelings.
- The importance of theory as the foundation for the counseling process.
- The importance of values and their influence on the counseling relationship.
- The modern person-centered counselor's role.
- The essential characteristics of a person-centered counseling relationship and an example of its application.
- The group counseling movement and the person-centered perspective on its theory and application.

• The application of person-centeredness through play therapy.
• The difficulties and opportunities surrounding evaluation.
• A person-centered perspective on the process of counselor education.
• Four therapeutic opportunities that are available outside the field of counseling.

We have struggled with the paradoxical dimensions of a person-centered eclecticism and the challenge of articulating an eclecticism which is coherent, meaningful, and consistent with person-centered therapeutic principles. Whether we have accomplished our goal, we leave it for you, the reader, to determine.

In the evolution of our eclecticism we have drawn not only from the contemporary literature of counseling and psychotherapy but also from the rich, vibrant, and eloquent history of client-centered theory and practice. We choose not to be ahistorical but to draw deeply from the historical roots of person-centered counseling. We hope you will resonate to this blend of the contemporary and the historical.

And finally, throughout this book, we share our personal beliefs and values which have emanated from our experience and reflections upon that experience. We share these beliefs and values with you in the hope of stimulating a silent dialogue between us and you, the reader. You may agree, disagree, approve, or be infuriated. Whatever your response, we hope we engage you and that the engagement will advance your goals in reading this book.

REFERENCES

Barrett-Leonard, G. T. (1999). *Carl Rogers' helping system: Journey and substance.* London: Sage.

Cohen,D. (1997). *Carl Rogers: A critical biography.* London: Constable.

Hutterer, R., Pawlowsky, G., Smid, P. F., & Stipsits, R. (Eds.). (1996). *Client-centered and experiential psychotherapy: A paradigm in motion.* Frankfurt am Main: Peter Lang.

Kahn, E. (1996). The intersubjective perspective and the client-centered approach: Are they one at their core? *Psychotherapy, 33,* 1, 30-42.

Lietaer, G., Rombauts, T., & VanBalen, R. (Eds.). (1990). *Client-centered and experiential psychotherapy in the nineties.* Leuven: Leuven University Press.

Mearns, D. (1994). *Developing person-centered counseling.* London: Sage.

Mearns, D. (1997). *Person-centered counseling training.* London: Sage.

Mearns, D., & Thorne, B. (1999). *Person-centered counseling.* London: Sage.

Merry, T. (1995). *Invitation to person-centered psychology.* London: Whurr.

O'Leary, C. J. (1999). *Family therapy and the person-centered approach.* London: Sage.

Prouty, G. F. (1994). *Theoretical evolutions in person-centered/experiential therapy: Applications to schizophrenic and retarded psychoses.* Westport, CT: Praeger.

Rennie, D. (1999). *Psychotherapy inside out.* London: Sage.

Thorne, B. (1992). *Carl Rogers.* London: Sage.

Thorne, B. T., & Lambers, E. (Eds.). (1999). *Person-centered counseling: A European perspective.* London: Sage.

Angelo V. Boy
Gerald J. Pine

CONTENTS

A PERSON-CENTERED
FOUNDATION FOR COUNSELING
AND PSYCHOTHERAPY

Chapter 1

EXPANDING PERSON-CENTERED COUNSELING

We have been identified with the person-centered literature of counseling since 1963 (Boy & Pine, 1963). Our deep commitment to person-centered counseling has not only been a visceral commitment, but the intellectual depth of the viewpoint has been reinforced in our own experience as counselors, by the human goals of the approach, the face validity of the process, and the objective research evidence that supports its effectiveness. Person-centeredness has been, personally and professionally, an enriching journey for us; but like other journeys, we have not yet reached our destination. The purpose of this book is to continue that journey and to formulate a more applicable approach to person-centered counseling. Hopefully, our current viewpoint will attract the intellectual interests of theoreticians, the application interests of counselors, and the curiosity of researchers.

We hope that this book serves as a transition from a traditional interpretation of person-centeredness to an eclectic application of the viewpoint. Our eclectic application does not mean that we have abandoned the traditional philosophic values of person-centeredness; these values are enduring. While retaining our commitment to these values, we also want the counseling process which reflects these values to be more flexible.

An effective theory of counseling is always developing, seeking an improved application model for assisting clients. We shall attempt to move the application model of person-centered counseling a notch forward with this book, but we realize that what we present may not be the ultimate outcome that we seek.

Person-centered counseling was founded and developed by Carl R. Rogers (1942, 1951, 1954, 1961, 1967, 1969, 1970, 1972, 1974, 1975, 1977, 1980). What began as a viewpoint that was originally developed to improve one-to-one counseling has become expanded to an ever-widening range of situations in which better interpersonal relations are crucial: teaching, organizational behavior, families, parenting, groups, marriage and its alternatives, leadership, pastoral and interpersonal relations in general. The impact of the Rogerian view has been immense in enabling a person to become self-actualizing, and thereby influencing the emergence of a self-actualizing behavior in others (Levant & Shlien, 1984).

Hart (1970, pp. 3-22) identifies three historic periods in the development of person-centered counseling:

> *Period 1* (1940-1950): The nondirective period in which the counselor created a permissive noninterventative atmosphere essentially forming a relationship with the client based upon acceptance and clarification.
>
> *Period 2* (1950-1957): The reflective period in which the counselor essentially responded to the client's underlying feelings by reflecting those feelings back to the client rather than simply semantically rephrasing what the client said.
>
> *Period 3* (1957-present): The experiential period in which the counselor created Rogers' necessary and sufficient conditions moving beyond reflecting the client's feelings and engaging in a wider range of responses in order to meet the needs of the client.

Corey (1996:III) has added a fourth phase (1970 to mid-1980s) which "...encourages an eclectic spirit in using a wider variety of methods rather than being restricted to listening, reflecting, and communicating understanding."

In this book, we attempt to develop a view that incorporates the major emphases within the four periods in an effort to produce a unified and more flexible application of person-centered theory.

We are essentially adding to the long-standing tradition of person-centered counseling. Rogers never intended that the person-centered viewpoint be an inflexible system of application. A fundamental thrust of person-centered-counseling has been its willingness to change, its openness to experience and to research data. As Rogers (Rogers & Wood, 1974.213) has said: "The incorporation of this element in changingness has set it apart, almost more than anything else I know, from other orientations to therapy."

Corsini (1973:123) observes that the changing character of person-centered counseling is due to Rogers' insistence on looking at the facts and altering the theory and methods whenever experience and research so dictated. A rigid interpretation of person-centered counseling would be in contradiction to the developmental nature of both Rogers and the theory: "Fortunately there has not grown up around Rogers the kind of orthodoxy that would require his formulations to be the last word on any issue. Rogers certainly would not welcome this kind of blind devotion and would in fact view it as a failure in actualization" (Wexler and Rice: 9). Person-centered counseling is a viewpoint that is still in the state of emergence. It is a set of tentative principles rather than dogma (Corey, 1986).

Our eclectic application of person-centered counseling aims to fit Patterson's (1985:v) view of eclecticism as "the selection and orderly combination of compatible features from diverse sources." We agree with Patterson (Watkins & Goodyear 1994: 181) that "the basic conditions of client-centered therapy—empathy, respect, genuineness—have been generally incorporated by most approaches" and "to the extent that these conditions have been accepted, one may say all therapy is some what client centered." We believe that the methodologies of other theories of counseling can be compatible with person-centered counseling when they do not violate the underlying and fundamental philosophy and values of person-centered counseling. We believe that counselors can be person-centered in their values and attitudes, and not violate those beliefs when applying a technique or approach from another theory of counseling. We don't feel that person-centered theory is ever compromised when these other methodologies are collaboratively applied to serve client needs which have been identified by clients themselves. Carl Rogers (1986) captures the spirit of our viewpoint when he says:

> Over the years I have become more and more aware of an aspect of the client-centered/person-centered approach that sets it apart. The approach is paradoxical. It emphasizes shared values yet encourages uniqueness. It is rooted in a profound regard for the wisdom and constructive capacity inherent in the human organism—a regard that is shared by those who hold this approach. At the same time it encourages those who incorporate these values to develop their own special and unique ways of bring, their own ways of implementing this shared philosophy.

Our person-centered approach accommodates the viewpoints of existentialism, humanism, and theology since certain aspects of these viewpoints contribute important parallel concepts regarding human nature, behavior, and the goals of existence. The person-centered viewpoint has traditionally dealt with human freedom, self-actualization, the necessity of a congruence between the ideal self and the actual self, acceptance, openness, socialization, the internal locus of evaluation, genuineness, nonpossessive love, and empathy. Parallel viewpoints regarding the preceding have also emerged from existentialism, humanism, and theology in their treatment of free will, humanity's desire for peace and goodwill, personal honesty and responsibility, respect for the dignity and worth of others, the desired congruence between a person's personal and social consciousness, the person's natural inclination to transcend the self, and guidelines for moral behavior that sustain the self and serve others.

Person-centered counseling is the core of our viewpoint, but existentialism, humanism, and theology can be viewed as enriching that core. We choose to identify with the person-centered viewpoint because it fulfills the requirements of a valid theory of counseling; has a substantive theory of personality that undergirds its application; has an established, effective, and flexible application model with enough range so that it can be translated into practice in a wide variety of settings, possesses both qualitative and quantitative research evidence supporting its effectiveness; and has been confirmed in our own experience as persons and as professionals.

THE CONTEXT FOR EXTENDING THE
PERSON-CENTERED VIEWPOINT

Since the publication of the first edition of this book in 1990, there has been a marked trend toward integration in theory and eclecticism in counseling practice (Arkowitz, 1992; Barrineau, 1992 & 1996; Bohart,1995; Bradley, Parve, & Gould, 1995; Beutler & Consoli, 1992; Cottone, 1992; Duncan et al., 1992; Goldfried, 1995; Kelly, 1991; Kelly, 1994; Kelly, 1996; Kelly, 1997; Kleinke, 1994; Kottler, 1991; Kottler & Brown, 1996; Lazarus & Beutler, 1993; Norcross & Goldfried, 1992; Prochaska & Norcross, 1994; Safran, 1990a; Safran 1990b; Safran & Segal, 1990; Wachtel, 1991). The trend toward theory integration and eclecticism has been accompanied by efforts to find common theoretical ground among various counseling philosophies and theories (Becvar & Becvar,1997; Coghlan & McIlduff, 1995; Day & Matthes, 1992; Kahn, 1996; Lumbelli, 1997; Moreira, 1993; Sanford, 1993). This body of work provides an intellectually rich and theoretically supportive context for extending person-centered theory and for laying the foundation for person-centered eclecticism. For example, Kahn (1996), based on his review of the relevant literature, has concluded that at their core, Rogers's person-centered approach and Kohut's self psychology approach to psychotherapy are one. Safran (1990a and 1990b) has developed a refinement of cognitive therapy in light of interpersonal therapy. Day and Matthes (1992) have identified numerous similarities between person-centered, Gestalt, and Jungian approaches to group therapy. Barrineau (1992 & 1996) has proposed a model of dream work which reflects the principles of person-centered therapy and calls for expansion or modification in our understanding of person-centered therapy.

Reservations and Tensions about Person-Centered Theoretical Integration and Eclecticism

While the current context is favorable for nurturing and advancing the theoretical and practical extensions of the person-centered approach, this is not to suggest that there is total enthusiastic embrace for such integration and eclecticism. Kelly (1997) notes that despite the advances toward theory integration and eclecticism in general, there are person-centered, existential, and humanistic formulations which are averse to integrating technical elements into counseling and technical formulations, especially in cognitive/behavioral procedures which focus so heavily on cognitive and behavioral techniques that the humanistic therapeutic relationship is diminished. Specifically, in regard to person-centered theory and practice, Temanar-Brodley (1993), Patterson (1993), and earlier Shlien (1986) and Raskin (1987) have expressed strong concerns about the extension of client-centered counseling. Patterson (1993:132) summarizes his concern about the new directions in person-centered therapy when he says, "If it ain't broke don't fix it" and Temanar-Brodley (1993:142) joins him when she says, "Watch out. If you think you're fixing it, be careful you don't break it." Shlien (1986: 348) finds that he has had to separate himself from person-centered therapy and remain client-centered because the extensions of the client-centered theory, under the name of person-centered, proceed thoughtlessly beyond the theory: "the person-centered approach invites extensions that outreach the theory of client-centered therapy." And Raskin (1987: 460) notes that "each of the neo-Rogerian methods takes something away from the thorough-going belief in the self directive capacities that is so central to client-centered philosophy."

Thorne (1992:92-94), in his biography of Carl Rogers, describes the emergence of two camps in the person-centered community—*orthodoxy and heresy*. Representing the "purist" approach are Bozarth and Temanar-Brodley— "who would believe that attempts to add other therapeutic methods to client-centered therapy are a betrayal of the approach" (Thorne,1992:93) and unequivocally oppose the idea that client-centered therapists have the choice to integrate skills drawn from other approaches. Representing the heretical approach is Reinhold Tausch who believes that the incorporation of other methods is a *"client-centered necessity."* He recommends (Thorne,1992:93) "as desirable supplementations, relaxation techniques, non-systematic behavioral counseling, problem analysis, medical treatment, and recommending books on philosophical, religious, and spiritual issues." Thorne (1992:93) summarizes the differences in a viewpoint noting that "Bozarth believes that Rogers work is of unique importance and that its essence is immediately contaminated if other methods are introduced and control is any way removed from the client. Tausch, one of the most prolific researchers of psychotherapy outcomes in the world, believes, on the other hand, that in many cases where pure client-centered therapy seems not to work the therapist should have no hesitation in offering other posssible strategies to his client."

Reflecting on these opposing concerns, Cain (1993:137) argues that, "there is nothing in client-centered theory that precludes or discourages diversity in practice. Although Rogers practiced in a manner compatible with his personality, he was fully aware that the practice of client-centered counseling might take different forms."

Recent analyses of verbatim transcripts of Rogers's sessions with a variety of ten clients (Farber, Brink, Raskin, 1996) reveal that his response repertoire was extensive and that he used a number of different interventions to actualize his guiding therapeutic ideals of genuineness, empathy, and caring. Brink and Farber (1996:15-24) listed these interventions as: providing orientation, affirming his attention, checking understanding, reflecting feelings, acknowledging client's unstated feelings, providing reassurance, interpreting, confronting, directly questioning, maintaining or breaking silences, and self-disclosing. They concluded that while Rogers consistently demonstrated fidelity to person-centered principles and values, he did so flexibly through a variety of techniques suited to the individuality of his clients. Bowen (1996:85), commenting on Rogers's 1983 session with Jill, writes:

> He uses interpretation; he uses the client's body cues to bring her to the here and now; he uses metaphors, humors her, and exaggerates and repeats her self-deprecating comments to accentuate their absurdity and promote greater accuracy in her self-evaluations. Second, he allows himself to be directive. He forms hypotheses about the source of problems and very openly checks his hypothesis. Moreover, he introduces topics, he breaks silences.

Bowen concludes, that over a forty-five year span, Rogers changed by adhering less closely to a nondirective approach, demonstrating that he trusted his clients more, considering them to be less fragile and less easily damageable by the therapist's comments and responses. Farber (1996:11) agrees:

> The point is that for Rogers, being truly person-centered meant not losing the flexibility demanded by the uniqueness of individuals. During one post-workshop discussion, a participant said to Rogers, "I noticed you asked questions of the client. But just last night a lecturer told us we must never do that." Rogers responded, "Well I'm in the fortunate position of not having to be Rogerian." (Brink, personal communication, 1990)

Resolving the Reservations and Tensions:
Kelly's Conceptual Framework.

Kelly (1997) has made a significant contribution to theoretical integration and eclecticism in advancing the the idea of relationship-centered counseling, a development in the humanistic and client-centered tradition. He offers a higher order conceptual framework that bridges the major principles of predominantly humanistic theories such as client-centered and existential theories and predominantly technical theories such as cognitive and behavioral theories. Kelly (1997:339-340) summarizes the basic principles of relationship-centered counseling in seven "rationally derived propositions":

1. The primary ontological ground of being and becoming is inherently relational.....personal subjectivity is grounded in relationality, and the individual person develops and functions within relationships.

2. The primary purpose of counseling—across all specific therapeutic objectives and technical procedures—is to enhance clients' humanity as characterized by the distinctively human qualities of reflective self-consciousness, intrinsic freedom, purposefulness or intentionality, social relatedness, ethical responsibility, and transcendent meaningfulness.

3. A corollary of the first two propositions is that the therapeutic relationship is the primary, integrative core of counseling.

4. ...(a)Technical expertise constitutes the secondary instrumental component of counseling, and (b) the therapeutic relationship does not exist apart from technical expertise. The therapeutic relationship extends its humanizing potential by way of technical expertise, which is the expressive enhancement of in-depth humanness.

5. A major in-depth, operational effect of the humanizing relationship in counseling is the inherent mutuality of the counselor-client relationship.....the fundamental focus of counseling is not the self center but the relational center, in which the individual can access not just the self but multiple human resources for personal self-devlopment."

6. The operational practical effect of this relational focus is that the core facilitative conditions of this relationship must be construed relationally as embracing both counselor and client.

7. ....the whole range of cognitive and behavioral techniques that have been identified as effective across a variety of client problems are legitimate, instru-

mental expressions of technical expertise that extends the humanizing force of the counseling relationship.

Kelly's contribution, which is more fully discussed in his 1994, 1995, and 1997 publications, is a compelling, well grounded, and thoughtful integration of theory and eclecticism and parallels our extension of the person-centered viewpoint which we first published in the 1990 edition of this book.

AN EXTENSION OF THE PERSON-CENTERED VIEWPOINT

Our person-centered eclecticism proposes that there are two basic phases to an effective person-centered counseling relationship. In Phase One, the counselor becomes involved in building a therapeutic, facilitative, collaborative, and substantive relationship with the client. Building such a relationship is the foundation from which future eclectic interactions with the client can be made productive. When a counselor has an authentic caring relationship with a client, that client responds to the relationship by participating in the counseling process as an active partner in a journey of self-discovery and growth. The counselor's person-centered attitude and ability to counsel become the catalyst for the client's positive participation in the counseling process (Egan, 1994; Patton & Griffin, 1974).

When the counselor has been effective in the relationship-building first phase of counseling, developing a working alliance, then what the counselor says or does in the second phase of counseling tends to produce a positive, collaborative, and participatory way of being on the part of the client. What is done in Phase Two, then, becomes effective essentially because the client has trust in the counselor and the counseling process, a trust that was initiated and facilitated by the counselor in Phase One. Therefore, if the counselor concentrates on the core conditions of counseling in Phase One, and in Phase Two with the client collaboratively centers on the needs of the client, then the outcomes of counseling will tend toward the positive.

A variety of methodologies can become more effective when the counselor delays the application of these methodologies until the core conditions of the relationship with the client have been established. Often these methodologies are "too much too soon" for the client to accept and absorb. Counselors diminish the potential of eclectic methodologies when they apply them too quickly and in a noncollaborative way. The typical client is not ready to accept a counselor who is overly assertive or confrontative in the beginning phase of counseling. Initially, the client's expectation is to be received as a person, to be accepted and understood on the client's terms and from the client's internal frame of reference.

Diverse counseling methodologies will yield more positive results when their application is preceded by the development of a close, human, and empathic relationship with the client during Phase One. It is the existence of such a relationship that improves the potential for Phase Two to be an effective heuristic collaboration in healing and growth.

Clients respond to counselors who possess observable human qualities. When the counselor is able to establish an affective bond with the client in the first phase of counseling, it is the durability of this bond that enables the second phase of collaboration to be effective. If counselors *first* create the fundamental conditions of person-centered counseling, they will more likely increase the effectiveness of eclectic methodologies in the second phase of counseling.

The development of an effective relationship requires that the counselor possess identifiable positive attitudes that can be communicated to clients through the counselor's verbal and nonverbal behavior. A modeling of these attitudes by the counselor will influence the development of a substantive relationship, so crucial in the first phase of counseling. Without the demonstrated possession of these attitudes, the counselor cannot expect the second phase of counseling to be productive.

Relationship building between the client and counselor is one of four beneficial outcomes of Phase One. A second valuable outcome is the full and accurate assimilation of the client by the counselor. By assimilating or absorbing the client's personality, attitudes, values, and behavior, the counselor is able to gain an accurate understanding of the client's hopes, fears, desires, life-style, self-concept, defenses, and essence as a person. Such a full and accurate sensitivity to the client enables the counselor to help the client more accurately understand which approach will yield the best results for the client during Phase Two. In person-centered eclecticism, it is important not to proceed prematurely with procedures which are based upon a limited understanding of the client's personality, attitudes, values, and behavior. Phase One, characterized by a holistic understanding of the client, enables the counselor to assimilate the client; and such an assimilation by the counselor facilitates the collaboration between counselor and client in exploring and applying approaches that best meet the needs of the client.

Counselor and client collaboratively develop a more effective approach for addressing the client's concerns because of the counselor's more sharpened, focused, and empathic understanding of the client's full range of attitudes, values, and behaviors. Without this understanding, the counselor often deals with and reinforces the client's presenting problem while deeper and more incapacitating problems go unattended; they were never identified because of the superficiality of the relationship. Superficial relationships usually occur when counselors do not take the necessary time to penetrate and absorb the inner, deep, and more influencing dimensions of the client's personality, attitudes, values, and behavior.

A third valuable outcome of Phase One is that it enables the client to go beyond a presenting problem. Most clients, if given opportunity during Phase One, will move beyond the "safe" problem talked about in the initial stages of counseling. By focusing on clients as persons rather than on their presenting problems in Phase One, the counselor helps clients to move beyond the superficialities which typically characterize a presenting problem. Phase One helps the client to move therapeutically to higher levels of knowing, understanding, and experiencing.

Finally, the fourth valuable outcome of Phase One is that it gives the client an atmosphere in which subconscious and unconscious feelings and denied components of experience are given an opportunity to emerge into the client's conscious awareness. Sometimes, as clients feel more comfortable with Phase One, they realize that current behavior has some roots in feelings and denied experiences which they have not thought about before. They become amazed at the connection, talk about it, and sometimes the connection becomes the foundation for the resolution of a client's problem or for a new way of being.

The evidence currently available confirms the desire of clients to be treated as human beings rather than as objects. They respond positively when they have an equalized relationship with a counselor who is empathic, accepting, genuine, liberating, involved, and a sensitive listener. These counselor attitudes have proven to be effective in establishing the foundation for a productive counseling relationship. Indeed, for many clients these counselor attitudes are sufficient to produce attitudinal and behavioral changes (Patterson, 1986).

For other clients, however, person-centeredness may need to be complemented by other approaches. Clients respond well to the person-centered attitudes of the counselor, but often they also need to choose from other alternatives in Phase Two in order to have their individualized counseling needs met.

Clients outside the mainstream of society often need more than the empathic caring attitudes of counselors. They may need the assistance of counselors to achieve a basic need: an artificial limb, a job, access to governmental agencies, legal assistance, protective shelter, adequate housing, etc. These are clients who have seldom crossed the thresholds of counseling offices in decades past. Their needs often require fulfillment at basic survival levels before they can have the luxury of the time and energy necessary to become self-actualizing.

Phase Two of our person-centered approach enables the counselor to be more flexible and concrete in meeting client needs once the Phase One relationship has been established by creating the core conditions of person-centered counseling.

PHASE ONE AND THE CORE CONDITIONS

In Phase One the counselor's goal is to create a nonthreatening atmosphere of open inquiry which facilitates the client's tendency toward self-actualization and growth. The counselor has no preconceived agenda of specific outcomes. The client is free to move in any direction, pursue any question, seek any goal, or present any data. The counselor creates this nonthreatening atmosphere of openness through the attitudinal core conditions of person-centered counseling—empathy, unconditional positive regard, and genuineness.

Barrineau and Bozarth (1989:470-471) suggest that these attitudinal core conditions create the atmosphere for open inquiry critical for heuristic research. They define the core attitudinal conditions not only as they apply to therapy but also to research.

> **Genuineness** refers to the therapist or investigator being a real person who is not playing a role. In therapy and research, this augments the relationship and enhances open responsiveness. The therapist as investigator is "a congruent, genuine, and integrated person. It means that within the relationship he is freely and deeply himself, with his actual, experience accurately represented by his awareness of himself" (Rogers, 1957:97)
>
> **Unconditional positive regard** refers to the prizing of the client (or subject) in a way that the person is free to "be whatever immediate feeling is going on—confusion, resentment, fear, anger, love, or pride. Such caring on the part of the therapist is non-possessive" (Rogers, 1980:116). The researcher holds this attitude toward the subject and the data. Subjects are totally affirmed in this way, which frees them to present the truest data. This attitude of unconditional positive regard may be held regarding the data per se. That is, the data related to the phenomenon are allowed to be, to unfold, and to evolve in empirical reality and in the growing experience of the research.
>
> **Empathy** refers to the understanding of the person's world as if the therapist (or researcher) were the other person. The biases and views of the empathizer are virtually eliminated with this stance. In therapy, such understanding promotes growth. In research, it promotes the ideal climate for open inquiry.

These core conditions are permeated by the counselor's profound belief in the person's ***actualizing tendency***. Rogers consistently referred to the actualizing tendency as the powerful inherent motivational force for positive change in each individual. Within each client there is the capacity for transcendence, a tendency toward positive, constructive, purposeful behavior, and optimal functioning which not only enhances the self but others as well. Rogers (1959:196) defined the actualizing tendency as:

> the inherent tendency of the organism to develop all its capacities in ways which serve to maintain or enhance the organism....this general tendency toward actualization expresses itself also in the actualization of that portion of the experience of the organism which is symbolized in the self.

Ford (1991:101), in his clarification of Rogers's construct of self-actualization, suggests that Rogers's propositions regarding the actualizing tendency, are "heuristic navigational stars." We agree! Without the counselor's intellectual and visceral belief in the person's actualizing tendencies the application of the core conditions will not be authentic nor sufficient for therapeutic change.

These core conditions distinguish Phase One and establish the foundation for Phase Two as an integrated process of counseling and heuristic study. In Phase One, the counselor, by creating the core conditions and attending to the client's experiential world in a focused and disciplined manner, not only develops a therapeutic relationship but also lays the groundwork for heuristic collaborative inquiry in Phase Two. In each counseling relationship, the heuristic collaborative inquiry of Phase Two "is a unique, creative challenge aimed at revealing the intimate nature of reality and thus requiring methods that fit the particular investigation" (Douglass & Moustakas 1985:42). The eclectic methodologies and approaches of Phase Two are a function of the dedication, commitment, and collaboration of the counselor and the client in finding the truth of the client's situation and world. Phase Two is both inquiry and therapy: a search for truth and healing based upon truth.

PHASE ONE COMMUNICATION

The counselor's basic response pattern in developing a productive counseling relationship in Phase One is ***reflection of feelings***. Clients expect to be understood, accepted, and able to reveal feelings and attitudes in a liberating atmosphere; they expect the counselor to be empathic, a sensitive listener, authentic, have a sense of presence in the relationship, equalize that relationship, and create a pattern of communication that will encourage the growth of the client as a person. Clients want the counselor to be a receiving person, one who is able to understand the client, as a person, and on the client's terms.

Counselor attitudes and behaviors that hinder Phase One are those which occur when the counselor functions as a moralist ("Living by these values will only cause you harm"), advisor ("The best thing you can do is find another job"), judge ("I think it was a poor decision"), guide ("Why don't you try living in another community"), questioner ("How many times has it happened?"), and diagnostician ("This current behavior is related to your past inability to accept parental authority"). When the client hears such statements the client clearly understands that the counselor is not really interested in understanding the client's problems from the client's viewpoint.

Reflecting the client's feelings enables the counselor to enter the client's private perceptual world; to understand and empathize with what it means to be *this* client with *this* background, undergoing *this* set of experiences, with *this* set of attitudes, feelings, and behaviors. When the counselor communicates empathy to the client through the process of reflecting the client's feelings, the client experiences the emergence of previously unexpressed feelings. When previously unexpressed feelings become expressed, the client has a feeling of closeness to the counselor who enables this to occur. The client develops a sense of trust for the counselor and feels comfortable and natural within the counseling process. The client feels receptive to counseling because finally, in a fast moving and technological society, there is someone who cares enough to listen and empathize with the client's set of perceptions and feelings. The client values catharsis and the counselor enables it to occur by reflecting the client's feelings—not the words, but the feelings beneath the words.

In reflecting the client's feelings, the counselor assumes the internal frame of reference of the client, perceives experiences as the client perceives them, and identifies with the feelings beneath the experiences. When the counselor identifies (empathizes) with the feelings of the client, the counselor then translates that identification into words that accurately represent the feelings of the client and mirrors back to the client those feelings so that the client may become aware of them, release them, understand them, and draw meaning from them.

When the counselor invests in the first phase of counseling by concentrating on reflecting the client's feelings, then what follows in the second phase will be naturally developed by the counselor and the client. In Phase Two, the counselor, in collaboration with the client, bases the helping process on clearly identified client needs; and these needs are accurately known by the counselor and the client as an outcome of Phase One.

Because of the importance of the process of reflecting the client's feelings, it will be clarified in detail in Chapter 2. At this point, we merely want to highlight the importance of the reflection process as the foundation for Phase One.

THE TRANSITION FROM PHASE ONE TO PHASE TWO

Thus far, we have basically featured the traditional elements of person-centered counseling which characterized its development through the first two periods of its history, from 1940 through 1957 (Hart, 1970: 4-22). In the first historic period, the person-centered counselor essentially focused on developing the relationship with the client. In the second historic period, the counselor stimulated the development of that relationship by reflecting the client's underlying feelings back to the client rather than simply rephrasing what the client said. These two historic periods are still viable and effective and correspond to Phase One in our eclectic application of person-centered counseling.

Our modification of person-centered counseling occurs in Phase Two, and Phase Two is consistent with the experiential third period identified by Hart (1970) and the eclectic fourth period identified by Corey (1996). Phase Two is experiential and eclectic in that it enables the person-centered counselor to respond to the client in a variety of ways rather than being restricted to reflecting the client's feelings. In Phase Two, the counselor adopts a pattern of responses that meets the needs of the individual client. When the counselor has the flexibility to respond to the needs of different clients in different ways, the counseling process becomes individualized and person-centered counseling matures into becoming more enriched, expanded, and accurate by being congruent with the specialized needs of different clients.

The identification of client needs in Phase One is an assessment that enables the counselor and client to determine which specific process will best assist the client in Phase Two. Without an investment in Phase One, the counselor and client are unable to know what clearly has to be done in Phase Two. Phase One enables the communication between the client and counselor to be honest, authentic, and open and this enables Phase Two to be accurate in meeting client needs. In Phase Two the counselor and client have a number of process alternatives available and a particular alternative can be matched with, and congruent with, the needs of the client. The process alternatives available in Phase Two are (1) the procedures available from existing theories of counseling compatible with person-centered values, (2) creative procedures, and (3) logical and natural eclectic procedures.

This essentially means that in Phase Two the counselor can continue with the person-centered approach started in Phase One because this approach best meets the needs of this particular client, or the counselor can incorporate another approach consistent with person-centered values because it best meets the needs of another client. In Phase Two, the counselor has the flexibility to more precisely meet the needs of individual clients and engage the client as a partner in choosing alternative approaches.

The person-centered counselor need not stay aloof from procedures which have proven themselves to be effective. If these procedures more accurately meet the needs of clients in Phase Two, why not use them? Today's counselor works with a more diverse client population than ever before. This diversity indicates that the core conditions of the person-centered approach may not be sufficient to meet the needs of all clients in Phase Two. Person-centered counseling must have the flexibility to accurately meet the needs of clients if it is to truly live up to the responsibility of being person-centered.

The need for this kind of flexibility is encouraged by Cain (1990) who indicates that the paradox of the person-centered approach is that while it acknowledges and values the uniqueness of persons, it does not specify how these unique differences in clients might affect counseling practice. He argues that while the emphasis of the person-centered approach on discovery learning may fit many persons it is clearly not appropriate to all. He goes on to say that the person-centered approach will not realize its full potential until it more fully recognizes the compelling reality that unique and important differences in clients require diversity in therapist responses, if they are to be maximally effective in helping their clients. We are in deep accord with Cain's view and resonate with him when he says (1990: 98-99):

> I have a deep appreciation for the wide range of individual differences that exist in people. Sometimes these differences astonish, puzzle and, occasionally, flabbergast me. And while the most human of experiences may well be those that are most universal, I have come to believe that the variety of ways in which people comport themselves and learn are crucial factors in the process of therapeutic change. Therefore, a guiding question I ask of myself and of my client is, "Does it fit?" It has become increasingly clear to me that people can be relied upon to recognize that which suits them and that which does not. Sometimes what fits a given client is readily evident to the client and therapist. Sometimes it is not. In the latter case the client can be asked directly. At times when the answer is not clear, further exploration may be necessary to determine what does fit. Regardless of how the therapist and client determine what is right for the client, doing so is an essential part of serving and assisting the client to meet his or her needs.

In Phase Two, the person-centered counselor might make use of many creative ways to meet client needs. Since these more creative ways exist, why not make use of them if they meet the needs of clients and are compatible with person-centered values? Some of these more creative procedures are the creative arts (Agell, 1979; Cockle, 1994; Silverstone,1997), contracting (Worall, 1997), photographs (Amerikaner, Schauble & Ziller, 1980), bibliotherapy (Bellows & Gerlet, 1982), poetry (Berger, 1969; Gladding, 1979), metaphors (Brink, 1982), psychodrama (Coven, 1977; Marques-Teixeira, 1993), games (Crocker & Wroblewski, 1975), the expressive arts (Feder & Feder, 1981), music (Harper, 1985), creative writing (Mitchell & Campbell, 1972), multimodal therapy (Akande & Akande, 1994); play therapy (Lefebvre, 1986; Landreth, 1991; Goetze, 1994; Frick-Helms,1997), cartooning (O'Brien, Johnson, & Miller, 1978), hypnotherapy (Mason 1995), transcendental meditation (Brooks & Scarano, 1985), and dream work (Barrineau 1992,1996; Jennings, 1986). A significant number of these approaches have been explicitly incorporated into the person-centered therapeutic approach and framework. It is important to bear in mind that these procedures and approaches are always applied with a person-centered ethos and behavior. They can be regarded as ***affordances*** (Gibson, 1979 as cited in Bohart & Tallman, 1996)—processes that afford opportunities for certain kinds of experiences.

Bohart and Tallman (1996:19) indicate these affordances can be used by the client in different ways:

> Because the client who uses the technique is a whole person, the client may be able to approach his or her problems from a multiplicity of productive directions, gaining insight into the unconscious (psychodynamic), exploring feelings and values (humanistic), practicing skills (Behavioral), or changing conditions (cognitive). It is the whole person—the active client—who takes these various part processes and uses them in his or her self growth.

In Phase Two then, it is the client's choice of the procedure and use of the procedure which is central in the relationship. "The client uses it to make something new. Two clients using the same technique may use it in quite different ways" (Bohart & Tallman, 1996:19).

A natural, eclectic, and common sense approach can also be applied in Phase Two. For example, helping homeless clients to find affordable housing, helping hungry clients to have access to food, and helping other clients to learn how to read and write, understand laws which protect minority rights, identify rights under workman's compensation laws, have contact with job training opportunities, and develop contacts with support groups which deal with alcohol and substance abuse.

The length of time that it takes a counselor to build Phase One with a client varies according to the human credibility, authenticity, and empathy of the counselor. Counselors with observable human qualities can have a successful Phase One in a relatively short period of time. Other counselors may have to invest in several or more Phase One counseling sessions.

The counselor knows that Phase One has been achieved when the client:
1. Has achieved an emotional catharsis and is no longer overwhelmed by incapacitating feelings.

2. Is more open and honest in assessing the self and the attitudes and behaviors that constitute the self.
3. Shows a movement from emotionally-based communication to rationally-based communication.
4. Is motivated to solve or resolve a problem.

PHASE TWO: THE FREEDOM DILEMMA

Persons learn and grow in a variety of ways. Person-centered counselors recognize that their clients have the capacity to identify and choose the ways that promote their own growth and learning. Client determination of the direction of counseling and the selection of approaches which best suit the client are hallmarks of a collaborative relationship in which the client is an active partner in the diagnosis and remediation of his or her problems (Cain, 1989).

Phase Two of counseling begins when counselor and client feel free to interact in ways that may or may not include nondirectiveness. Cain (1989:131) articulates the freedom dilemma when he observes that while person-centered counselors share a fundamental value and desire to empower their clients their conscious intention not to direct or control another person sometimes has a constraining instead of a freeing effect. He comments:

> By adhering to strongly ingrained values of nondirectiveness, person-centered practitioners sometimes lose sight of the fact that they too need to feel free and act freely if they are to offer or create optimal conditions for growth in their clients. Our clients are not likely to experience any manipulative or controlling intention on our part if whatever we offer (e.g., exercises, strategies, tools, and techniques, information, structures) derives from our understanding of their individual needs and is done in a manner that clearly communicates that 'this is an option you may wish to consider." If we truly trust our client's capacity to recognize and choose what they need to move forward in their lives, then we are more likely to feel free to offer our personal and professional resources to them.

It is critical that in Phase Two, clients have the opportunity to consider and choose options in counseling procedures. The person-centered counselor in essence communicates "here are some resources and approaches which I can offer which may be helpful to you." Clients are capacitated to choose options when they are viewed holistically as persons and enabled to engage in an ongoing process of self-diagnosis rather than limiting themselves to understanding a problem in isolation. As collaborative partners in the counseling process clients achieve the freedom to function as coassessors and as users of their individualized findings (Fischer, 1989). As a result Cain (1989:280) notes:

> Clients are more likely to continue to assess the meaning of their experiences and to transform it into personal knowledge that can be applied to present and future problems. Clients who have participated in collaborative approaches will tend to want to develop individualized remediational programs for themselves rather than accept remedies in which "one approach fits all." They are likely to feel satisfied about the active and significant role they have played in the remediation of their problems and less likely to feel (or become) dependent on their professional caretakers.

The issues of power and control are fundamental concerns in conceptualizing Phase Two of the counseling relationship. From beginning to end the person-centered counseling relationship is a collaborative process between the counselor and the client. The direction for the relationship is guided by client's choices and needs. Authority about the client lies in the client and not in the counselor. This is a fundamental premise of the person-centered approach. Bozarth and Temanar (1986) indicate that the counselor's belief in the importance of rejecting the pursuit of control or authority over other persons is central to the whole practice of person-centered counseling. This belief cannot be compromised or abandoned for the sake of eclecticism, otherwise one would not be able to practice person-centered counseling as we define it in this book. In Phase Two, "this implies an ever watchful attentiveness to any imbalance between counselor and client and a constant seeking to equalize power through any procedures, whether verbal or otherwise, which can remedy such imbalance" (Mearns & Thorne, 1988: 18).

In Phase Two, the counselor is not free to intervene unilaterally in the name of eclecticism. Counselor and client are engaged in a dialogical and heuristic investigation into the nature and meaning of a unique human experience. O'Hara (1986: 177-179) in describing this heuristic process, indicates that the function of the therapist becomes more like that of a research assistant in a scientific laboratory:

> The therapist's contribution is to help bring pieces of the puzzle to awareness. Using faculties of perception and discernment to enlarge the client's awareness of existent realities, the therapist helps the client to put into words vague, unclear ideas, feelings, and sensations. In this way, the therapist helps draw attention to overlooked elements of the puzzle. Using expressive capacities to communicate as clearly as possible, offering faith that there is an order in the unfolding picture even if it is currently hidden, the therapist makes a whole-

hearted commitment to the other's search. This last challenge is demanding, delicate, and not without risk for the therapist.

Counselor and client function as collaborators in a shared inquiry to diagnose and remediate the client's problem or to help the client discover new ways of being. In this collaboration the counselor need not, and indeed cannot, assume the role of healer. Any discoveries made by the counselor are offered to the client for acceptance, rejection, or further exploration. Even incorrect interpretation by the counselor can point the way toward deeper awareness and understanding if the counselor and client have entered into a journey together.

In Phase Two, the counselor views the client holistically, is more person-centered than problem-focused, attends as much to what is right with the client as to what is wrong, places observation of immediate experience above explanation, and enables the client to engage in a continuing process of self-discovery rather than attending to discrete problems (Cain, 1989b: 179-180). The role of the counselor is one of service to the client's inquiry which means that in Phase Two, the selection of an approach, procedures, or experience is directed by the client.

The success of Phase Two eclecticism and integration depends upon the collaborative working relationship between the counselor and client and reflects the basic person-centered value that authority, control, and power reside in the client. Cain (1989b: 180) describes this essential feature of person-centered eclecticism when he says:

> A major strength of the collaborative approach is that it helps create in clients a new consciousness about the significant and crucial role they can play in determining the nature and quality of care afforded to them. It enables them to realize that they are the best judge of their need—physical, psychological, and otherwise—and that they can learn to take more charge of and influence the course of their lives, even in areas in which they have relatively little "expertise." Clients are more likely to insist that any remediations proposed to them by experts are compatible with what they know (or have learned) about themselves and with their values.

Unlike the medical model which is built upon external diagnosis and prescription conducted by the doctor as a medical expert, person-centered eclecticism is based upon the unfolding personal knowledge and expertise of the client who decides what actions and prescriptions are to be implemented. In the Phase Two collaboration between counselor and client, the counselor may suggest an approach to facilitate client growth and change, but the client is always informed about the approach and its purposes and the client is free to reject the approach.

Guiding the counselor and the client in the selection of eclectic approaches in Phase Two are person-centered beliefs (Mearns & Thorne, 1988: 18).

The Person-Centered Counselor's Creed

The person-centered counselor believes:
• that every individual has the internal resources for growth;
• that when a counselor offers the core conditions of congruence, unconditional positive regard, and empathy, therapeutic movement will take place;
• that human nature is essentially constructive; that human nature is essentially social;
• that self-regard is a basic human need; that persons are motivated to seek the truth; that perceptions determine experience and behavior;
• that the individual should be the primary reference point in any helping activity;
• that individuals should be related to as whole persons who are in the process of becoming;
• that persons should be treated as doing their best to grow and to preserve themselves given their current internal and external circumstances, that it is important to reject the pursuit of authority or control over others and to seek to share power.

In summary, then, in Phase Two, the counselor and the client enter into a shared search together jointly studying the rich, mysterious, and unique world of the client (O'Hara, 1986). In their search, counselor and client open themselves to the variety of approaches and ways in which the client can learn and grow. They free themselves from the ideology and orthodoxy that "one approach fits all" and thus are empowered to choose from a diversity of healing approaches.

AN EXAMPLE OF A PHASE TWO APPLICATION: DREAM WORK

A clear example of a Phase Two counseling approach can be found in the work of Barrineau (1992; 1996) who has developed a model of dream work which reflects the assumptions, principles, and practices of the person-centered approach. His model expands on the work of Jennings (1986) and suggests that it is possible to explore the meanings and symbols of client dreams in an approach that is consistently person-centered. The proposed model calls for an expansion of person-centered therapy and for further inquiry on the nature and value of the unconscious as it relates to dreams, and recommends that a delicate differentiation between content expertise and process expertise is required to maximize person-centered therapeutic effectiveness for clients who choose to explore their dreams in therapy.

In person-centered dream work, the therapist consistently demonstrates unconditional regard for the dreamer and the dream, strives to be genuine in the encounter with the dreamer and to balance this authenticity with empathic understanding and responses, and endeavors to enter the word of the dreamer and the dream in order to empathically understand that world as completely as possible, and to reflect this understanding to the client.

Phase Two in person-centered dream work begins when the client presents a dream for exploration. Barrineau (1992:95) describes the phase two process when he says:

> The client is explicitly saying to the therapist: 'Here is my dream. I do not know what to make of it. Please help facilitate my exploration of it.' The decision to explore a dream's meaning is the client's alone, having been made aware of the therapist's interest in facilitating the exporation. The client may 'bring in a dream' to a traditional therapy interview for exploration, or the therapist and client may meet for the stated purpose of dream exploration. In either event, the decision about which dream to present for exploration, or whether to present one at all, is the client's. The responsibility for this choice never rests with the therapist, because the explorative work to be done is the dreamer's.

After the client makes the decision to enter dream work, the therapist facilitates the discovery of the meaning of the dream as the client presents it and the client's present experiencing of the dream by using different types of questions and responses. *Clarification questions* facilitate the therapist's understanding of what the client has presented in the dream: *exploratory questions* facilitate the client's exploration of the waking life meaning of some elements of the dream. These questions are seen as invitations for the client to explore dreams further, and they emanate from the therapist's understanding of the dream work process and his or her therapeutic skills.

Barrineau points out that, on the surface, questioning the client about his or her dreams would seem to be inconsistent with person-centered philosophy and principles, because person-centered theory indicates that the locus of control for the direction, pace, and style of therapy lies within the client. Barrineau (1992:97) notes, however:

> The tension is resolved by the assumption that (a) when there is an explicit agreement between client and therapist to engage in dream exploration, as opposed to traditional therapy, the client has explicitly invited the therapist to

enter the dream and to become a co-explorer of its meaning, and (b) the dream facilitator holds some expertise about the process of dream work.

The client decides which dream to present based on criteria unknown to the therapist, the therapist "assumes that the client has made the best decision and honors this choice because the therapist prizes the client," the locus of expertise about the content of the dream resides with the client. The model requires the therapist to provide the necessary conditions and attitudinal qualities defined by Rogers (1957): empathy, unconditional positive regard, and genuineness. These person-centered conditions define Phase One of the relationship and continue throughout Phase Two of the relationship when clarification and exploratory questions are raised.

Other examples of explicitly developed Phase Two applications in person-centered counseling include art therapy (Cockle, 1994, Silverstone, 1997), contracting (Worall, 1997), psychodrama (Marques-Teixeira, 1993), multimodal therapy (Akande & Akande, 1994), and hypnotherapy (Mason, 1995).

PERSON-CENTERED ECLECTICISM: A CONCLUDING NOTE

Our eclectic application of person-centered counseling meets the criteria of eclecticism identified by Patterson (1986:460): "Eclecticism, thus is, or should be, a systematic, integrative, theoretical position."

Examples of the *systematic characteristics* of our eclectic application of person-centered counseling are:
1. Phase One is the foundation for applying Phase Two. Phase Two does not occur unless it is preceded by Phase One.
2. Phase One requires the counselor to systematically reflect the feelings of clients and is characterized by the person-centered therapeutic values of congruence, empathy, and unconditional positive regard.
3. The purposes of Phase One are to enable the therapeutic quality of the relationship between client and counselor to develop; to enable the client to express previously unexpressed feelings; to enable the counselor to assimilate the client's attitudes, values, and behavior, to give the client the time necessary to go beyond a presenting problem; and to give the client the time to be in contact with subconscious and unconscious causes of behavior, if they exist, and to enable the client to be less defensive and more open.
4. Phase Two occurs only after the client has achieved an emotional catharsis and is no longer overwhelmed by incapacitating feelings, is more open and honest in assessing the self and the attitudes and behav-

iors that constitute the self, shows a movement from emotionally based communication to rationally-based communication, and is motivated to solve or resolve a problem.

Examples of the *integrative characteristics* of our eclectic application of person-centered counseling are:

1. Phase One is integrated with Phase Two. Phase Two may involve the counselor in approaches that are different from Phase One, but they are an integrated extension of Phase One.
2. Phase One is integrated with the universal needs of clients to be treated with respect and dignity, to be accepted, and to be understood.
3. Phase Two is integrated with the specific needs of clients that are identified in Phase One.
4. There is an integration between what the counselor does in Phases One and Two, the counselor's personal/professional values, and the client's needs.

Examples of the *theoretical characteristics* of our eclectic application of person-centered counseling are:

1. The counselor accepts the person-centered concept of personality and behavior, but it is accepted as a viewpoint rather than as dogma. No theory of personality and human behavior can identify all of the causes for human behavior. These causes are phenomenologically unique.
2. The theoretical foundations for the counselor's behavior in Phase One remain the same for the counselor's behavior in Phase Two. There is no compromising of the person-centered view as the counselor works with the client in Phase Two. Empathy, unconditional positive regard, and genuiness pervade throughout Phase Two.
3. The specific goals of counseling are unique to each client and are a reflection of the client's needs which were identified in Phase One.
4. The counselor's role during the counseling process reflects the person-centered view regarding therapeutically effective interpersonal communication. That communication is always person-centered and never counselor-centered or theory-centered. It is primarily characterized by the counselor attitudes of empathic understanding, respect and warmth, genuineness, and unconditional regard. These attitudes remain constant during Phases One and Two although the approaches applied may change in Phase Two. These Phase Two approaches may vary from client to client, but they are always activated and influenced by the counselor's human qualities and adherence to the person-centered values of empathy, conguence, and unconditional positive regard.

REFERENCES

Agell, G. L. (1979). The history of art therapy education. In P. B. Hallen (Ed.). *The use of the creative arts in therapy*. Washington, DC: American Psychiatric Association.

Akande, A., & Akande, B. E. (1994). On becoming a person: Activities to help children with their anger. *Early Child Development and Care, 101*, 31-62.

Amerikaner, M., Shcauble, P., & Ziller, R. (1980). Images: The use of photographs in personal counseling. *Personnel and Guidance Journal, 59*, 68-73.

Arkowitz, J. (1992: 261-303). Integrative theories of therapy. In D.K. Freedheim, et.al. (Eds), *History of psychotherapy: A century of change*. Washington, DC: American Psychological Association.

Barrineau, P. (1992). Person-centered dream work. *Journal of Humanistic Psychology, 32*, 1, 90-105.

Barrineau, P. (1996) A reexamination of the role of dreams from a person-centered perspective: practical implications for mental health counselors. *Journal of Mental Health Counseling, 18*, 1, 3-15.

Barrineau, P., & Bozarth, J. D. (1989). A person-centered research model. *Person Centered Review, 4*, 4, 465-474.

Becvar, R., & Becvar, D. S. (1997). The client therapist relationship: A comparison of second order family therapy and Rogerian therapy. *Journal of Systemic Therapies, 16*,2,181-194.

Bellows, E., & Gerlet, E. R., Jr. (1982). Helping books for children: A multimodal project for the school library. *Elementary School Guidance and Counseling, 16*, 296-303.

Berger, M. (1969). *Poetry therapy*. Philadelphia: J. B. Lippincott, 75-87.

Beutler, L. E., & Consoli, A. J. (1992). Systematic eclectic psychotherapy. In J. C. Norcross & M. R. Goldfried (Eds.), *Handbook of psychotherapy integration*. (264-199). New York: Basic Books.

Bohart, A. C., & Tallman, K. (1996). The active client: Therapy as self-help. *Journal of Humanistic Psychology, 36*, 3, 7-30.

Bohart, A. C. (1995). The person-centered psychotherapies. In A. S. Gurman, & S.

Bowen, M. V. (1996:) The myth of non-directiveness: the case of Jill. In Farber, B.A.;

Brink, D.C.; & Raskin, P.M. *The psychotherapy of Carl Rogers: Cases and commentary* (84-94). New York: Guilford Press.

Boy, A. V., & Pine, G. J. (1963). *Client-centered counseling in the secondary school* Boston: Houghton Mifflin.

Bozarth, J., & Temanar-Brodley, B. B. (1986). *The core values and theory of the person-centered approach*. Paper presented at the First Annual Meeting of the Association for the Development of the Person-Centered Approach, Chicago.

Bradley, L. J., Parve, G., & Gould, L. J. (1995). Counseling and psychotherapy: An integrative perspective. In D. Capuzzi & D. R. *Gross, Counseling and psychotherapy: Theories and interventions*. Columbus, OH: Merrill.

Brazier, D., et al. (Eds.). (1993). *Beyond Carl Rogers*. London: Constable Publishers.

Brink, N. E. (1982). Metaphor creation for use within family therapy. *American Journal of Clinical Hypnosis, 24*, 258-265.

Brink, D. C., & Farber, B. A. (1996). A scheme of Rogers's clinical responses. In B.A. Farber, D. C. Brink, & P. M. Raskin. *The psychotherapy of Carl Rogers: Cases and commentary* (15-24). New York: Guilford Press.

Brooks, J. S., & Scarano, T. (1985). Transcendental meditation in the treatment of post-Vietnam adjustment. *Journal of Counseling and Development. 64,* 202-215.

Burks, M. M, Jr., & Stefflre, B. (1979). *Theories of counseling.* New York: McGraw-Hill.

Cain, D. (1989a). The paradox of nondirectiveness in the person centered approach. *Person-Centered Review, 4,* 2, 123-131.

Cain, D. (1989b). The client's role in diagnosis: three approaches. *Person-Centered Review, 4,* 2, 171-182.

Cain, D. (1990) Further thoughts about non-directiveness and client-centered therapy. *Person-Centered Review, 1,* 98-99.

Cockle, S. (1994) Healing through art: the self portrait technique. *International Journal of Play Therapy, 3,*1,37-55.

Coghlan, D., & McIlduff, E. (1996). Process consultation and the person-centered approach: Schein and Rogers on the helping process. *Organization Development Journal, 13,* 3,45-56.

Corey, G. (1996). *Theory and practice in counseling and psychotherapy* (5th ed.). Monterey, CA: Brooks/Cole.

Corsini, R. (1973). *Current psychotherapies.* Itasca, IL: F. E. Peacock.

Cottone, R. R. (1992). *Theories and paradigms of counseling and psychotherpy.* Boston: Allyn and Bacon.

Coven, A. B. (1977). Using Gestalt psychodrama experiments in rehabilitation counseling. *Personnel and Guidance Journal, 56,* 143-147.

Crocker, J. W., & Wroblewski, M. (1975). Using recreational games in counseling. *Personnel and Guidance Journal, 53,* 453-458.

Douglass, B. G., & Moustakas, C. (1985) Heuristic inquiry: the search to know. *Journal of Humanistic Psychology, 25,* 3, 39-54.

Duncan, B. L., et. al. (1992). *Changing the rules: A client directed approach to therapy.* New York: Guilford Press.

Egan, G. (1994) *The skilled helper* (5th ed.). Pacific Grove, CA: Brooks/Cole.

Farber, B. A., Brink, D. C., & Raskin, P. M. (1996). *The psychotherapy of Carl Rogers: Cases and commentary.* New York: Guilford Press.

Farber, B. A. (1996). Introduction. In B. A. Farber, D. C. Brink, & P. M. Raskin, *The psychotherapy of Carl Rogers: Cases and commentary* (1-14). New York: Guilford Press.

Feder, E., & Feder, B. (1981). *The expressive arts therapies.* Englewood Cliffs, NJ: Prentice-Hall.

Fischer, C. T. (1989). A life-centered approach to psychodiagnosis: attending to lifeworld, ambiguity, and possibility. *Person-Centered Review, 4,* 2, 163-170.

Ford, J. G. (1991). Rogerian self-actualization: A clarification of meaning. *Journal of Humanistic Psychology, 31,*2,101-111.

Frick-Helms, S. B. (1997). "Boys cry better than girls": Play therapy behavior of children in a shelter for battered women. *International Journal of Play Therapy, 6,* 1, 73-91.

Gibson, J. J. (1979). *The ecological approach to visual perception.* Boston: Houghton Mifflin.

Gladding, S. T. (1979). The creative arts of poetry in the counseling process. *Personnel and Guidance Journal, 57,* 285-287.

Goetze, H. (1994). Processes in person-centered play therapy. In J. Hellendoorn & R. van der Kooij (Eds.). *Play and intervention.* Albany, NY: SUNY Press.

Goldfried, M. R. (1995). *From cognitive-behavior therapy to psychotherapy integration.* New York: Springer.

Harper, B. L. (1985). Say it, review it, enhance it with a song. *Elementary School Guidance and Counseling, 19,* 218-221.

Hart, J. (1970). The development of client-centered therapy. In J. T. Hart & T. M. Tomlinson (Eds.), *New directions in client-centered therapy* (3-22). Boston: Houghton Mifflin.

Jennings, J. (1986). The dream is the dream is the dream: A person centered approach to dream abnalysis. *Person-Centered Review, 1,* 310-333.

Kelly, E. W., Jr. (1994). *Relationship centered counseling: An integration of art and science.* New York: Springer.

Kelly, E. W., Jr (1995). *Relationship-centered counseling: The integrative interaction of relationship and technique.* Paper presented at the 103rd Annual Convention of the American Psychological Association.

Kelly, E. W., Jr. (1997). Relationship-centered counseling: a humanistic model of integration. *Journal of Counseling and Development. 75,* 337-345.

Kelly, K. R. (1991). Theoretical integration is the future for mental health counseling. *Journal of Mental Health Counseling, 13,* 106-111.

Kleinke, C. L. (1994). *Common principles of psychotherapy.* Pacific Grove, CA: Brooks/Cole.

Kottler, J. A. (1991). *The compleat therapist.* San Francisco: Jossey Bass.

Kottler, J. A., & Brown, R. W. (1996). *Introduction to therapeutic counseling.* (3rd. ed.). Pacific Grove, CA: Brooks/Cole.

Lazarus, A. A., & Beutler, L. E. (1993). On technical eclecticism. *Journal of Counseling and Development, 71,* 381-385.

Lefebvre, N. R. (1986). Creative activity and action oriented play therapy. *New Hampshire Journal for Counseling and Development, 14,* 17-19.

Levant, R. F., & Shlien, J. M. (Eds.). (1984). *Client-centered therapy and the personcentered approach: New directions in theory, research and practice.* New York: Praeger.

Lumbelli, L. (1997). Gestalt theory and Carl Rogers's interviewee-centered inter view-das verden of the interview climate. *Gestalt Theory, 19,* 2, 90-99.

Marques-Teixeira, J. (1993: 217-226) Client-centered psychodrama. In D. Brazier, et al. (Eds.). *Beyond Carl Rogers* (217-226). London: Constable Publishers.

Mearns, D., & Thorne, B. (1988). *Person-centered counseling in action.* Beverly Hills: Sage Publications.

Merry, T. (1995). *Invitation to person-centered psychology.* London: Whurr Publishers, Ltd.

Messer B. (Eds.), et al. *Essential psychotherapies: theory and practice.* New York: Guilford Press.

Mitchell, D. W., & Campbell, J. A. (1972). Creative writing and counseling. *Personnel and Guidance Journal, 50,* 690-691.

Moriera, V. (1993). Beyond the person: Merleau-Ponty's concept of "flesh" as redefining Carl Rogers's person-centered theory. *Humanistic Psychologist, 21,2,* 138-157.

Norcross, J. C., & Goldfried, M. R. (Eds.). (1992). *Handbook of psychotherapy integration.* New York: Basic Books.

O'Brien, C. R., Johnson, J., & Miller, B. (1978). Cartooning and counseling. *Personnel and Guidance Journal, 57,* 55-56.

O'Hara, M. (1986). Heuristic inquiry as psychotherapy: The client-centered approach. *Person-Centered Review, 1,* 2, 172-184.

Patterson, C. H. (1985). *The therapeutic relationship: Foundations for an eclectic psychotherapy* Monterey, CA: Brooks/Cole.

Patterson, C. H. (1986). *Theories of counseling and psychotherapy* (4th ed.). New York: Harper and Row.

Patton, B., & Griffin, K. (1974). *Interpersonal communication in action.* New York: Harper and Row.

Prochaska, J. O., & Norcross, J. C. (1994). *Systems of psychotherapy* (3rd ed.) Pacific Grove, CA: Brooks/Cole.

Rogers, C. R. (1942). *Counseling and psychotherapy.* Boston: Houghton Mifflin.

Rogers, C. R. (1951, renewed 1979). *Client-centered therapy.* Boston: Houghton Mifflin, 483-522.

Rogers, C. R. (1959). A theory of therapy, personality, and interpersonal relationships, as developed in the client-centered framework. In S. Koch (Ed.), *Psychology: a study of a science. Vol.3. Formulations of the person and the social context* (185-256). New York: McGraw-Hill.

Rogers, C. R. (1961). *On becoming a person.* Boston: Houghton Mifflin.

Rogers, C. R. (1967). The conditions of change from a client-centered viewpoint. In B. Berenson & R. Carkhuff (Eds.), *Sources of gain in counseling and psychotherapy.* New York: Holt, Rinehart and Winston.

Rogers, C. R. (1969). *Freedom to learn.* Columbus, OH: Merrill.

Rogers, C. R. (1970). *On encounter groups.* New York: Harper and Row.

Rogers, C. R. (1972). *Becoming partners: Marriage and its alternatives.* New York: Delacorte.

Rogers, C. R. (1975). Empathic: An unappreciated way of being. *The Counseling Psychologist, 5,* 2-10.

Rogers, C. R. (1977). *On personal power.* New York: Delacorte.

Rogers, C. R. (1980). *A way of being.* Boston: Houghton Mifflin.

Rogers, C. R. (1986). A comment from Carl Rogers. *Person-Centered Review, 1,* 3-5.

Rogers, C. R., & Dymond, R. F. (1954). *Psychotherapy and personality change.* Chicago: University of Chicago Press.

Rogers, C. R., & Wood, J. (1974). Client-centered theory: Carl Rogers. In A. Burton (Ed.), *Operational theories of personality.* New York: Bruner/Mazel.

Safran, J. D. (1990a). Towards a refinement of cognitive therapy in light of interpersonal theory: I. Theory. *Clinical Psychology Review, 10,* 87-105.

Safran, J. D. (1990b). Towards a refinement of cognitive therapy in light of inerpersonal theory: II. Practice. *Clinical Psychology Review, 10,* 107-121.

Safran, J. D., & Segal, Z. V. (1990). *Interpersonal process in cognitive therapy.* New York: Basic Books.

Sanford, R. (1993). From Rogers to Glieck and back again. In D. Brazier, et al. (Eds.), *Beyond Carl Rogers* (253-273). London: Constable Publishers.

Silverstone, L. (1997). *Art therapy: The person-centered way* (2nd ed.). Philadelphia: J. Kingsley Publishers.

Thorne, B. (1992). *Carl Rogers.* London: Sage.

Wachtel, P. L. (1991). From eclecticism to synthesis: Toward a more seamless psychotherapeutic integration. *Journal of Psychotherapy Integration., 1,* 43-54.

Watkins, C. E., Jr., & Goodyear, R. K. (1994). C. H. Patterson: Reflections on client-centered therapy. *Counselor Education and Supervision. 22,*3,178-186.

Wexler, D. A., & Rice, L. N. (Eds.). (1974). *Innovations in client-centered therapy.* New York: John Wiley.

Worall, M. (1997). Contracting within the person-centered approach. In C. Sills, et al. (Eds.), *Contracts in counseling: Professional skills for counselors* (65-75). London: Sage.

Chapter 2

THE REFLECTIVE PROCESS

The previous chapter introduced the reader to an eclectic application of person-centered counseling. In this chapter, we present the most fundamental element of that process, reflection of feelings, and give it the detail necessary for its successful application in Phase One of counseling. Phase One is basically built upon the process of reflecting the client's feelings in which the counselor assimilates the needs of the client, builds an affective and facilitative relationship, enables the client to go beyond a presenting problem, and lays the foundation for counselor-client collaboration regarding which approach or procedure will best meet the needs of the client in Phase Two.

Through this chapter we hope that counselors will be better inclined to apply the reflective process with sensitivity, facilitative attitudes, and accuracy. If applied with empathy and genuineness, reflection of feelings will enable the counselor to fundamentally improve Phase One of the counseling process. Reflection of feelings is a basic channel for developing the fundamental conditions of effective counseling(Hansen, Stevic, and Warner, 1986)

One of the classic misunderstandings and stereotypes of the person-centered approach is that it consists of mechanical reflection of feelings. Indeed, over the years, Rogers (1986) became more and more allergic to the use of the term. His unhappiness with "reflection of feelings" was that it came to be viewed as a technique and too often was applied in a wooden and technical way. Rogers' disenchantment with the term revealed itself in his earlier work (1957) when he indicated that although reflection of feelings could provide a technical channel by which sensitive empathy and unconditional positive regard could be communicated, it was by no means an essential condition of therapy, e.g., feelings could be reflected in ways which would indicate a lack of therapist empathy.

We have found in our experience that reflection of feeling can be a complex, multidimensional, facilitative, and richly empathic response. We also have found that reflection of feeling can be taught as a technique, learned and acquired as a skill, internalized as an attitude, and eventually synthesized as an intuitive, insightful, and empathically sensitive response which significantly advances therapeutic movement and new ways of being for the client. For the new counselor, reflection of feeling begins and is learned as a way *of doing*, with maturity and experience it eventually emerges as a way *of being*.

In our opinion, the power, richness, depth, and complexity of reflection of feelings in fostering client growth, learning, and change have been greatly underestimated. Reflection of feeling has not been appreciated and valued as it might have been if the concept had not been denigrated and devalued in the person-centered literature. When the term—reflection of feeling—was dismissed in an effort to counter the abuses of its application we threw the baby out with the bath water. An overcorrection was made. Based on our experience we believe reflection of feeling warrants renewed attention and serious reconsideration as a central feature of person-centered counseling.

Shlein (Rogers, 1986) captures the situation regarding reflection of feelings in a letter he wrote to Rogers:

> Reflection is unfairly damned. It was rightly criticized when you described the wooden mockery it could become in the hands of incentive people, and you wrote beautifully on that point. But you neglected the other side. It is an instrument of artistic virtuosity in the hands of a sincere, intelligent, empathic listener. It made possible the development of client-centered therapy, when the philosophy alone could not have. Undeserved denigration of the technique leads to fatuous alternatives in the name of congruence.

FEELINGS INFLUENCE THINKING AND BEHAVIOR

We like to think of ourselves as very rational and in control of our behavior. Very often, however, we are not. Intellectually, we know how we should respond but somehow we don't end up responding the way that we should. We know that excessive speed on our highways is an invitation to death, but we insist on exceeding speed limits. We know that children should be emotionally nourished and physically protected, but the statistics tell us of the increasing rate that children are being abused. We know what constitutes proper schooling, but we insist on providing students with second-rate learning experiences. We know what humanism considers to be noble, good, rational, and beautiful, but we persist in behaving in ways that are in conflict with these values. Why?

One clearly emerging answer to the "why" of our overt behavior lies in the covert world of our feelings. We do not behave in a vacuum. We often behave as a response to our subconscious feelings that have developed in a certain way over a period of time. Feelings that have been nurtured and influenced by an entire range of life's experiences and events. An employer may insist on badgering an employee not because the worker is inefficient but because the employer has subconscious autocratic feelings which must be expressed and the worker is a convenient target. A student may act out in class not because the learning experience is inadequate but because of unresolved, angry feelings toward siblings at home. An adolescent boy may engage in abusive sexist language because he has unresolved feelings about his own maleness. A university president may engage in patriarchal behaviors because of a lack of respect for the capabilities of others.

We are not the rational persons that we think we are. The potential for us to be rational exists, but that potential is often not realized because feelings interfere. Too often these feelings interfere with the use of our intellect and prompt us to behave in ways that are not good for ourselves or others. Life would be good, simple, and clear if our thinking could be free from obstructive feelings and simply based upon a rational analysis of the facts. We would have a world free from the threat of nuclear war, child abuse, murder, rape, and countless other crimes. We might someday have that kind of a world, but meanwhile we must first take a serious look at how our subconscious feelings influence our rational behavior and learn how to identify and get rid of obstructive feelings so that our intellect is free to make decisions that are truly objective instead of having those decisions influenced by an undercurrent of unknown but destructive feelings (Boy, 1982).

We all have the potential to use our minds well and reach logical conclusions, conclusions based upon the evidence of objective facts. But our ability to reach logical conclusions is influenced by feelings which interfere with the mind's ability to function logically. A teacher may logically explain the importance of studying mathematics to a student, but the student's feelings of intellectual inadequacy will prevent the teacher's message from being objectively received. The student's feelings of inadequacy prevent the assimilation of the logical message that mathematics is a necessary life skill.

Feelings Affect Thinking

We all want to think well—to gather the facts, analyze those facts, and reach logical conclusions. But the thinking process is influenced bv feelings. Clear thinking emanates from a person whose feelings are known and under control. Faulty thinking emanates from a person who is unaware of how feelings influence our ability to reason well.

If the logic of a work situation dictates that an employee should have an open and frank discussion with an employer, a subconscious fear of authority figures will result in that discussion never taking place. If logic dictates that one should not smoke cigarettes, the feelings which nourish the desire to smoke overpower the logic of not smoking.

We are not what we appear to be. As persons, we are supposed to be logical and rational. But leaf through the pages of any daily newspaper. There you will read stories about destructive and self-defeating human behaviors that serve as prime evidence that we do not think well. But if these stories were examined in detail, we would find persons who engaged in destructive behavior not because they lost the ability to think but because their subconscious and unresolved feelings obstructed the mind's ability to be logical.

Feelings Affect Behavior

Feelings affect thinking and thinking affects behavior. One's behavior is not random. It is caused by something. We often look at negative behavior and conclude that it is due to poor thinking. "If he had only used his head he wouldn't be in this mess!" This statement is true, but we often fail to identify what caused the person to think as he did.

Feelings lead to good or faulty thinking and the quality of that thinking leads to good or faulty behavior. Simply stated, feelings influence thinking and thinking influences behavior. Good behavior is preceded by good thinking which is influenced by good feelings; poor behavior is preceded by faulty thinking which is influenced by negative feelings.

The quality of our feelings influences the quality of our thinking and the subsequent behavior. This chain reaction is put in motion bv our feelings. When they are positive, then the thinking and behavior will be positive. When they are negative then our thinking and behavior will be negative.

When examining any behavior and attempting to determine the cause of that behavior, we must avoid examining superficial causes (i.e., home conditions, physical handicap, learning disability, cultural deprivation, etc.). The person may be a product of these conditions, but the deeper cause for the behavior is the person's subconscious or unconscious feelings about these conditions. It is these feelings which caused the thinking which caused the behavior.

Repressing Feelings Leads to Interpersonal Conflict

Many of us keep our feelings bottled up inside. We smile, do our daily work, and try to come across as friendly and reasonable people. But too many others have unexpressed, antagonistic feelings toward others. We often tolerate an insensitive employer, spouse, parent, or politician. We do that by putting on a front. But if these negative feelings persist, they must eventually find expression. When they are expressed, they often come out in a torrent of bitterness, anger, resentment, and rage. In some cases these repressed feelings eventually find their expression through some act of violence.

Some people attempt to deal with their repressed feelings through physical activity or fantasy. Runners and joggers often release a buildup of negative and angry feelings through their physical activity. Other people find solace in their fantasies of a better life. In both cases these persons may develop an ability to cope with life. But they may not. In far too many cases, when repressed feelings have built up over a period of time, they must be expressed more directly. This direct expression is most often toward another person and usually takes the form of "clearing the air." The benefit of doing this is enormous. But far too many people fear this exchange and prefer to hide behind a mask. They prefer to keep negative feelings to themselves. They are afraid to come out into the open because of a fear of the consequences. This fear, however, adds to the buildup of tension. And eventually that tension may reach a point where it has to be expressed and it sometimes becomes expressed in dehumanizing ways.

Repressing Feelings Leads to Negative Physical Consequences

When feelings are continually repressed, the result can be nagging backaches, stomach disorders, depression, migraine headaches, or low levels of energy. These are the less severe consequences. Medical research has produced evidence which links psychological problems to heart attacks and various forms of cancer. This is a logical outcome for the person whose life is filled with repressed feelings. Feelings were repressed in childhood, during adolescence, during marriage, and on the job. This buildup of unexpressed feelings, over the years, can only result in the eventual deterioration of the body and its normal functioning.

Medical research also indicates that a large percentage of patients who appear in a physician's office do not have physical problems which can be medically treated. They have psychological problems which produce pseudophysical symptoms that have no medically discernable basis.

We pay little attention to our feelings since we cannot see or touch them. We do pay attention to the swollen breast, the limp, the back pain because they are obvious. Feelings, however, are hidden from sight and touch. They're there, but we often label them as moods and figure that what we can't see or touch can't harm us. The consequences of negative feelings, however, are far more incapacitating than a broken leg. The leg can fully mend in a few months. Negative feelings, however, are not that easily mended. They linger, grow, cause us anxiety and tension, and affect not only our interpersonal behavior but our physical well-being.

Expressing Feelings Involves Risk

Repressed feelings often cause us to feel isolated, lonely, angry, and not understood. We would like to turn to people in our lives in an effort to get help, but we often feel that they're too involved with their own problems to give us the time and empathy we need. Furthermore, getting help from them requires an enormous risk that we're often not willing to take. If we do express our feelings to relatives, coworkers, and friends, there is the possibility that our human frailties will not be understood or accepted. Instead of risking the expression of how we feel, we turn inward. We keep those feelings inside since there is less apparent risk involved. The risk, however, of keeping those feelings inside is far greater than the risk of expressing them. Bottling up feelings can lead to psychological and physical consequences that can be far more painful and long lasting than the risk involved in expressing those feelings. The decision, however, for most of us is not to say anything. To survive each day. To protect those feelings from being expressed to others.

Expressing Feelings Enables Us to Examine Motives

A person expressing previously inhibited feelings, however, feels a release from the bonds of such feelings. He or she feels free from the negative consequences of not having expressed feelings in the past. Free from the anguish that accompanies not having responded to persons, situations, and events that require a feeling response. As the person begins to engage in the process of expressing feelings there also occurs an inclination to examine the motives which prompted the development of these feelings. The person basically is asking, "Why do I do these things? Why do I feel this way? Where did all of this come from?"

This self-examination of motives usually leads one to examine situations and events which influenced the development of certain feelings. Such an examination enables one to recall experiences that influenced the development of current feelings. The person often says, "Now I know why I feel as I do!" By recalling the situations and events which caused current feelings, one is able to determine the rhyme and reason for those feelings. Current feelings are understood more deeply, especially the motives which prompt those feelings to exist.

There are motives for feeling as we do and these motives are usually linked to situations and events in which we felt either enhanced or diminished as persons. Those debilitating experiences, especially, whether they occurred yesterday or many years ago, leave us with psychological scars—

repressions of feelings about what transpired and how we emotionally responded. We want to know what happened and why we responded as we did. We want to identify the motives which influence certain feelings.

Expressing Feelings Serves as a Release

If the feelings that we have accumulated over a period of time do not have the opportunity to be released, we create a reservoir of feelings that will eventually overflow its banks. The victim in such an overflow is often ourself and those around us. We cannot expect to repress feelings and live a life that is free from tension, anxiety, and physical consequences. The bottling up of feelings, for too long, can only lead to negative physical and psychological consequences. The price that one pays for inhibiting feelings is too high.

When feelings are siphoned off as they begin to form, they are released. They no longer have the power to build up and incapacitate us. They no longer have the power to make us uncertain and insecure. By their release, feelings have an opportunity to evaporate. Their expression releases us from the tension, anxiety, and anguish that retaining them requires. Keeping feelings inside requires an enormous effort. We have to carefully plan what we say, to whom, and the circumstances in which we'll say anything. Just saying how we feel does not require the same planning. We merely say it, feel better about having said it, and cleanse ourselves of feelings that have no opportunity to build up inside.

If we merely said what we feel, then we would all be far more psychologically stable. But we don't. We repress saying what we feel. We figure that the risks involved in being emotionally open are far greater than the positive outcomes. But the loser is the one who represses feelings because such repressions will eventually take their toll.

Expressing Feelings Leads to Self-Responsibility

A person who has learned to express feelings gains in self-responsibility. There is an enormous responsibility involved in expressing feelings. It is the dual responsibility toward self and others. Certainly the expression of feelings can be a therapeutic experience. The person will feel unburdened of the necessity of hiding certain feelings and the psychological and physical tensions that accompany such a repression. But the person will also develop a responsibility to examine feelings. To determine whether these feelings are legitimate and emanate from an objective situation or event or whether they are more related to a subjective need to feel angry, misunderstood, lonely, or unloved. Often we express feelings toward a person today that are totally unrelated to what that person is saying or doing. The feeling expressed often doesn't feel right and we know it. It is often more related to a past experience with *another* person, but we wait until today to express that feeling to an innocent bystander.

Being in touch with our feelings gives us an opportunity to examine their accuracy. The more practice we have with expressing our feelings, the better able we are to monitor their expression so that they will be expressed to the right person in the right situation. We become less random in expressing feelings. We know more accurately how we feel and the persons to whom those feelings should be expressed. We become more responsible because we have a more accurate understanding of how we feel, why we feel that way, and identify the most appropriate person who needs to hear our feelings.

Expressing Feelings Leads to Personal Freedom

Persons who have learned how to express their feelings are in contact with an important ingredient of personal freedom. They feel alive, liberated, and whole. They feel connected to the psychologically wholesome life. They have freed themselves from the chains of unexpressed feelings. They can make free choices and decisions based upon the logic of what should be done rather than having those choices and decisions influenced by unexpressed feelings.

Clearly, an important outcome for the person who has expressed feelings is the movement toward increased personal and psychological freedom. The motives for certain choices and decisions are unrelated to unexpressed feelings. A certain house or car is purchased because of reasonableness rather than being related to the subconscious need to impress others. A special cause is supported because of the nobility of the cause rather than being a symbol of unexpressed feelings. Choices and decisions are made because they are logically the best rather than being symbols of certain unexpressed subconscious feelings.

Personal freedom is not a luxury for the chosen few. It is available to anyone who has learned to understand feelings, express them, and identify the relationship of this expression to one's sense of freedom and comfort in interpersonal relationships.

INTERACTION BETWEEN COGNITIONS AND EMOTIONS

While we believe the free expression of feelings in the safety of the counseling relationship is important in facilitating the client's learning and growth, it is equally important that the counselor attend to the client's cognitions. In viewing the client holistically, the counselor recognizes that cognitions and emotions are intertwined. With few exceptions, one does not appear without the other. Exclusive focus on either cognitions or emotions fractionate the client's expression of being in the counseling relationship. Patterson, reflecting on client-centered therapy, in an interview with Watkins, Jr. and Goodyear (1994:179), observes:

> You can't separate affect and cognition; all behavior includes both. While the therapist attends to affect, he or she is simultaneuously aware of the client's cognitions. These aspects are present in clients to greater or lesser degrees and, also, they are present in the therapist. Therefore, you cannot attend to affect without doing so for cognition and vice versa. Essentially, the helper attends to the whole person rather than focusing on one domain exclusively.

Tausch (1988:284) in a thoughtful examination of the relationship between cognitions and emotions, suggests several possible disadvantages when the counselor tends to focus predominantly on empathic understanding of emotions.

1. Cognitions that trigger emotions may remain hidden for both counselor and client resulting in the client paying little attention to them.

2. Clients with strong psychological disturbances attend predominantly to their negative emotions. This may reinforce their negative emotions.

3. Some psychotherapists encourage clients to "let out aggressions." This frequently leads to a reduction of tensions. However, the emotions are not really admitted into consciousness. Therefore, the clients do not develop an understanding of the relationship between their emotions and their origin, the cognitions. As a result, there is rarely a lasting change.

4. Clients' intensive and predominant attention to their emotions makes them more open and sensitive to their emotions. If, however, their emotions are experienced as something frightening and disturbing and/or other persons reinforce this, psychological disturbances in the client may be stronger after psychotherapy than before since the client is more open and vulnerable.

Tausch goes on to indicate that "intensive empathic response to the client's emotions tends to lead to a prolongation of the therapy and to less change particularly since most of the emotions that clients express are mainly burdening emotions" (285-286). He proposes several advantages in focusing on empathic understanding of clients' emotions that are connected with their cognitions (287): (1) When clients' feelings are deeply understood, positive relationships are facilitated with their therapists. Further, when the client feels that the therapist has really understood his or her emotions, a state of relaxation often occurs. If clients can relax while they explore their cognitions, they are less likely to become rigid, which in turn increases the possibilities for change. (2) Changes in cognitions may lead to changes in emotions, which the client may then perceive more consciously. In turn, changes in emotions may facilitate a change in cognitions. (3) As a result of the therapist's attention to both cognitions and emotions, clients are more likely to attend to both. Consequently, clients may become more conscious of instances where they wrongly attributed specific emotions to particular cognitions. (4) If the therapist addresses both cognitions and the appropriate emotions, there is less danger that the client will overemphasize the importance of thoughts or feeling states. (5) Because of the continuous attention to both cognitions and their appropriate emotions, there is no need for the therapist to guide the client in any way. Clients are then free to explore and examine their cognitions largely on their own. (6) The therapist's empathic understanding and acceptance of the client's emotions increases the accessibility of the corresponding cognitions. If emotions that have been denied or ignored are now admitted into consciousness, the possibility for altering the corresponding cognitions is increased. (7) Since emotions are usually more conscious and easily accessible to the client than cognitions and appraisals, the client has an identifiable framework from which to identify the related cognitions.

Tausch (1988:288) concludes that empathy for both cognitions and emotions appears to be more beneficial than exclusive or predominant attention to either. What the most effective balance is remains open to questions which may be answered by research. One significant implication for person-centered counseling is that the client's journey of self-discovery can be viewed as a discovery of the connection between cognitions and emotions, and of any contradictions between them. If the counselor accepts and reflects the client's emotions and cognitions, then the client may evaluate them less negatively, thus increasing the possibility for change in distorted perceptions or in emotions that are a function of faulty cognitions.

It is clear then that reflection of feelings involves reflection of the cognitions embedded in feelings. One cannot accurately reflect feelings without resonating to the underlying or more visible cognitions. This indicates that reflection is a difficult, complex, and subtle counselor expression of empathic understanding—the kind of robust understanding Schlein (1987:467) describes when he says:

> In our view, understanding is more than warm soup. It is not love or comfort. Those may be motives or consequences, empathic understanding is active, rational, cognitive. It is consciousness expanding. It restores the sanity lost through isolation or misunderstanding. It supplies the energy, attention, and

reflection to facilitate new levels of thought and intelligence. It involves more brain, more knowing, more vision. Those valued positive emotions or attitudes, such as trust, self-esteem, and the like, are happy by products.

Reflection is more than technique—it is a way of being in which the counselor through verbal and nonverbal expressions conveys indwelling in the client. "Indwelling is the immersion of oneself in the subject at hand in order to 'know' it in a way that is impossible with detached observation.... Through intense contemplation one pours oneself into the subject. One participates completely in that which one contemplates. This does not imply observation or control of the subject, but rather living in it, surrendering oneself to it. As clients in psychotherapy, the framework we are trying to dwell in and make useful is ourselves. As psychotherapists in psychotherapy, the framework we are trying to dwell in is the client" (Sims 1989:32).

THE ROOTS OF THE REFLECTIVE PROCESS

Reflection of feelings has been traditionally used by many counselors and psychotherapists in their work with clients. It was first identified as a powerful therapeutic process in the landmark book by Carl R. Rogers, *Counseling and Psychotherapy* (Rogers, 1942). This book was the foundation for the development of other humanistic concepts of counseling and it still serves as a fundamental viewpoint for the successful application of counseling. Through the years, the process of reflecting feelings has also been applied to improving interpersonal communication in teaching, administration, organizational behavior, marriage and its alternatives, parenting, race relations, the building of community, conflict resolution, social action, the physician/patient relationship, and interpersonal relations in general. Rogers has identified an expanded application: as a foundation communication process which can lead to international understanding, so vital to harmony and peace among nations (Rogers, 1982).

Rogers (1942:133), in his first major contribution to our understanding of reflection of feelings, tells us that the process is not easy:

Probably the most difficult skill to acquire in counseling is the art of being alert to and responding to the feeling which is being expressed .

Rogers (1942:37-38) also helped us to understand that reflecting a feeling is not responding to the logical content of what a client is communicating.

If the counselor is to accept these feelings, he must be prepared to respond, not to an intellectual content of what the person is saying, but to the feeling which underlies it.

In his second book, Rogers (1951:29) added to our understanding of the process of reflecting feelings by indicating that the counselor's function is to assume:

> . . . the internal frame of reference of the client, to perceive the world as the client sees it, to perceive the client himself as he is seen by himself, to lay aside all perceptions from the external frame of reference while doing so, and to communicate something of this understanding to the client.

Rogers (1951:289) elaborated further when he said:

> Essentially what the therapist attempts to do is to reconstruct the perceptual field of the individual, at the moment of expression, and to communicate this understanding with skill and sensitivity .

Rogers (1951:352) concluded that the counselor:

> . . . tries to adopt the internal frame of reference of the other person, to perceive what the other person perceives, to understand what is in the central core of the speaker's conscious awareness—in a sense, to take the role of the other person .

Those who represent other counseling theories also recognize the importance of reflection of feelings as a foundation process. George and Cristiani (1981:70) indicate that after the counselor has accurately perceived the client's feelings, the counselor then:

> . . . feeds back to clients, as accurately as possible, the feelings they are expressing. The counselor hopes that the clients will be able to view these feelings more objectively .

Hansen, Stevic, and Warner (1986) concur with the preceding and reinforce the therapeutic importance of any helper's ability to reflect the client's feelings.

WHY REFLECT FEELINGS?

Brammer and Shostrom (1977:189-191) have identified the advantages accruing to the counseling process when the helper is able to successfully reflect the client's feelings. Their view is summarized as follows:

1. Reflection helps the individual to feel deeply understood.

2. Reflection helps to break the so-called neurotic cycle, often manifested in marital counseling and expressed by such phrases as, "She won't understand me, and therefore I won't understand her."

3. Reflection impresses clients with the inference that feelings are causes of behavior.

4. Reflection causes the locus of evaluation to be in the client.

5. Proper reflection gives . . . the feeling that (the client) . . . has the power of choice.

6. Reflection clarifies the client's thinking so that . . . the situation (can be seen) more objectively.

7. . . . It helps communicate to the client the idea that the counselor does not regard him (or her) as unique and different. (The counselor is not shocked.)

8. Reflection helps clients to examine their deep motives.

An inner core of feelings contributes to our self-concept and it is our self-concept which influences us to think and behave as we do. If our inner feelings about ourselves are positive, then our self-concept will be positive. We will think well of ourselves and have confidence that we can improve the quality of our psychological life experiences. A positive self gives us a sense of personal power and decreases the possibility of being psychologically victimized. On the other hand, a set of negative feelings about ourselves will produce a self-concept which feels powerless in its ability to control reactions to threatening psychological life experiences. We then perceive ourselves as victims who have no control over what happens to us.

Feelings have an enormous impact upon our thinking and behavior. They form the critical core which influences our thinking and behavior. Therefore, in any effective counseling the client's inner world of feelings must be entered in order to understand how these feelings influence the client's thinking and behavior and contribute to the formation of the client's problem. The process of reflecting feelings enables the counselor to enter the client's inner world of feelings.

CONDITIONS FOR REFLECTING FEELINGS

The process of reflecting feelings is both an attitude toward the client and a learnable skill. As an attitude it emanates from the counselor's identification with the human principles of person-centered counseling. Rogers (1975) believed that when the counselor is truly committed to respecting the client as a person, and believes in the client's capacity to improve and change, to move toward values which enhance one's personhood, manage behavior, make decisions, and solve problems, then the counselor forms a helping relationship characterized by an empathic understanding of the client's inner world of feelings. With an attitude of empathy as the foundation for the helping process, the counselor easily moves toward the skill of reflecting feelings since the skill is a natural expression of an empathic attitude. Once the reflective process is understood and learned, its application occurs in a natural, human, and facilitative manner, it flows easily. If the counselor is attitudinally empathic with clients, then the ability to reflect feelings is not awkward. It is a way of entering the client's inner world of feelings, feelings that influence the behavior that others see and respond to. Being attitudinally empathic and caring makes reflecting feelings a natural process.

Another counselor without a commitment to the importance of empathy and caring can still use the reflective process. It can be used as a therapeutic technique or skill rather than as a natural application of one's empathic and caring attitude. As a technique, the reflective process will lose some of its strength, but it will still work in eliciting feelings. The client will have a better and deeper response to its empathic and natural application but will respond to its application as a technique. Reflection will serve either counselor but not as well when it is used as a technique.

Reflection not only facilitates the establishment of a counseling relationship but also enables the counselor and client to learn about the client's inner world of motives, values, attitudes, and behaviors which have contributed to the development of the client's way of being. Empathically reflecting the client's feelings, then, produces clear results. It enables the counseling relationship to develop, the counselor to assimilate the client's way of being, and the client to uncover subconscious or unconscious material.

In order for feelings to be reflected well, certain conditions must first be met. The effectiveness of the reflective process occurs in proportion to the existence of these conditions. If they exist optimally, then the counselor is able to apply the reflective process in a natural way. If these conditions exist minimally, then the reflective process loses its potential to be effective. Following are those conditions:

Be Convinced that the Client Has the Capacity to Change

Reflecting feelings occurs easily and well when the counselor is convinced that the client has the capacity to change attitudes, values, thinking, and behavior. When the counselor is convinced of this, the reflective process is applied because of the counselor's conviction that it will produce positive results. The client will change. The client needs to feel the stimulus of the reflective process in order to talk about those feelings which are influencing behavior. Once the client realizes the contribution of these feelings to behavior, the client is in a position to do something about that behavior; and changing one's behavior will mean that the client needs to change the feelings which cause the behavior. Understanding and improving those feelings is the catalyst for understanding and improving one's behavior.

Be Convinced that Feelings Influence Thinking and Behavior

Once the counselor realizes the powerful influence of the client's feelings upon thinking and behavior, the counselor becomes committed to utilizing reflection of feelings as a process for helping the client get in touch with those feelings. Once the client becomes sensitive to how feelings influence thinking and behavior, the client can begin to change those feelings; and once those feelings change, the client's thinking and behavior will also change, much like a chain reaction.

In order for the counselor to be sensitive to feelings, two pitfalls must be avoided. The first is the temptation to be an analyst, the tendency to try to analyze the client's feelings and put them in some known diagnostic framework and explain the meaning of these feelings to the client. The second is the temptation to be solution oriented, to listen to and reflect the person's feelings for a while and then revert to offering a solution to the problem. Both temptations are indicative of our natural desire to want to do something to help the client, but doing either or both will interfere with the client's movement toward the necessary understanding of how one's feelings are affecting one's thinking and behavior. This realization puts the client in control of doing something about these feelings rather than waiting for the counselor to solve the problem. Self-resolution of a problem is deep and long-lasting. Other than-self resolution is superficial and short-term.

Be Aware of the Veracity of the Client's Presenting Problem

Too many counselors hear the client's presenting problem and quickly begin to work on that problem and its solution. Even if a solution is developed that appears reasonable, the problem solved is often superficial. Clients tend to begin a counseling relationship with superficial concerns. They try to present themselves as reasonable people who don't possess serious problems. They typically talk about a class "D" problem. They sometimes do this because all they are aware of is the class "D" problem. The counselor who quickly responds and begins helping with the class "D" problem may appear to be efficient. In reality, however, this client has not been given the opportunity to move beyond a class "D" problem toward a class "A" problem. The counselor moved so quickly toward responding to the class "D" problem that the client didn't have the time to identify and talk about the existence of a class "A" problem.

Experienced counselors realize that what the client talks about in the early stages of counseling is not what the client talks about in the middle or later stages of counseling. Clients need a period of time to warm up, to feel comfortable with the counseling process. After they've warmed up, they feel inclined to talk about more serious class "A" problems. Other clients don't realize that they have a class "A" problem until they are well into a counseling relationship. As they begin to peel away layers of feelings, they typically go from class "D" to "C" to "B" to "A" problems. It takes time for the client to get in touch with the deepest of experiences and feelings which affect current thinking and behavior; especially those experiences and feelings which are repressed in the subconscious and unconscious recesses of our minds.

Be Attitudinally Empathic

The counselor who is genuinely empathic is able to enter the deeper recesses of a client's inner world of feelings. Empathy is that quality which enables a counselor to feel, just as deeply as the client, the very same feelings that the client is feeling (Gordon, 1980). Egan (1994) identifies two levels of empathy: *primary level empathy* and *advanced level accurate empathy*. In primary level empathy, there is an interchangeability between the cleint's statements and the counselor's reflections indicating that the counselor understands the client's attitudes, feelings, and thoughts. Primary level empathy is the foundation for advanced level empathy in which the counselor's empathic responses facilitate the deeper exploration of critical issues in the client's life. A counselor cannot do this as well when the reflective process is used as a technique. As a technique, there is some penetration of the client's inner world of feelings, but the penetration is superficial when compared to what the client experiences when working with a counselor who is attitudinally empathic (Rogers, 1975).

Seemans (1986:231) notes that the research findings strongly indicate that the nonverbal correlates of judged empathy are more significant than verbal correlates. This finding is consistent with Carl Rogers' view that empathy is first and foremost an attitude. Seemans observes (p. 231) "the finding also causes me to wonder about the ways of enhancng empathic ability in counselors, and particularly about the risk of confusing empathy with verbal-technical skills."

The attitudinally empathic counselor penetrates the client's feeling more deeply because the reflective process is being used in a natural rather than a mechanical manner. What to say next is easily known by this counselor. And what is reflectively said is congruent with what the client is feeling and prompts the client to examine those feelings with greater depth and a closer scrutiny.

Empathic understanding has been identified as a powerful helping attitude. Reflection of feelings is the counselor's vehicle for expressing empathic understanding. All counselors consider themselves to be empathic, to a degree. Feeling empathy is one thing; expressing empathy is another. Empathy expressed within the disciplined and vigorous framework of the reflective process enables the counselor to be empathic from the beginning of the counseling relationship to its conclusion. Feeling empathic toward the client without a process (reflecting feelings) for expressing that empathy leaves the counselor frustrated. The empathy is not expressed and its therapeutic potential lies dormant. Empathy toward the client needs a vehicle for its expression, and the most scientifically accurate and humanistic vehicle for its expression is the reflective process.

Unfortunately, with the advent of managed care approaches, short-term psychotherapy, and the growing popularity of "manualized approaches" for some counselors, *empathy* has lost its therapeutic potency, fading into the background while other quick and financially profitable counseling tactics have surged ahead. They regard empathy as helpful but not necessary for therapeutic successs. Bohart and Greenberg (1997) not only reject such extravagant claims but affirm empathy's central place in therapy and offer a new and powerful vindication of the role of empathy—not as one ingredient but as the special and extraordinary *sine qua non* that fosters heightened interactions, and ultimately the development of the client's key life skills. They document that empathy sensitively expressed through caring reflection is the core component of most therapeutic orientations.

Possess an Affective Vocabulary

Many counselors who are attitudinally empathic and understand the reflective process still experience difficulty in expressing that empathy. This is a simple technical problem that can be overcome by expanding one's affective vocabulary.

Most people have reasonable cognitive vocabularies. We can easily discuss, clarify, and reach conclusions about a rational topic. Schools, families, and society have trained us to do this reasonably well. We do, however, have difficulty in expressing affect or feelings. Schools, families, and society have been deficient in expanding our affective vocabularies, perhaps not purposely deficient but deficient all the same. So much of life is concrete that we become conditioned to use words and phrases which represent that concrete reality. To many, the vagueness of feelings prompts us not to have much experience in using words which accurately describe feelings. We prefer to use concrete words since they appear to describe a precise reality. We tend not to use abstract words, the words which convey feelings, simply because such words often sound vague.

The counselor who expects to reflect feelings well, however, must devote time and energy to expanding one's affective vocabulary since the possession of such a vocabulary will facilitate the process of reflecting feelings. Danish, D'Augelli, and Hauer (1980:40-42) have produced a list of 377 words designed to help expand one's affective vocabulary. Some time spent with such a list will improve the counselor's ability to reflect feelings. Categories of affective words are provided in the last section of this chapter.

Be Patient with the Reflective Process

Some counselors have said, "I tried the reflective process and gave it up. It didn't work." The authors' observation is that the process will work if the counselor gives it the time to work. You can't expect to apply reflection of feelings for ten minutes and see magnificent results. You must patiently and steadily apply it over a series of meetings before the process begins to produce results. It takes time to apply the reflective process and it takes time for the client to respond to the process.

We live in a society in which "doing it quickly" is too often the goal. We are surrounded by fast food enterprises, microwave ovens, jet travel, quick divorces, and computers that promise to work more quickly than their competitors. If we apply this attitude of quickness to reflecting feelings, then the process will fail. Reflecting feelings requires the utmost of patience in steadily applying it and making it work. There are no shortcuts, gimmicks, or tricks which will speed up the process. It takes time to do it well.

The time required to reflect feelings well and produce results should not be surprising if one looks at the typical problems possessed by clients. Those problems didn't develop yesterday or the day before. Client problems are basically interpersonal and have developed over a period of time. It seems logical, then, that time will be needed for the client to identify the cause of a problem and the best way to solve it. A client's problem that has developed over a period of two years will not be resolved by a counselor in one reflective counseling session.

THE PROCESS OF REFLECTING FEELINGS

Once the counselor has internalized the preceding conditions for reflecting feelings, the process can begin. Internalizing these conditions alerts the counselor to focus on the feelings of the client. The process cannot be effectively implemented until the counselor is attitudinally ready to hear the feelings which accompany the words, but it is this special kind of listening which enables the reflective process to occur. Following are some important elements of that process.

Read the Client's Feelings Accurately

Beneath almost everything that a client says is a set of feelings. These feelings are not often well verbalized, but they exist. Regardless of what the client may choose to discuss, feelings accompany that discussion. Even what appears to be an innocuous statement about snowfall will, more often than not, also contain feelings about the snowfall. The client may either feel elated about the snowfall because of the opportunity to "get away from it all and go skiing," or the client may be terrified about driving conditions.

Almost everything we say has two dimensions. The content dimension and the feeling dimension. The content dimension consists of the facts contained in a client's statement. The client may say, "I'm five feet two inches tall, weigh 175 pounds, and live in a three room apartment on Elm Street. If I could lose some weight, I'd feel a lot better about myself." The facts contained in the client's statement are the client's height, weight, size of apartment, and its location. The feeling contained in the client's statement is the dissatisfaction regarding being overweight and the effect of that added weight upon the client's self-concept. The reflective counselor pays no attention to the facts contained in the client's statement but pays full attention to the feeling contained in the statement. The client's feeling is read, absorbed, and internalized by the counselor and reflected back to the client with a statement approximating the following: "You don't feel good about your body image. You'd like to be able to lose some weight." Such a reflective statement will prompt the client to continue talking about feelings. Such a continuation will give the counselor additional feelings to reflect and will prompt the client to explore the same feeling more deeply or move on to discuss other related feelings. Each time that the client makes a statement containing a feeling, the counselor acknowledges the existence of that feeling by reflecting it. Reflecting feelings can be viewed as a conditioning process whereby the client is encouraged to express feelings because of the stimulus provided by the reflective responses.

The reflective counselor must hear what the client is feeling rather than what the client is saying, and those feelings must first be identified before they can be reflected. An accurate reading of the client's feelings will enable the counselor to make accurate reflections.

Be Sensitive to Same, New, or Conflicting Feelings

The reflective counselor stays attentive to the client's feelings. Those feelings often remain the same, especially at the beginning stages of counseling, but as counseling progresses, those feelings often undergo either obvious or subtle changes. The counselor must be alert to these changes.

A woman in counseling may spend a number of meetings expressing feelings or disappointment about her marriage. She may spend much time unraveling the feelings which reinforce that disappointment. At one meeting she may focus on her husband's financial irresponsibility, at another on his sexual disinterest, and at another, she may express disappointment about his lack of interest in being a good father. The feelings throughout these counseling sessions are constant: disappointment about her husband's attitudes and behavior. Toward the middle stages of counseling her feelings shift from disappointment to a new set of stronger feelings which revolve around anger toward her husband. The reflective counselor must be alert to the emergence of these new and stronger feelings, read them, and reflect them back to the client. As the counseling relationship continues, the client may begin to present conflicting feelings. Although she is angry about her husband's attitudes and behaviors, she also feels conflict because of a simultaneous and mysterious resurgence of the love she experienced at the beginning of her marriage. Such different feelings must be recognized by the counselor and reflected back to the client. There has been a change in the client's feelings and the counselor sensitizes the client to this change throughout the reflective process.

The client's movement from feelings of disappointment, anger, and renewed love does not occur in one meeting. These changes in feelings become expressed over a series of meetings. The last feeling, that of renewed love, is reached after having first worked through the feelings of disappointment and anger.

The preceding example is not presented as being the normal progression of feelings in counseling. It is merely presented as a example of how one client might process her feelings with a reflective counselor. A different client, with the same initial feelings and working with the same counselor, may move through an entirely different set of feelings about her marriage and husband and terminate counseling not with a renewed sense of love but with a clear determination to terminate the marriage. These different solutions can occur because the reflective process enables different clients to have different solutions to their problems. The solutions are individualized because of the application of the reflective process. The reflective process will produce as many different solutions as there are clients. The reflective process will stimulate individualized solutions. It focuses on the client's feelings and what the client wants to do about those feelings.

Each client has a unique set of feelings and gets in touch with them in very individualized way with a reflective counselor. The counselor must be sensitive to the fact that clients do move from one set of feelings to another and must be prepared to respond to these changes throughout the reflective process.

Reflect Primarily, But Also Clarify

When the counselor has achieved a reflective tempo in response to the client's feelings, that tempo has to be maintained in order for the client to receive help. When the counselor is able to steadily reflect the client's feelings, the client will have a release from those feelings and become able to move toward rational thoughts regarding how to solve a problem. Along the way, however, the client sometimes stumbles, becomes confused, and can give the counselor feelings which are confusing, complex, and contradictory. Some inexperienced counselors, who are overly committed to the reflective process, feel that every expression of feeling must be matched with an appropriate and accurate reflective response. Not all statements of feeling, however, are made with full clarity. Some feelings are couched in hesitation and uncertainty. Others are characterized by being ambiguous and contradictory. When the client is expressing feelings which fall into these categories, the experienced reflective counselor asks the client to clarify the intended feelings with statements like. "I don't quite understand that," "You're confusing me . . . please help me understand what you're feeling," "You're not quite certain how you feel and so am I," and "I'm confused . . . I don't know whether you feel good or bad about that."

If the client leads the counselor down a path of hesitant, uncertain, ambiguous, and contradictory feelings, and the counselor follows, then we have two confused participants in the counseling process. When confusing feelings are heard, the counselor realigns, refocuses, and expedites the reflective process by requesting that the client clarify these feelings (Egan, 1994).

Be Sensitive to Client Corrections of Reflections

Reflection of feelings is virtually a failproof process. The counselor can afford to be occasionally inaccurate when reflecting because the counselor's greatest ally for improving or correcting the accuracy of a reflection is the client.

After the counselor has established a reflective response pattern, the client begins to listen very carefully to what is being reflected. The client is essentially monitoring the counselor's reflections and judging his or her empathic accuracy. When the client hears the counselor responding with an inaccurate reflection, the client usually responds with, "That isn't quite what I feel. What I'm feeling is.... " Such corrections serve the reflective process well. They enable the counselor to improve or correct the accuracy of a reflective statement.

In recognizing this capacity of the client to refine, sharpen, and to align the counselor's response with the client's affective experiencing, Rogers recommended that the therapist response should not be labeled "Reflection of Feelings" but "Testing Understandings" or "Checking Perceptions." Every reflection of feeling can be regarded as a test of an affective empathic hypothesis in which the counselor tries to determine if the counselor's understanding of the client's inner world is correct. Rogers (1986) describes this testing of understanding :

> Each response of mine contains the unspoken question, "Is this the way it is in you? Am I catching just the color and the texture and flavor of the personal meaning you are experiencing right now? If not I wish to bring my perception in line with yours.

It is crucial for the counselor to be highly accurate with reflective responses at the beginning of a counseling relationship. Once the client begins to understand what the counselor is trying to accomplish through the reflective process, the client will make corrections when the counselor's reflections are inaccurate.

Be Disciplined in Applying Reflective Responses

In reflecting the client's feelings, the counselor assumes the internal frame of reference of the client and perceives experiences as the client perceives them.

When the counselor identifies with the feelings of the client, the counselor translates that identification into words that accurately represent the feelings of the client and mirrors back to the client those feelings so that the client may take a look at what they mean.

When the counselor accurately identifies with the feelings of the client and wants the client to know this, the counselor prefixes the reflection of feeling with such phrases as:

You are saying. . .
You feel. . .
If I understand you correctly. . .
I'm not sure I follow you, but is this it. . .
I gather that you mean. . .

Some counselors so deeply identify with the feelings of a client that their reflections of feelings gradually move from saying, "You feel that. . . " to "I feel that. . . " This kind of transition takes place when the counselor develops such a deep and empathic identification with the feelings of the client that it becomes more natural to use "I feel. . ." rather than "You feel. . ." when responding. Using "I" rather than "You" is a quantum step forward for the counselor; but when the step is taken, it occurs in a natural manner when the counselor feels so closely drawn to the feelings of the client that the most natural response involves the use of "I." The following *counselor* reflections of feelings convey the depth of empathic identification that can occur when responding to the feelings of clients by the use of "I":

I never could speak to her. . . I was always afraid that I'd be criticized.
It's hard to be me. . . I want to but I never seem to be able to say what's on my
   mind.
I wish I could get mad. . . but somehow I just don't think that I would be heard.
I feel myself moving toward becoming a more likable person and it's exciting!
I wish I could stop being my own worst enemy. . . sometimes I feel that if I
   could like me then things would begin to improve.
I'm confused. . . I was never like this before. . . before I seemed to have an idea
   of what to do.
If I could only do it then maybe my nervousness wouldn't be so bad.
There are times when I don't even understand myself. . . times when about all
   I know about me is my name.

Once again, the preceding statements are counselor responses to the feelings of clients. They represent reflections of client feelings; they are responses that counselors can comfortably make after they have accurately read the feelings of clients.

REFLECTING FEELINGS: EXPANDING ITS EFFECTIVENESS

Concrete Reflections

Prouty (1994) has made a significant contribution to the theory and practice of the reflective process through his work with clients suffering from schizophrenia and retarded psychoses. Noting that one of the six necessary and sufficient conditions for therapeutic personality change stated by Rogers (1957:96) "that two persons are in psychological contact," Prouty conceptualized *pre therapy* as a person centered methodology for therapists to help clients with severe communication impairments develop psychological contact with the World, Self, and Other (Merleau Ponty, 1962 as cited in Van Werde, 1994). The therapist establishes contact with the client on a very basic level of client experiencing through five different forms of therapeutic reflections. Through the following forms of reflection the therapist reflects back concrete client behavior and/or salient aspects from the surrounding environment (Van Werde,1994: 122-123):

Situational Reflections (SR) people, places, things, and events are reflected, for example, "The sun is shining," "we are in my office." These reflections facilitate the client's contact with his or her immediate environment.

Facial Reflections (FR) relect the emotion that is implicitly present on the face of the client, for example, "You smile," "Peter looks angry." These reflections facilitate the client's contact and expression of pre-expressive feeling.

Body Reflections (BR), reflect the client's movements or body postures by means of words or by empathically mirroring them, for example, "Your arm is up"; or perhaps the therapist rocks in his or her seat the same manner as the client. These reflections facilitate the client's immediate sensing of his/her body and help to form "here and now" reality contact.

Word-for-Word Reflections (WWR) mirror back to the client those words, sounds or sentences that are socially comprehensible or which seem meaningful for the client. These reflections facilitate the client's experiencing self once again as an expressor and communicator and work towards restoring functional speech.

Reiterative Reflections (RR) repeat previously successful reflections in order to strengthen the contact established and further facilitate the experiencing process, for example, "I said floor and you looked at me."

Van Werde (1994: 124) notes these reflections can be applied in " any relationship between two persons where one is in a vulnerable state and functioning on a pre-expressive level and the other is empathically present with the intention to enable the first person to come back from contact-loss into the world of feeling and communicating."

Incorporating Additives in the Reflective Process

Reflecting the client's feelings also has another potential–it can incorporate "additives," a procedure that has been explored by Carkhuff (1973), Egan (1994), and Turock (1978) and has been found to be effective as an expander of the reflective process. That is, a pure reflection of the client's feelings can be expanded to include an additive that is confrontative, interpretive, or challenging. When well timed, such additives can give the client an added dimension of self-awareness not typically included in a standard reflection of feeling. For example, a standard reflection by a counselor might be: "You feel discouraged and lonely during this period of your life."

A counselor additive that is *confrontative* would be: "You feel discouraged and lonely during this period of your life *and have lost the courage to do something about it.* " An additive that is *interpretive* would be: "You feel discouraged and lonely during this period of your life *and would feel much better if you only knew that your parents cared for you.*" An additive that is challenging would be: "You feel discouraged and lonely during this period of your life *and you are content to stay this way.*"

Reflecting the client's feelings can be done in a basic way or with additives that can be tacked on to a basic reflection. An additive can be used on certain occasions when such an additive gives the client a new insight that could not be achieved if the counselor's response was confined to just a basic reflection.

To Continue or Limit the Reflective Process?

Many clients achieve progress in solving their problems when the counselor does nothing else but empathically reflect their feelings. When the counselor only uses reflection of feelings throughout a counseling relationship, that process represents the application of the traditional and well-established, person-centered approach to counseling. To be traditionally person-centered is to follow a counseling theory for which there is more than ample research evidence indicating its effectiveness (Corey, 1996). If the counselor, however, decides that with another client the reflecting process has taken the client just so far and the client needs to go beyond that point, then the counselor can apply a different approach because that different approach better serves the needs of the client. The following guidelines, which were introduced in Chapter 1, are repeated here in order to reinforce when to move beyond the reflection of feelings in the counseling process. The counselor does this when the client:

1. Has achieved an emotional catharsis and is no longer overwhelmed by incapacitating feelings.

2. Is more open and honest in assessing the self and the attitudes and behaviors which constitute the self.

3. Shows a movement from emotionally-based communication to rationally-based communication.

4. Is motivated and willing to energize the self toward solving or resolving a problem.

This chapter represents our clarification of the foundation process of reflecting feelings. Its sections have dealt with the roots of the reflective process, the rationale for reflecting feelings, the conditions necessary for the reflective process to occur, and the process itself.

The counselor's attitudinal commitment to, and accurate application of, the reflective process has enormous potential. When applied well, the reflective process will improve a counselor's ability to help clients solve and resolve psychological problems on a deeper and more permanent basis. For the counselor who learns how to qualitatively apply the reflective process, the ultimate beneficiaries will be those clients who profit from its application. They will, perhaps for the first time in their lives, face their unexpressed negative feelings and denied experiences and by expressing them, enhance their ability to think and behave in positive and growth producing ways.

CATEGORIES OF AFFECTIVE WORDS*

Some time spent going over the words in each of the following categories will help expand one's affective vocabulary and improve the range of affective words used in reflections of feelings.

ASSERTIVE

aggressive	forceful
attacked	forward
baited	hostile
battered	independent
belligerent	mad
bitchy	responsible
brave	scold
bristling	self-centered
dominated	selfish
domineering	strong
eager	sure
esteemed	

Adapted from Danish, D'Augelli, and Hauer (1980).

COLD

accused
aloof
bored
empty
repulsed
repulsive
resistant

smug
stubborn
stupid
tired
ugly
uncomfortable

HAPPY

accepted
adventurous
agreeable
alive
amused
appreciative
approved
beautiful
bubbly
calm
ecstatic
elated
enticed
exhilarated
fortunate
friendly
funny
gay

grateful
happy-go-lucky
healthy
high
hopeful
independent
joyous
lively
overjoyed
proud
relieved
satiated
satisfied
silly
stimulated
successful
terrific
tickled
thrilled

HATEFUL

bitter
greedy
insulted
intolerant
jealous
malicious
mean
nasty
raped

ravished
revengeful
rotten
screwed
spiteful
tainted
unfriendly
violent

HOPELESS

abandoned	lost
alienated	moody
anguished	out-of-control
apart	powerless
beaten	removed
betrayed	ruined
boxed-in	shot down
bound-up	scared
distraught	smothered
doomed	squelched
dreadful	stifled
exposed	suffocated
hollow	trapped
hung-up	wiped out
incomplete	zapped
irresponsible	

HOT

burned	real
enthusiastic	tremendous
hyper	voluptuous
important	wild

IRRITATED

bugged	peeved
burned-up	perturbed
enraged	quarrelsome
exasperated	resentful
frustrated	scorned
furious	sickened
irate	tricked
irked	violated
ornery	

LOVING

affectionate	lustful
alluring	open

aroused
attached
attentive
attractive
enraptured
flattered
full
generous
giving
intimate
involved

responsive
seduced
seductive
sympathy
tender
tolerant
trustful
understanding
valuable
valued
willing

SAD

aching
aggravated
agony
alone
angry
annoyed
apologetic
apprehensive
argumentative
badgered
bereaved
down
grief
grim

grouchy
grumpy
hurt
left-out
lonely
miserable
offended
put-down
regretful
rejected
sinking
sorry
unhappy

SURPRISE

amazed
astonished
breathless
fascinated
horrified
impressed
numb

paralyzed
shocked
snowed
spontaneous
stunned
unaware

WARM

aware
genuine

smart
soft

helpful
patient
peaceful
perceptive
pleased
quiet
refreshed
safe
secure

soothed
sweet
under control
understood
useful
whole
wishful
wonderful
worthy

WHIMPY

belittled
broken-up
bruised
burdened
embarrassed
foolish
forced
frightened
hesitant
humiliated
ignorant
impotent
incompetent
innocent
insignificant
insincere
loose
misunderstood

pampered
phony
self-conscious
shy
sneaky
strangled
subdued
submissive
timid
unapproachable
unimportant
unstable
vulnerable
weak
whipped
withdrawn
wounded

WORRIED

anxious
awestruck
bothered
careful
distressed
distrustful
double-crossed
edgy
guarded

overwhelmed
panicky
petrified
pressured
pulled apart
puzzled
shattered
tense
terrified

impatient	tight
insecure	tormented
jittery	torn
mystified	tortured
nervous	uncertain
obsessed	uptight

REFERENCES

Bohart, A. C., & Greenberg, L. (1997). *Empathy reconsidered: new directions in psychotherapy.* Washington, DC: American Psychological Association.

Boy, A. V. (1982). Feelings influence thinking and behavior. *Religious Humanism.* 20.

Brammer, L. M., & Shostrom, E. L. (1982). *Therapeutic psychology: fundamentals of counseling and psychotherapy.* Englewood Cliffs, NJ: Prentice-Hall.

Carkhuff, R. R. (1973). *The art of problem solving.* Amherst, MA: Human Resources Development Press.

Corey, G. (1996). *Theory and practice of counseling and psychotherapy.* (5th ed.) Pacific Grove, CA: Brooks/Cole.

Danish, S. J., D'Augelli, A. R., & Hauer, A. L. (1980). *Helping skills: A basic training program.* New York: Human Sciences Press.

Egan, G. (1994) *The skilled helper* (5th ed.). Pacific Grove, CA: Brooks/Cole.

George, R. L., & Cristiani, T. S. (1981). *Theory, methods, and processes of counseling and psychotherapy.* Englewood Cliffs, NJ: Prentice-Hall.

Hansen, J. C., Stevic, R. R., & Warner, R. W., Jr. (1986). *Counseling: Theory and Process* (4th ed.) Boston: Allyn and Bacon.

Mearns, D. (1994). *Developing person-centered counseling.* Thousand Oaks, CA: Sage.

Prouty, G. (1994). *Theoretical evolutions in person-centered/experiential therapy: Applications to schizophrenic and retarded psychoses.* Westport, CT: Prager.

Rogers, C. R. (1942). *Counseling and psychotherapy.* Boston: Houghton Mifflin.

Rogers, C. R. (1951). *Client-centered-therapy.* Boston: Houghton Mifflin.

Rogers, C. R. (1975). Empathic: An unappreciated way of being. *The Counseling Psychologist, 5,* 2-10.

Rogers, C. R. (1982). Nuclear war: A personal response. *Monitor, 13,* 6-7.

Rogers, C. R. (1957) The necessary and sufficient conditions of therapeutic personality change. *Journal of Consulting Psychology, 21,* 2, 95-103.

Rogers, C. R. (1980) *A Way of Being.* Boston: Houghton-Mifflin.

Rogers, C. R. (1986). Reflection of feelings and transference. *Person-Centered Review. 1,*4, 375-377.

Schlein, J. (1987). Further thoughts on transference. *Person-Centered Review, 2,* 4, 455-470.

Seemans, J. (1986). Book Review of Empathy by A. P. Goldstein and G. Y. Michaels. Lawrence Erlbaum, Associates, Hillsdale, NJ (1985) in *Person-Centered Review, 1,* 230-232.

Sims, J. M. (1989). Client-centered therapy: The art of knowing. *Person-Centered Review, 1*, 27-41.

Tausch, R. (1988). The relationship between emotions and cognitions. *Person-Centered Review*, 33-54, 277-291.

Turock, A. (1978). Effective challenging through additive empathy. *The Personnel and Guidance Journal, 57*, 144- 149.

Van Werde, D. (1994). An introduction to client-centered pre-therapy. In D. Mearns, *Developing person-centered counseling* (121-124). Thousand Oaks, CA: Sage.

Watkins, C. E., Jr., & Goodyear, R. (1994). C. H. Patterson: Reflections on client-centered therapy. *Counselor Education and Supervision, 22*, 3, 178-186.

Chapter 3

THE IMPLICATIONS OF PERSON-CENTERED COUNSELING THEORY

Combs, Avila, and Purkey (1971) state that utilizing a theory has a useful function because a theory provides the helper with ". . . guides to action and makes his behavior more likely to be consistent and efficient."

Shertzer and Stone (1980:233) reinforce the importance of theory in their identification of a theory's major functions. They state that a theory:

1. Synthesizes a particular body of knowledge.
2. Increases the understanding of a particular body of knowledge.
3. Provides the tools by which predictions can be made.
4. Encourages further research into the area.

Kottler and Brown (1996:94) , in their discussion of theory construction, suggest that:

A theory....is a blueprint for action. The counselor's choices for interventions, reactions, analysis, and understanding all flow logically from a theoretical model of what people are like, what is good for them, and what conditions are likely to influence them in a self determined , desirable direction.

Through the careful examination and evaluation of a counseling theory, one can appreciate how practical a theory is. Theory has a number of useful functions:

Theory helps us to find relatedness, or some degree of unity, among diverse observations and experiences particularly as these occur in counseling and living situations. For example, counselors can bring some unity to their counseling when they are able to identify those counselor attitudes that are helpful to clients. Those helpful attitudes serve to improve counseling when they are the type that can be repeated in other counseling relationships. Implementing facilitative attitudes is made easier when the counselor has a theoretical foundation which gives meaning to those attitudes.

Theory compels us to observe relationships that we had previously overlooked. When counselors feel that a theoretical base for counseling is unimportant, each day is merely a series of unrelated events. Sally cried, Ted shouted, Henry became more withdrawn, Debbie was more evasive, Ann was anxious again. Counselors who possess a theoretical base see these client behaviors as having a relationship to each other. Theory can help us to understand the common affective foundation for each of these client behaviors.

Theory provides operational guidelines that help us in making provisional evaluations of the directions and desirability of our development as counselors. Counselors who possess a theoretical base move themselves toward decisions and solutions that are logical outcomes of their theory. They rarely find themselves in a blind alley in the decision-making process. They realize that one's theory will guide the counselor toward an appropriate decision. The strength of the decision will be in proportion to the strength of one's theory.

Theory focuses our attention on relevant data by telling us what to look for. Counselors who function from a theoretical base use primary and substantive facts in order to help clients. They don't rely on personal whims. Because these counselors think conceptually, they are able to see the wholeness of a problem as well as the necessity of assisting the client in developing a whole solution. They are able to conceptualize and behave in wholes because their theoretical base is whole.

Theory provides us with guidelines for helping clients modify their behavior more effectively. Counselors who function from a theoretical base are, intellectually and attitudinally, deeply involved. They are always seeking to deepen and widen their approaches and results. They look upon their theory as the most reasonable but they are also cautious. They realize that it can be improved. They know that the better they understand their theoretical base, the better will be its application.

Theory helps us to construct new approaches to counseling and point to ways of evaluating old ones. Counselors who possess a theoretical base have an awareness of the impact of their counseling behavior. They are also freer to be creative in their counseling because their theory motivates them to seek ways to improve rather than being static and content. As their theoretical base expands and evolves, their counseling behavior is also influenced to expand and evolve.

Kelley (1963:22) has pointed out that a theory provides a basis for the freedom needed to assess events:

> Theories are the thinking of men who seek freedom amid swirling events. The theories comprise prior assumptions about certain realms of these events. To

the extent that the events may, from these prior assumptions, be constructed, predicted, and their relative courses charted, men may exercise control and gain freedom for themselves in the process.

Recently, there have been profound changes in the ways we view the theoretical frameworks which frame our thinking about counseling and psychotherapy. Constructivism, multiculturalism, and feminist theory are significant intellectual, cultural, and social forces which are reshaping the theory and practice of counseling. Kottler and Brown (1996:96) observe that, historically, foundational counseling theory was primarily constructed by white, upper-middle class men and consequently reflected their biases. However, they indicate that constructivism and feminism have expanded the theoretical structures of counseling and psychotherapy to counter these biases.

Constructivist theoretical formulations (Anderson 1990; Efran, Lukens, &Lukens, 1990; and Gergen, 1991) propose that theory needs to be adapted to reflect the individual values, culture, gender, langauge, and perceptions of each client. "Rather than approaching our clients with our preconceptions about what their experiences might mean, we work instead to help them create their own meanings based on their cultural and perceptual background" (Kottler & Brown, 1996:96). Feminist theoretical formulations of counseling (Burstow, 1992; Cook, 1993; Enns, 1993) propose that theories be adapted to place a greater balance on values other than those emphasized by the dominant male culture. "This means that any of the theories...must take into consideration differences in gender roles, as well as diversity and complexity in human experiences" (Kottler & Brown, 1996:96).

Advocates for multicultural counseling focus on the value of diversity, argue that all counseling theories and relationships are formed and influenced by cultural norms and values, and call for counselors to become more sensitive, conscious, and understanding of their own cultural biases as well as the cultural contexts and values which influence their clients (Altarriba & Bauer, 1998; Atkinson, Morton, & Sue, 1993; Atkinson & Hackett, 1995; Axelson, 1993; Carney and Kahn, 1984; Casas & Pytluk, 1995; Cross, 1995; Helms, 1995; Ivey & Ivey, 1998; Kerwin & Ponteretto, 1995; Rowe, Behrens, & Leach, 1995; Lee, 1995; Pederson & Carey, 1994; Sabnani, Ponteretto, & Borodovsky, 1991; Sodowsky, Kwan, & Pannu, 1995; Sue, Ivey, Pederson, 1996; Sue & Sue, 1990).

Counseling theory is not constructed in a vacuum nor is it free of historical, cultural, and social conditions and forces. Theories are not static nor are they written in stone. They are best regarded as ongoing tentative hypotheses always subject to critical examination and change. Viewed in this way, theory offers us a foundation for constructing new counseling approaches which reflect changes in our knowledge and understanding of the human condition.

JUDGING A THEORY OF COUNSELING

When does an approach or concept of counseling possess enough substance to be legitimately classified as a theory? Should a counselor utilize a theory just because the counselor has a homemade idea regarding the best way to counsel? If a counselor counsels from a purely subjective base, how does the counselor objectively justify such a process?

A professional in any field must go beyond a personal bias in selecting and applying a theory. One of the behaviors characterizing any professional is the professional's sense of personal responsibility and public accountability in selecting and applying a theory. Certainly, we would not want a physician to treat us according to personal biases or hunches. We would instead want that physician to engage in a medical procedure that is based upon a set of objective standards that go beyond personal bias. We would want a physician to base treatment on a theory or set of procedures for which there is objective evidence indicating its effectiveness.

Experimentation in all fields is crucial if there is to be an advancement of knowledge. But experimentation must confine itself to experimental settings before it is publicly applied. All professionals possess the obligation to be certain that a theory has a reasonable chance of working before publicly applying it; and during an experimental period, there must be an adherence to standards and procedures so that the well-being of persons participating in the experimentation will be protected (American Psychological Association, 1982 & 1992).

Therefore, the professional counselor is obligated to apply a theory of counseling that meets the criteria for being a theory, rather than engaging in the practice of applying a personal bias. Counseling is both an art and a science and although the effective counselor is sensitive to the artful dimensions of counseling that rely on the counselor's personality, the effective counselor also pays attention to the scientific dimensions of counseling. Science rests on objectivity, and the effective counselor proceeds beyond self-serving needs and identifies objective criteria that support a legitimate theory.

What are the criteria that will enable a counselor to know when a theory is legitimate and has the potential to be successfully applied? Stefflre and Grant (1972: 4-7) offer the following criteria for judging whether or not a counseling theory has legitimacy as a theory. A theory should possess:

1. Assumptions regarding human nature
2. Beliefs regarding learning theory and changes in behavior
3. A commitment to certain goals of counseling
4. A definition of the role of the counselor
5. Research evidence supporting the theory.

Patterson (1986) identifies the following criteria for judging whether or not a counseling theory can be classified as a bona fide theory. A bona fide theory possesses:
1. Importance
2. Preciseness and clarity
3. Simplicity
4. Comprehensiveness
5. The ability to be applied
6. Empirical validity and verifiability
7. A stimulating substance.

Hansen, Stevic, and Warner (1980) focus on the following criteria for ascertaining the credibility of a counseling theory. They state that a theory must:
1. Be clear
2. Be comprehensive
3. Be stated in terms that are explicit enough to generate research
4. Relate means to desired outcomes
5. Have utility.

A legitimate theory of counseling should meet certain criteria, but no theory should lock the counselor into a fixed and mechanical set of procedures and responses. Although the counselor follows the general framework of a particular theory and operates within it, a theory should also enable the counselor to possess individuality and flexibility so that process judgments can be made that meet the individualized needs of clients. Dimick and Huff (1970:59) reinforce the view that a theory should provide individuality and flexibility for the counselor:

> A useful theory is molded for the individual and is well thought out, practical, and consistent with the behavior of the individual counselor. At the same time it is flexible enough to incorporate change by the individual counselor.

WHY PERSON-CENTERED COUNSELING?

A churchgoer who participates only in the rituals of a religion never really knows what is believed or why it is believed. This person's religious participation is often social and the whole matter of belief becomes a mixture of mysticism, auctions, bean suppers, incense, and sweet-smelling flowers. The practices of a person's religion become confused unless that religion is based upon some objective and subjective beliefs that give substance to its practice. *Something* has to serve as a rationale for one's religion, otherwise the practice of a religion becomes a hollow experience.

A religion that bases itself upon superficialities cannot hope to retain the commitment and belief of its followers over an extended period of time, because people need more than superficialities in order to achieve an *internal* feeling of belief. They need a spiritual awareness that enables them to deal with the fundamentals of life long after the sweet scents and appetizing foods have become victims of nature.

A counselor's adherence to a theory of counseling is very similar to a person's adherence to a religion. Some counselors believe only in superficialities, techniques, and rituals, while others believe because of the interplay of objective and subjective judgments that give depth to the belief and make it operational in one's work and life.

In this section, we will attempt to identify those objective and subjective reasons that have influenced us to support the theory and practice of person-entered counseling, in both its traditional form and in our eclectic extension.

Person-centered theory possesses a positive and affirming philosophy of the person. Person-centered counseling views the person as having basic impulses of love, belonging, and security, having the internal resources for growth, and as essentially cooperative, constructive, trustworthy, forward moving, rational, social, and realistic. These human qualities tend to become actualized in environments that encourage their emergence and tend to be dormant in environments that inhibit their emergence. Counseling, then, is the process of liberating a capacity that is inherent to the individual but has been stifled. The counselor enables this liberating to occur by genuinely owning attitudes toward the client that focus on respect, the individual's capacity and right to self-direction, and a prizing of the worth and significance of each individual (Patterson, 1986).

Person-centered theory articulates heuristic propositions regarding human personality and behavior. These propositions regarding human personality and behavior (Rogers, 1951: 483-524; Rogers1959: 184-256) form and reflect the philosophic core of person centered counseling and provide the counselor with a general conceptual framework for understanding human motivation. These propositions view the person as:

1. Being the best determiner of personal reality
2. Behaving as an organized whole
3. Desiring to enhance the self
4. Goal-directed in satisfying perceived needs
5. Being behaviorally influenced by feelings that affect rationality
6. Best able to perceive the self
7. Being able to be aware of the self
8. Valuing
9. Interested in maintaining a positive self-concept
10. Behaving in ways that are consistent with the self-concept

11. Not owning behavior that is inconsistent with the self-concept
12. Producing psychological freedom or tension by admitting or not admitting certain experiences into the self-concept
13. Responding to threat by becoming behaviorally rigid
14. Admitting to awareness experiences that are inconsistent with the self if the self is free from threat
15. Being more understanding of others if a well integrated self-concept exists
16. Moving from self-defeating values toward self-sustaining values.

We are attracted to person-centered counseling because we are congruent with its theory of human personality and behavior that serves as the foundation for the process of counseling and makes it understandable and applicable.

Person-centered theory possesses achievable human goals for the client. The goals of person-centered counseling are very personalized and human goals for *the client* rather than being goals designed to simply support the theory, society, or its institutions; but in achieving these personalized goals, the client will behave in ways that contribute to the well being of society and its institutions. Although the goals of person-centered counseling are general, they are interpreted and translated by the individual client and can become applicable to the client's life outside of counseling. Person-centered counseling is aimed at helping the client to:

1. Engage in behavior that liberates, actualizes, and enhances the self
2. Engage in the discovery of previously denied feelings and attitudes
3. Become more acceptant and trustful of the self
4. Engage in self-assessment
5. Engage in reorganizing the self
6. Become more self-reliant
7. Become more responsible for the self
8. Engage in self-determined choices, decisions, and solutions
9. Achieve individuality while being conscious of social responsibilities
10. Become sensitive to the process of becoming a person that involves a new and self-actualizing way of being.

Our experience as counselors indicates that these client goals represent a process that can bring the client closer to an optimum level of psychological stability. We have experienced clients' achieving these goals in proportion to the quality of the person-centered counseling that was offered.

Person-centered theory possesses a definition of the counselor's role within the counseling relationship. The counselor's person-centered attitude toward the client finds its expression in the following behaviors. The counselor is understanding, liberal, acceptant, empathic, a sensitive listener, authentic, and possesses a sense of involvement while equalizing the relationship.

While identifying the necessary counselor behaviors for effective counseling, the person-centered viewpoint also indicates counselor behaviors to be avoided. The counselor is not a moralist, questioner, or diagnostician.

An enlightening aspect of person-centered counseling is that it defines the counselor's role in terms of attitudes and behaviors that will both facilitate and inhibit the client's progress in counseling. Our experience as counselors confirms that when we exhibit the desired counselor attitudes and behaviors our counseling is beneficial to clients, and when we exhibit undesirable attitudes and behaviors, the outcome is to inhibit the client's movement toward improved behavior.

In Phase Two of our eclectic application of person-centered counseling, the counselor tends to be more concrete and open to personal reactions to the client and is comfortable in expressing these reactions to the client; but these reactions are always focused on the person-centered concept of client needs rather than being expressions of the counselor's need to be a moralist, questioner, or diagnostician.

Person-centered theory has research evidence supporting its effectiveness. Although person-centered counseling, like all other theories of counseling, is more an art than a science, we feel that any theory of counseling must also satisfy the requirements of science by possessing both qualitative and quantitative research evidence that objectively confirms the effectiveness of the theory. In this area, person-centered counseling does not let us down. It does possess the desired research evidence that supports its effectiveness. In fact, it goes far beyond the requirements in this area. As Patterson (1986:412) has observed: ". . . it must be noted that the client-centered approach has led to, and is supported by, a greater amount of research than any other approach to counseling or psychotherapy."

Corey (1996:113) also acknowledges the attention that has been paid to developing the research evidence that supports person-centered counseling: "Perhaps more than any other single approach to psychotherapy, client-centered theory has developed through research on the process and outcomes of therapy."

From our own investigations and research into the effectiveness of person-centered counseling (Arbuckle & Boy, 1961; Boy & Pine, 1963, 1968) and its application to learner-centered teaching (Pine & Boy, 1977), plus the far more voluminous investigations and research by others, we feel that person-centered counseling has more than met its obligation to be supported by research evidence.

Person-centered theory is comprehensive. Person-centered counseling has the needed substance to be applied beyond the one-to-one counseling relationship. The comprehensive nature of the person-centered view is seen in its application to teaching, organizational behavior, family relationships, parenting, groups, marriage and its alternatives, leadership, pastoring, and inter-personal relationships, in general.

Another indication of its comprehensiveness is that the same principles of person-centered counseling can be applied to all persons– "normals," "neu-rotics," and "psychotics" (Corey, 1996). The comprehensiveness of person-centered counseling enables it to be applied by counselors in a variety of set-tings dealing with a wide range of human problems: mental health centers; elementary, middle, and high schools; colleges and universities; rehabilita-tion agencies; prisons and halfway houses; pastoral counseling centers; mar-riage and family centers; human development centers; employment service agencies; youth centers; religious seminaries; and professional schools of law, medicine, and dentistry.

From our experience, the depth and range of the person-centered view-point enables it to be applied in any agency that deals with human problems. We have been able to apply it to our individual and group counseling, con-sultation, staff relations, teaching, family living, friendships, administrative functions, interpersonal relationships, and recreational and spiritual experi-ences. Whenever it has been well applied, we possessed an attitudinal and behavioral congruence with the philosophy and process of person-centered counseling. Whenever we stumbled or failed, it was because we were attitu-dinally and behaviorally detached from its philosophic and process cores. We sense that the person-centered theory is comprehensive enough to be applied in interpersonal relations and encounters that have yet to be identi-fied.

Person-centered theory can be applied. Person-centered counseling is clear and precise enough so that it can be applied. At the process level, the coun-selor's reflections of the client's feelings is an understandable concept that is applicable in proportion to the counselor's grasp of why it is done and how such reflections contribute to the client's self-awareness and needs. We see no difficulty in applying person-centered counseling when the counselor is *atti-tudinally* person-centered. When a counselor is not *attitudinally* person-cen-tered, then that counselor has difficulty in intellectually absorbing and apply-ing reflections of the client's feelings. Such a counselor typically reflects the surface content of what the client is saying rather than reflecting the feelings below the surface. When the counselor does this, the results are innocuous, bland, and ineffective, and the counselor gives up the application of person-centered counseling. But this counselor doesn't give up person-centered counseling because the counselor never applied it. What the counselor applied was a misinterpretation of the person-centered approach rather than the approach itself.

To us, the process of reflecting feelings appears to be simple while actual-ly being quite complex. A counselor's ability to accurately reflect feelings depends upon his or her ability to read and absorb those feelings, the ability to accurately represent those feelings back to the client, and a vocabulary range that can reflect a core feeling to a client in a number of descriptive ways. And once again, the quality and depth of a counselor's reflections are proportional to the degree to which the counselor is *attitudinally* person-centered.

Phase Two of our eclectic application of person-centered counseling becomes effective in proportion to the quality of Phase One. If Phase One was qualitative and if the relationship between the counselor and client is interpersonally solid and equalized, then Phase Two takes place in a natural sequence of events.

The only danger in our concept of Phase Two is *that the counselor's* personal needs for domination, moralization, or righteousness could impinge upon and influence the counselor's responses, and the result could be the creation of a forum for the counselor's expression of personal ideologies rather than the development of a Phase Two which meets the needs of the client. But once again this will not occur if the counselor is *attitudinally* person-centered.

Our experience in the preparation of counselors indicates that our eclectic application of person-centered counseling is both teachable and applicable, and becomes teachable and applicable only in proportion to the degree to which we are able to model the attitudes and behaviors that characterize both phases.

Person-centered theory has an expansive intellectual and attitudinal substance. Intellectually, person-centered counseling keeps us alert to better understand its philosophy, process, goals, and outcomes. On some days, there are rays of intellectual insight that give wholeness to the viewpoint, while on other days, a personal experience, or the experiencing of another very different viewpoint, causes us to wonder about the veracity of person-centeredness. From these insights and uncertainties a clarity or synthesis emerges that serves to energize our intellectual understanding of the theory. We are always alert to, and challenged by, the ability of person-centeredness to be intellectually stimulating. It possesses an intellectual *gravitas* which can sometimes exceed our grasp, but we respect the viewpoint's ability to keep our brain cells curious and electrified.

Another intellectually stimulating aspect of person-centeredness is its congruence with other past and present systems of thought. The writings of existentialists, humanists, phenomenologists, theists, rationalists, and politicians take on a clarity because we have a person-centered point of reference from which to better understand these other views. Without this point of reference, our understanding would be superficial and partial.

Attitudinally, person-centeredness gives us a process by which our spiritual tendencies can be expressed. Those who possess spiritual inclinations often have difficulty identifying a career in which that spirituality can be expressed. Person-centeredness appears to be the bridge that connects our spiritual tendencies to the real world of interpersonal relationships; it enables us to express those values that deal with truth, honesty, beauty, justice, love, human rights, and peace. The congruence between person-centered counseling and our spiritual tendencies gives us a feeling of unity.

Person-centered theory focuses on the client as a person rather than on the client's problem. Person-centered counseling has much to say about the improvement of the human condition. It is person-centered rather than technique-centered, process-centered, or counselor-centered. It fundamentally focuses on *the client as a person* rather than on the client's problem, and this, to us, is where the focus should be.

When the counselor is able to assist a client to become a more adequate and better functioning person, this improvement will enable the client to solve current and future problems. When the client becomes psychologically stable, that client is able to deal with problems because that stability leads to affective and rational solutions. From psychological stability come insights and attitudes that produce behaviors designed to overcome identified problems.

Other theories of counseling focus on the client's problems rather than the psychological stability of the client and produce a short-range and temporary solution to a problem while often neglecting to affect the cause of the problem—the client as a person.

Since person-centered counseling focuses on the person rather than the problem, it possesses a deeper potential for assisting a person to become more adequate, *as a person*, in dealing with a range of problems that we all have to face in life. The stronger the personhood of the client, the better able the client is to deal with, and find solutions to, specific problems.

Person-centered theory focuses on the attitudes of the counselor rather than on techniques. The counselor's facilitative attitudes all flow from the personhood of the counselor. If we desire clients to develop themselves as persons, then we must also expect the counselor to do the same if he or she is to be influential in affecting behavioral change among clients. We cannot expect the client to become a more adequate and better functioning person if the counselor does not model attitudes that enable these behaviors to emerge from the client.

The personhood of the counselor, when expressed through a qualitative counseling relationship, becomes the primary influence that prompts the client to move toward more satisfying and sustaining behavior. Some counseling approaches have given little focus to the therapeutic influence of the counselor as a person giving more attention to the development of mechanical techniques to induce behavioral change. These techniques can sometimes be useful (role playing, Gestalt empty chair, confrontation, goal identification) if they are used as *an adjunct* to the personhood of the counselor. In too many cases, however, such techniques are the core of the counseling process and the therapeutic influence of the *counselor as a person* is neglected.

If one listens to clients describe how a counselor has helped them, one will hear these clients describe the counselor's personhood as the *primary influence* rather than the techniques the counselor employed.

Person-centered theory provides the counselor with a systematic response pattern. Most theories of counseling make insightful statements regarding their philosophy, goals, process, and outcomes. Their philosophic, goal-oriented, and outcome statements are often noble and sometimes border on the poetic when describing the human condition and its improvement. But most counseling theories do not present the student-counselor or practitioner with a systematic response pattern whereby the counselor is able to assist the client in moving toward these philosophically noble goals and outcomes. These theories address themselves to the "why" of counseling but provide the counselor with little regarding the process or "how" of counseling.

Person-centered counseling presents the most clear and well defined response pattern to guide the counselor in the process of counseling: empathically reflecting the client's feelings and establishing core conditions of genuineness and unconditional positive regard. This response pattern enables the counselor to assimilate the client's perceptions, values, and attitudes and how these affect the client's behavior; it enables the client to develop an awareness of how these perceptions, values, and attitudes affect behavior; it enables the client to go beyond a presenting problem; it gives the client the time to get at subconscious or unconscious material; it enables the client to perceive the counselor as a caring person who is able to understand the client's problem from the client's viewpoint; it serves to free the client to communicate values and attitudes that the client was not able to disclose in other interpersonal relationships; and it serves to establish the client/counselor trust needed for effective counseling.

Although reflecting the client's feelings may be sufficient and effective throughout a counseling relationship and has the potential to influence behavioral change, Phase Two of our eclectic application of person-centered counseling enables the counselor to go beyond reflecting feelings *if such help more adequately meets the needs of clients.* Further, if in this transition from Phase One to Phase Two progress and therapeutic movement do not occur for the client, the counselor is able to return to reflecting the client's feelings in order to better clarify the client's perceptions, values, and attitudes, thereby developing a more accurate understanding of the client's problem which can lead to a more accurate and effective Phase Two. Reflecting the client's feelings, then, offers the counselor a systematic empathic response pattern that serves as the core of the counselor's responses in Phase One but is not the only response pattern available to the counselor in Phase Two.

Person-centered theory provides flexibility for the counselor to go beyond reflection of feelings. In the first two historic periods of person-centered counseling, perhaps some person-centered counselors were in a verbal straightjacket when they only reflected the client's feelings. During these two periods, however, there were some other person-centered counselors who felt free and comfortable with reflecting the client's feelings and saw evidence that such a process was therapeutically effective.

We believe in, and have continually experienced, the therapeutic effectiveness of reflecting feelings. Reflecting the client's feelings does not have to be bland; the process can be lively, penetrating, and expanding in proportion to the counselor's ability to read the feelings of clients and the counselor's disciplined commitment to the process. A pure reflection of the client's feelings does possess therapeutic impact in that it prompts the client to investigate previously denied feelings and bring them into awareness.

In the third (Hart, 1970) and fourth (Corey, 1996) historic periods of person-centered counseling, person-centered counselors have engaged in behaviors, mostly counselor self-disclosure, which have gone beyond just reflecting the client's feelings. In Phase Two of our eclectic application of person-centered counseling, the counselor has five choices: (1) the counselor can continue to engage in pure reflections of feelings if doing this best meets the therapeutic needs of the client; (2) the counselor can make additives to basic reflections of feelings if doing this best meets the therapeutic needs of the client; (3) the counselor can incorporate techniques from nonperson-centered theories of counseling if doing this best meets the therapeutic needs of the client; (4) the counselor can make use of the helping procedures contained in the creative arts; and (5) the counselor can make a natural and responsible judgment to do something natural, intuitive, and eclectic if this best meets the therapeutic needs of the client. As Rogers (1980:5) has said, "sometimes a feeling rises up in me which seems to have no particular relationship to what is going on. Yet I have learned to accept and trust this feeling in my awareness and try to communicate it to my client."

Person-centered counseling is not a set of static and hardened principles. It gives the counselor a high degree of flexibility if one is willing to absorb the implications of what it means to be person-centered. In our opinion, this means that the counselor's behavior is within the bounds of the theory when it is person-centered and meets the needs of the client, and the counselor's behavior is outside the bounds of the theory and is counselor-centered when it instead meets the needs of the counselor.

Person-centered theory can be individualized according to the particular needs of a client. Person-centered counseling's ability to be flexible enables it to more accurately meet the particular needs of clients. It should not be viewed as a fixed theory that does not have the malleability to be shaped toward a client's unique needs. Person-centeredness can be individualized to meet client needs and this is one of its inherent strengths.

Some clients can become manipulated by the requirements of a theory rather than having their needs met. If a theory requires that clients behave realistically, then clients *must be* molded to behave realistically; if a theory sees the problems of adulthood rooted in the experiences of childhood, then the client *must be* prompted to recall those inhibiting childhood experiences; and if a theory postulates that repressed anger is the cause of a client's problem, then the client *must be* confronted in order to release that anger. Counseling according to a narrow theoretical bias can result in a particular theory being thrust on all clients, regardless of their individualized needs or problems. The client whose problem is far from the need to be realistic is molded to be realistic; the client whose problem is situational and far removed from childhood is prompted to delve into childhood experiences; and the client whose problem is far removed from the need to express anger is confronted to release a nonexistent anger.

The flexibility of the person-centered approach enables it to be individualized according to the needs of the client. The theory has no grandiose message that the counselor has to deliver to clients. What the theory does require is the development of a collaborative relationship in which *the client* can identify the problem and a relationship and in which *the client* can choose the behaviors that will enable the problem to be solved. A person-centered relationship is open and flexible because the client is the one who determines the scope, depth, and intensity of a problem, and once this recognition has occurred, the client is in the best best position to determine the process through which the problem will be solved. Such an individualization of the counseling process enables person-centeredness to be directly joined to client needs.

Person-centered theory enables client behavior to change in a natural sequence. A client who enters a counseling relationship typically has an interpersonal communication problem with a person or persons in their lives. The cause of the problem is usually that the client is unable to honestly communicate with that person or persons and, as a result, has repressed a large number of negative feelings. Such a repression of feelings often produces tension, behavioral confusion, and physical symptoms.

In Phase One, the counselor establishes a relationship with the client in which these repressed feelings can become expressed. The counselor accomplishes this essentially by reflecting whatever feelings the client may present. If the counselor's reflections are accurate, the client becomes more comfortable in the relationship and feels secure enough to go more deeply into these feelings and also explore other feelings.

Once a client has expressed previously repressed feelings and feels released from the debilitating effects of such feelings, the natural inclination is for the client to begin to seek a solution to the conflict that initially brought the client to counseling. At this stage, because the client feels emotionally cleansed, the client moves away from emotionally-based attitudes and reactions and toward identifying a rational solution to the problem. Because the client is no longer in an emotional knot, the client can begin to work toward an objective rational solution. The resources of the client's intellect, clouded by emotions in the past, are now free to function and move toward a rational solution. All persons are both emotional and rational, and problems often develop because our emotions overpower our ability to think. Once we have released and tamed our emotions, we free our intellect to function clearly and bring us to a reasonable solution.

In our eclectic application of person-centered counseling, the counselor can follow this natural sequence of events by basically reflecting the client's feelings in Phase One. In Phase Two, as the client becomes more rational, the counselor can begin to respond to the client by using more rational and objective responses.

An important aspect of effective counseling, regardless of theory, is that a counselor should respond affectively to an emotionally burdened client and should respond rationally to a client who communicates rationally. Our viewpoint is that clients are generally emotional at the beginning and middle stages of counseling and are more rational during the later stages of counseling. Therefore, the counselor's response pattern should parallel the client's emotionality or rationality if counseling is to be effective.

Person-centered theory can draw from the process components of other theories of counseling and human development. We wish to emphasize that in Phase Two, the person-centered counselor in collaboration with the client can draw from other theories those procedures that possess potential for meeting the individualized and unique needs of clients. *Only three criteria have to be met in selecting the process components of other theories: the client is empowered to accept or reject the technique or approach, the approach or technique is compatible with person-centered values, and the selection is made to meet client needs.*

In some cases, person-centered counseling has failed to develop such eclectic procedures because they have been perceived to be inamicable with the relationship-centered philosophy of person-centered counseling; namely, that the *relationship itself* if it were of sufficient quality, could influence behavior change on the part of the client and that such procedures were too superficial and mechanical to be accommodated within the purity of an affective relationship and would, in fact, interfere with that relationship.

This perspective has resulted in person-centered theory not developing a usable set of diverse procedures. The one exception is the counselor's reflecting of the client's feelings, which some classify as a technique or procedure which can be applied regardless of the level of counselor empathy. Since the person-centered approach is basically without techniques and procedures and relies more on the counseling relationship itself for behavioral change, the counselor who is at Phase Two may need to look, with the client, to other theories in order to identify viable techniques or procedures such as role playing, fantasizing, desensitization, goal identification, modeling, encouragement, and confrontation. But if the person-centered relationship developed in Phase One is of sufficient quality, the counselor in collaboration with the client should be able to utilize modified versions of these techniques especially if they can accurately meet the individualized needs of clients and are consistent with person-centered values.

The counselor and client decision about what to do in Phase Two can also be concrete and based upon common sense as in the following illustration. The counselor had counseled a female client on a weekly basis for about nine months. The client had a poor self-concept and felt that she was physically unattractive and unable to feel comfortable in her relationships with peers. The client became isolated, lonely, shy, and depressed. The counselor responded to her feelings by reflecting those feelings, and although the client felt close to the counselor and appreciated the counselor's genuineness and warmth, there was no improvement in her self-concept and, hence, no improvement in her behavior. As the counseling relationship developed, the counselor took more notice of the client's decaying teeth as the client began to talk about herself negatively because of the condition of her teeth. The counselor made a common sense judgment to help the client improve the condition of her teeth. Since the client had no finances and came from an economically deprived family, she felt that she was forever doomed to carry a negative self-concept and to become more introverted as a result.

The counselor with the consent of the client decided to telephone a nearby dental school and inquire about the possibility of free dental work for the client. The dental school was cooperative, and, with the counselor's support, the client arranged to make a series of visits to the school's dental clinic which was staffed by interns. After the client completed her dental work, which necessitated the removal of all existing teeth and replacing them with full upper and lower plates, there was a dramatic improvement in her self-concept. She became friendly and gregarious and was no longer isolated, shy, and depressed. Her new appearance gave her confidence in meeting people and she became confident about what life held in store for her.

The person-centered counselor in this case could have complicated and inhibited the client's development of a positive self-concept by continuing to reflect her feelings, making additives to the reflections, or using a technique from another theory of counseling. The counselor chose not to do any of these in Phase Two, but instead made a common sense judgment that result-ed in a dramatic improvement in the client's self-concept.

Such common sense judgments are available in Phase Two when the per-son-centered counselor is not theory bound but instead is flexible and responsive and open in collaborating with the client to bend the theory toward the individualized needs of the client.

Person-centered theory is cross-cultural. Counseling theories are generic frameworks not specific to every potential client's aesthetic, behavioral, developmental, economic, emotional, cultural, psychological, psychosexual, physical, social, and spiritual need. Theories do not vary depending on whether the client is a man, a woman, an Asian American, or a person with a disability. (Weinrach & Thomas, 1998). Kottler & Brown (1996:274) note that:

> The same counseling skills are used with women as with men. Depression or anxiety does not feel qualitatively different to a Chicano, African, American, or Caucasian. Group dynamics operate in similar ways in groups of children, middle-aged adults, and older adults. Gay men and lesbian women feel loneli-ness frustration, or anger just as do heterosexuals. The delinquent, disabled, or drug addicted clients all respond to empathy, confrontation, and other thera-peutic strategies, depending on the counselor's finesse and sensitivity.

Person-centered theory is not bounded by culture. Empathy, uncondi-tional regard, and congruence reflect a respectful valuing of each person as unique and precious and a complex mixture of cultural influences and idio-syncratic characteristics and most important as a person better able able than the counselor to judge what is in her/his own best interests. In person-cen-tered counseling, it is the congruence between the counselor's values, beliefs, words, and behavior which constitute the psychological integrity essential to achieving and deserving a client's trust (Malcolm,1998). The facilitative and core conditions of person-centered counseling are transcendent reflecting the principle "that the most basic and common characteristic of humankind, indeed, of all living organisms, is the need to develop or actualize their potentials or abilities" (Watkins & Goodyear, 1994:184).

In summary, we believe that an effective person-centered counselor both believes and doubts. Within the framework of the theory of person-centered counseling, there is much that is applicable in the process of assisting clients; but there are certain other aspects of the theory we must be willing to doubt in order to shed new light not only on the theory itself but on the process of counseling. A competent counselor is one who believes in a theory but also maintains a flexibility regarding the theory and its application. This flexibil-ity is necessary in order to shape theory to meet the needs of clients rather than shaping clients to meet the needs of theory.

The flexibility needed by a counselor is aptly represented by the following two historic statements:

No scientific investigation is final; it merely represents the most probable conclusion which can be drawn from the data at the disposal of the writer. A wider range of facts or more refined analysis, experiment. and observation will lead to new formulas and new theories. This is the essence of scientific progress (Pearson, 1897).

Knowledge progresses by stages, so that the theory one holds today must be provisional, as much a formulation of one's ignorance as anything else, to be used as long as it is useful and then discarded. Its function is to organize the available evidence. It is really a working assumption which the user may actively disbelieve (Hebb, 1958).

REFERENCES

Altarriba, J., & Bauer, L. M. (1998). Counseling the Hispanic client: Cuban Americans, Mexican Americans, and Puerto Ricans. *Journal of Counseling and Development.* 76, 4, 389-396.

American Psychological Association. (1982). *Ethical principles in the conduct of research with human participants.* New York: APA.

American Psychological Association. (1992). *Ethical principles of psychologists, American Psychological Association.* New York: APA.

Anderson, W. T. (1990). *Reality isn't what it used to be.* San Francisco: Harper Collins.

Arbuckle, D. S., & Boy, A. V. (1961). Client-centered therapy in counseling students with behavior problems. *Journal of Counseling Psychology, 8,* 136-139.

Atkinson, D. R., Morton, G., & Sue, D.W. (Eds.). (1993). *Counseling American minorities: A cross cultural perspective* (4th ed.). Dubuque, IA: William C. Brown.

Atkinson, D. R., & Hackett, G. (1995). *Counseling diverse populations.* Dubuque, IA: William C. Brown.

Axelson, J. A. (1993). *Counseling and development in a multicultural society* (2nd ed.). Dubuque, IA: William C. Brown.

Boy, A. V., & Pine, G. J. (1963). *Client-centered counseling in the secondary school* Boston: Houghton Mifflin.

Boy, A. V., & Pine, G. J. (1968). *The counselor in the schools: A reconceptualization.* Boston: Houghton Mifflin.

Burstow, B. (1992). *Radical feminist therapy.* Newbury Park, CA: Sage Publishing

Carkhuff, R. R., & Berenson, B. G. (1967). *Beyond counseling and therapy.* New York: Holt, Rinehart and Winston.

Carney, C. G., & Kahn, K. B. (1984). Building competencies for effective cross cultural counseling: A developmental view. *The Counseling Psychologist, 12,* 111-119.

Casas, J. M., & Pytluk, S. D. (1995:155-180) Hispanic identity development: Implications for research and practice. In J. G. Ponteretto, J. M. Casas, L. A.

Suzuki, & C. M. Alexander (Eds.). *Handbook of multicultural counseling* (155-180). Thousand Oaks, CA: Sage.

Combs, A. W., Avila, D. L., & Purkey, W. W. (1971). *Helping Relationships: Basic concepts for the helping professions* (2nd ed.). Boston: Allyn and Bacon.

Cook, E. P. (Ed.). (1993). *Women, relationships, and power.* Alexandria, VA: American Counseling Association.

Corey, G. (1996). *Theory and practice of counseling and psychotherapy* (5th ed.). Pacific Grove, CA: Brooks/Cole.

Cross, W. E., Jr. (1995). The psychology of nigrescence: Revisiting the Cross model. In J. G. Ponteretto, J. M. Casas, L.A. Suzuki, & C.M. Alexander (Eds.), *Handbook of multicultural counseling* (93-122). Thousand Oaks, CA: Sage.

Dimik, K. M., & Huff, V. E. (1970). *Child counseling.* Dubuque, IA: Wm. C. Brown.

Efran, J. S., Lukens, M. D., & Lukens, R. J. (1990). *Language, structure, and change.* New York: W.W. Norton.

Enns, C. Z. (1993). Twenty years of feminist counseling and therapy. *Counseling Psychologist. 21*, 1, 3-87.

Gergen, K. J. (1991). *The saturated self.* New York: Basic Books.

Hansen, J. C., Stevic, R. R., & Warner, R. W. (1986). *Counseling: Theory and process* (3rd ed.). Boston: Allyn and Bacon.

Hart, J. (1970). The development of client-centered therapy. In J. T. Hart & T. M. Tomlinson (Eds). *New directions in client-centered therapy.* Boston: Houghton Mifflin, 3-11 (a).

Hebb, D. O. (1958). *A textbook of psychology.* Philadelphia: Saunders.

Helms, J. E. (1995). An update of Helm's White and people of color racial identity models. In J. G. Ponteretto, J. M.Casas, L. A. Suzuki, & C. M. Alexander (Eds.), *Handbook of multicultural counseling* (181-198). Thousand Oaks, CA: Sage.

Ivey, A. E, & Ivey, M. B. (1999) *Intentional interviewing and counseling: Facilitating client development in a multicultural society* (4th ed.). Belmont, CA: Brooks/Cole-Wadsworth.

Kelley, G. A. (1963). *A theory of personality.* New York: Norton.

Kerwin, C., & Ponteretto, J. G. (1995). Biracial identity development theory and research. In J. G. Ponteretto, J. M. Casas, L. A. Suzuki, & C. M. Akexander (Eds.), *Handbook of multicultural counseling* (199-217), Thousand Oaks, CA: Sage.

Kottler, J. A., & Brown, R. W. (1996. Introduction to therapeutic counseling (3rd ed.). Pacific Grove, CA: Brooks/Cole.

Lee, C. C. (1995). *Counseling for diversity.* Boston: Allyn Bacon.

Malcolm, D. D. (1998). Another counselor educator's personal observations about the Rogerian approach and cross cultural counseling. *ACES Spectrum. 58*,3, 12 &16.

Patterson, C. H. (1986). *Theories of counseling and psychotherapy* (4th ed). New York: Harper and Row.

Pearson, K. (1897). *The chance of death and other studies in evolution.* London: E. Arnold.

Pine, G. J., & Boy, A. V. (1977). *Learner-centered teaching: A humanistic view.* Denver: Love.

Polster, E., & Polster, M. (1973). *Gestalt therapy integrated: Contours of theory and practice.* New York: Bruner/Mazel.

Rogers, C. R. (1951, renewed 1979). *Client-centered therapy.* Boston: Houghton Mifflin, 3-4.

Rogers, C. R. (1959). A theory of therapy, personality, and interpersonal relationships, as developed in the client- centered framework. In S. Koch (Ed.). *Psychology: A study of science. Study I. Conceptual and systematic.* Vol. 3. *Formulations of the person in the social context.* New York: McGraw-Hill.

Rogers, C. R. (1980). *A way of being.* Boston: Houghton Mifflin.

Rowe, W., Behrens, J. T., &Leach, M. M. (1995). Racial/ethnic identity and racial consciousness: Looking back and looking forward. In J. G. Ponteretto, J. M. Casas, L. A. Suzuki, & C. M. Alexander (Eds.), *Handbook of multicultural counseling* (218-235). Thousand Oaks, CA: Sage.

Shertzer, B., & Stone, S. C. (1980). *Fundamentals of counseling* (3rd ed.). New York: McGraw-Hill.

Sodwosky, G. R., Kwan, K-l. K., & Pannu, R. (1995). Ethnic idnetity of Asians in the United States. In J. G. Ponteretto, J. M. Casas, L. A. Suzuki, & C. M. Alexander (Eds), *Handbook of multicultural counseling* (123-154). Thousand Oaks, CA: Sage.

Stefflre, B., & Grant, W. (Eds.). (1972). *Theories of Counseling.* New York: McGraw-Hill.

Sue, D. W., Ivey, A. E., & Pederson, P. B. (1996). *A theory of multicultural counseling and therapy.* Pacific Grove, CA: Brooks/Cole.

Sue, D. W., & Sue, D. (1990). *Counseling the culturally different* (2nd ed.). New York: Wiley.

Watkins, C. E. Jr., & Goodyear, R. K. (1994). C. H. Patterson: Reflections on client-centered therapy. *Counselor education and supervision.* 22,3, 178-186.

Chapter 4

PERSON-CENTERED COUNSELING VALUES

In this chapter, we would like to share our beliefs about values in the counseling process. Our beliefs have served as the foundation for our person-centered approach to counseling. While one may not agree with our beliefs, or will accept some and not others, we agree with Coombs (1986), that what makes an effective helper is a consequence of the helper's belief system. Based on an analysis of fourteen studies conducted since 1962, Coombs (1986a:57-58) found that several areas of belief seem to discriminate clearly between good and poor helpers:

1. *Beliefs about the significant data.* Good helpers are people-oriented. They seem to attend to internal personal meanings rather than external behavioral data. They choose their own behavior in light of the client's personal meanings. This is another way of saying that they tune in to how things seem from the point of view of those with whom they work. In behavioral terms, they are sensitive or empathic.

2. *Beliefs about people.* Effective helpers seem to hold more positive beliefs about the people they work with than do less effective helpers. They see them as trustworthy, able, dependable, and worthy. What one believes about people makes a lot of difference in how one behaves toward them.

3. *Beliefs about self.* Modern psychology has helped us understand the crucial importance of self-concept in all human activities. The helper's self-concept plays an important role in effective practice. A positive view or self-confidence in one's abilities, and a feeling of oneness with others are crucial factors for successful practice.

4. *Beliefs about purposes or priorities.* Helpers, like everyone else, behave in terms of what seems important. The beliefs helpers hold about the purposes of society, helping, relationships, practices, and so on determine their moment-to- moment goals, decisions, and methods.

Our most fundamental beliefs about what we do as counselors have a profound impact on the nature and character of our interactions with clients. Our interactions with clients force us to think and respond instantaneously.

To respond under such conditions in a helpful and facilitative way requires that we have in place a broad, accurate, consistent, defensible, and personally relevant belief system from which to select or create appropriate action (Coombs, 1986:73).

Nacmias (1990:1) suggests how our beliefs of what counseling is may influence our counseling behavior when he shares this story:

> I mentioned the story of the three stone cutters which tells of a cathedral building yard where three stone cutters were executing the same task; cutting stones to shape to build the cathedral walls. Asked individually what exactly they were doing, the first one replied: 'Simple, this is my way of earning a living." The second one said, "Obviously, I am cutting a stone." As to the third one, his reply was: "Well, I am building a cathedral." If they had been therapists, they might have said:
>   Therapist Nr. 1: "This is my job."
>   Therapist Nr. 2: "I am curing a suffering person.""
>   Therapist Nr. 3: "I am helping a human being to become a Person."

In creating our values, we create ourselves. What we authentically believe is what we are. It is difficult for persons to function or behave out of context with what they truly believe. Persons who live thoughtfully nourished values live fully and fearlessly; persons whose lives contradict their values live anxiously. The implications for counseling are clear. As Kottler (1993:115) warns: "If we do project our values during our work, what are the personal consequences for both client and therapist? We must shoulder the burden not only of relying on our clinical judgments and professional skills, but of knowing clients will adopt many of our personal beliefs. Are we really certain that the way we are living our lives is all that great for the rest of the world?" Kottler's question challenges us to examine the values we live in counseling. We bring who we are to the counseling process. We need to be sure that the way we live our lives in the counseling process reflects values which promote the growth and the learning of the client.

Over thirty years ago Rogers(1964:100) made an observation about the search for values which is still relevant today:

> There is a great deal of concern today with the problem of values. Youth, in almost every country, is deeply uncertain of its value orientation; the values associated with various religions have lost much of their influence; sophisticated individuals in every culture seem unsure and troubled as to the goals they hold in esteem. The reasons are not far to seek. The world culture, in all its aspects, seems increasingly scientific and relativistic, and the rigid, absolute views on values which come to us from the past appear anachronistic. Even more important, perhaps, is the fact that the modern individual is assailed from

every angle by divergent and contradictory value claims. It is no longer possible, as it was in the not too distant historical past, to settle comfortably into the value system of one's forebears or one's community and live out one's life without ever examining the nature and the assumptions of that system.

The client's searching and processing of values characterizes the client's movement in counseling. The process of counseling essentially involves the client's search for the true self. As the client becomes involved in this search, he or she comes to grips with the values that have been internalized and influence behavior. The client processes these values into hierarchy that allows certain values to influence behavior (Wrenn, 1973). "When people change in counseling and psychotherapy, it appears to be not simply because someone has educated them, but because they have come to what is often a rediscovery of basic values" (Curran, 1976:79).

We believe it is important to identify values that will enable the counselor to counsel more effectively. There are overlapping values held in common by counselors who provide clients with effective counseling relationships. These are the values we seek to articulate and discuss in the hope that we can bring a commonness of purpose to counseling and make it more effective. This is not to say that counselors must lose their individuality by developing a rigid set of values with which all must agree. It does indicate that we must become involved in identifying those values toward which we tend, individually and as a profession.

ATTITUDINAL VALUES

Values are part of a functioning counselor and developing a sensitivity to their existence and how they influence behavior is a necessary investigation for the counselor who desires to improve his or her counseling. Such an investigation will not only enable the counselor to develop a greater understanding of the values that influence behavior among clients, it will also enable the counselor to develop a keener sensitivity to how the counselor's personal values can either help or hinder clients.

Among person-centered counselors, there has been a movement away from value neutrality and a recognition that counselors must become more explicit regarding their values. Hart and Tomlinson (1970) indicate this when they state that: " . . . there has been a move away from insisting on a neutral value stand for the therapist toward an explicit recognition of the value commitments therapists must make" (p. 565).

General Attitudinal Values

The counselor who intends to be of service to clients must value their worth as persons (Boy & Pine, 1968: 26). When a counselor values power, personal recognition, or a superiority over others, the counselor has difficulty in valuing anything beyond the self. The counselor must value others and their existence; value those qualities that comprise the human personality; value the basic goodness of others and the factors that make behavioral improvement difficult; and must sense in others attributes and tendencies that ennoble the person and make human life the highest form of existence.

When the counselor values others, the counselor will move toward developing a sensitivity to the problems of living and deepen one's empathy toward others. Because the counselor cares, the counselor places the self in relationships that will enhance clients and not block their development. The counselor helps the client by providing a relationship based upon humanistic values. Because the counselor values clients, he or she doesn't retreat behind bureaucratic masks but is open to the self and how if affects client progress.

Without counselor respect for the dignity, worth, and integrity of the individual, the counselor can never hope to communicate at an empathic level. The counselor must welcome opportunities to assist others and provide clients with the therapeutic benefits of a truly warm and caring attitude.

The counselor who values the client has a fundamental respect for the client's freedom to know, shape, and determine personal attitudes and behavior. Clients have a human tendency to develop themselves toward a more self-enhancing existence (Boy & Pine, 1968: 28). If clients did not possess this quality, they would never have the capacity to overcome problems. Clients inherently visualize attitudes and behaviors that are more personally satisfying. Clients cannot eliminate this positive tendency, no matter how deep their discouragement or despair. When a client is pushed into the shadows of an emotional problem, the tendency is to move toward sunlight, toward a life that is more enriched and personally satisfying. This positive movement has been elegantly stated by Rogers (1995:21) :

> It has been my experience that persons have a basically positive direction. In my deepest contacts with individuals in therapy, even those whose troubles are most disturbing, whose behavior has been most anti-social, whose feelings seem most abnormal, I find this to be true.

> When I can sensitively understand the feelings which they are expressing, when I am able to accept them as separate persons in their own right, then I find that they tend to move in certain directions. What are these directions

which they tend to move? The words which I believe are most truly descriptive are words such as positive, constructive, moving toward self-actualization, growing towards maturity, growing toward socialization.

The human inclination is to move toward more self-sustaining attitudes and behavior. The counselor who is generally pessimistic about the forward thrust of attitudes and behavior will have difficulty forming a counseling relationship that respects this tendency and movement. This pessimistic attitude will foster counseling relationships in which the counselor attempts to control the client rather than thrust the client's ability for self-control and development. The creation of a liberating counseling relationship requires that the counselor not only have a fundamental belief in the client's tendency toward psychological stability but that the counselor create a counseling atmosphere in which this tendency is nourished (Arbuckle, 1975, Rogers & Stevens, 1975).

A person's free functioning not only tends toward a development of self; it also includes one's responsibility to other persons (Boy & Pine, 1968: 30). A person's social consciousness enhances personal existence and gives it a deeper meaning because the person defines existence not just in terms of the self, but in relation to others (Glasser, 1965; George & Christiani, 1995). At the beginning of a counseling experience, the client often thinks and talks, first and foremost, about the self. The client's dialogue is usually filled with self-serving statements and is not typically sensitive to how his or her behavior affects others. As the client becomes more open and receptive to the self, there is a decrease in self-serving statements and an increased awareness to the rights of others. The client becomes more acceptant of other persons, attempting to understand their perceptions, attitudes, and behavior. This does not mean that the client gives up individuality; the client certainly remains highly sensitive to the importance of individuality. But the client also goes beyond the self and develops a social consciousness; the client begins to own the concept that inner values, if they are to be personally appropriate, cannot be imposed upon others but must be in harmony with the rights of others (Glasser, 1972). There is a high degree of difference between doctrinaire individualism and socially conscious individuality. The psychologically stable person tends toward an individuality that is sensitive to others and their rights; there is a valuing of the self but, because of a conjoined awareness, others and their rights also become valued.

Rogers (1964:160) states that when a person chooses personally appropriate values, it is characteristic for the human organism to move also toward socialized goals that acknowledge the well-being of others:

> I find it significant that when individuals are prized as persons, the values they select do not run the full gamut of possibilities. I do not find, in such a climate

of freedom, that one person comes to value fraud and murder and thievery, while another values a life of self-sacrifice, and another values only money. Instead, there seems to be a deep and underlying thread of commonality. I believe that when the human being is inwardly free to choose whatever he deeply values, he tends to value those objects, experiences, and goals which make for his own survival, growth, and development, and for the survival and development of others. I hypothesize that it is *characteristic* of the human organism to prefer such actualizing and socialized goals when he is exposed to a growth promoting climate.

Rogers (1964:160) concludes with:

The psychologically mature person as I have described him has, I believe, the qualities which would cause him to value those experiences which would make for the survival and enhancement of the human race. He would be a worthy participant and guide in the process of human evolution .

Barnes (1962:182-183) indicates that before a person can come to respect and value the uniqueness of others, the person must first be self-valuing:

Ultimately, of course, the meaningful life is one which includes others. Existentialists have written much about the Mitsein or being-with-others. But I think one must begin with the solitary individual. In any case, one will not get far with an unhappy client by pointing out to him his duty to think of others or by telling him he ought to feel a sentimental glow when reflecting on his close relationship with them. A person is not capable of thinking with or for other people until he has learned to value himself. Once he knows how to choose for himself the kind of life he can honestly feel to be significant, then he is free to realize the importance of the other person's uniqueness and to find that a wholly different way of life may be profoundly interesting to him without threatening him.

The counselor values genuineness; the counselor's genuine attitude is so deeply a part of the counselor that it can be sensed and responded to by those with whom the counselor has contact. It is the genuineness of the counselor that is often the difference between effective and ineffective counseling (Boy & Pine, 1968:32). Clients react to counselor genuineness by communicating freely and openly. Genuineness can be sensed just as surely as one senses sunlight. Because of the counselor's genuineness, the client is able to communicate with ease; the client is able to delve into various aspects of personal behavior because the client feels that the counselor is authentic in caring for the client as a person (Egan, 1994; Eysenck, 1972).

Counselor genuineness in the counseling process enables clients to feel that they can be themselves, that they can involve themselves in a relationship that is characterized by a free exploration of why one acts and reacts in a particular way. Quinn (1993:17) argues for the primacy of counselor genuineness in psychotherapy contending that the practice of person centered-psychotherapy overemphasizes empathy and caring to the detriment of genuiness because of an overly optimistic belief in the actualizing tendency and the organismic valuing process.

> I do not believe that continuous listening, holding, and caring, will always be sufficient conditions for change. It is an essential, absolutely necessary part of therapy, but just as in the natural progression of development, there is often a need (usually later in the therapy) for some contradiction, some nudging, some confrontation, that is saying the hard truths that help a client move toward fuller functionality.

In closing his argument for the preminence of genuiness in the therapeutic relationship, Quinn (1993:22) states: "To the degree that we as therapists are deeply and consistently open to our inner selves, our behavior will be more trustworthily therapeutic." Graf (1994:90), in responding to Quinn, writes "Rogers never intended to restrict the client-centered therapist only to genuine expressions of empathy and acceptance" and warns that genuiness expressed in the form of counselor- centered confrontation is problematic. And Mearns (1994:96), in a cautionary note, observes: "There is considerable confrontation in person-centered counseling but it is achieved in a fashion which seeks to keep the client at the centre of his locus of evaluation rather than make the counselor the centre."

Braaten (1986) and Mearns and Thorne (1988) caution that genuineness is not always facilitative for the client. Counselor self-disclosure can be overdone in magnitude and kind. There is the danger that in the name of genuineness or congruence the counselor can impose counselor needs and fears on the client. The counselor needs to be alert to aspects of counselor needs and fears which might surface in the counseling relationship. This suggests that the freedom offered by genuineness is accompanied by the responsibility of the counselor to be continually involved in self-development because it is through such development that the counselor's needs and fears become less intrusive in the counseling relationship (Mearns & Thorne, 1988:90).

Mearns and Thorne note that the counselor cannot express whatever he/she is feeling in the moment on the grounds that one is being congruent; otherwise the counseling session becomes more focused on the counselor than on the client. They prescribe three guidelines which would generally govern the counselor's therapeutic use of congruence or genuineness (1988:81-82):

1. Congruence (genuineness) refers to the counselor's response to the client's experience. Among the counselor's flow of feelings and sensations it is only those which are in response to the client which are appropriate for expression.

2. The congruent (genuine) response must be one which is relevant to the immediate concern of the client.

3. The feelings which the counselor responds to tend-to be those which are *persistent* or particularly *striking*.

Braaten (1986:44) says most clients are very sensitive people who "have an uncanny awareness of all kinds of faking, role-playing, hypocrisy, attempts at taking the easy route, double-talk, and the incongruence between one's words and nonverbal cues." That is why genuineness on the part of the counselor is an essential core condition of person-centered counseling. The presence of genuineness makes it easier for the client to trust the counselor and the counseling process, it demystifies the counseling process, enhances the quality of the counselor's response to the client, and it models one of the generic goals of counseling, i.e., to help the client become more congruent or genuine (Mearns & Thorne, 1988:86-87).

Specific Attitudinal Values

The client possesses free will—he or she can be the determiner of a personal destiny. At the beginning of a counseling relationship, clients center on other persons as the causes of their problems. The tendency to blame others is certainly natural because when the cause of a problem can be projected toward someone else, the client can then escape the responsibility for personal behavior. Such clients begin counseling with statements like, "I can never change because my wife won't allow me the freedom to change"; The antiquated attitudes of society do not allow me personal freedom"; "I'll never feel comfortable unless my neighbor stops harassing me"; and "My mother won't allow me to grow up."

Effective counseling helps the client assume responsibility for behavior, to come to the realization that although other persons make some contribution to the development of a problem, the resolution of the problem occurs when the client senses that he or she possesses the free will to change personal behavior—to manage one's destiny, to control one's life and behavior—rather than leaning on the crutch of blaming others (deChardin, 1959; Frankl, 1970; Tillich, 1952; Van Kaam, 1966).

The client must arrive at this realization on his or her own terms. The counselor can't convince the client that the client possesses personal freedom. The client comes to this realization by existing in a counseling relationship that contributes to the natural realization that one does possess free will. Persons can intellectually realize personal freedom by first experiencing the emergence of their free will through an affective counseling process.

The client possesses an individual conscience and sense of morality that guides personal behavior. Some counselors insist on guiding the client because the client might falter, make inappropriate personal decisions, and generally increase the severity of a problem. Some counselors have a basic distrust of the client's sense of responsible behavior. Such counselors tend to prod their clients toward the counselor's sense of responsible behavior. They point out the inappropriateness of certain behavior, indicate the consequences of norm-violating behavior, and even dictate to the client the size and shape of one's conscience and sense of morality. What the counselor is saying to the client, explicitly or implicitly, is, "I don't trust your conscience to bring you to a truly moral decision."

The effective counselor creates a relationship with the client in which the client may explore a personal conscience and sense of morality (Mowrer, 1964). If the client is encouraged to encounter the self, to communicate openly about the rationale for personal behavior, the client can begin to sense the existence of a personal conscience and the degree to which it affects the morality of one's behavior. Morality is the relation of behavior to one's values. Person-centered counselors see human nature as essentially tending toward caring and cooperation. Values are seen as flowing from this nature and guiding behavior—that facilitates and enhances one's development as a person. If the client exists in a facilitative relationship with a counselor, the client will move toward more selfless, and hence more moral, behavior. A moral person is moral simply because the person has transcended selfish needs and reflects this tendency by becoming more selfless in behavior. Clients can become more selfless, more caring, and cooperative, and hence more moral, in proportion to the degree to which the counselor is selfless, caring and facilitating (Brander, 1971).

In commenting on the work of Chang and Page (1991), who found that both Rogers and Maslow believed that personal autonomy, self-acceptance, open communication and interaction, and the freedom to make choices are characteristics of self-actualized persons, Benjamin and Looby (1998:96) highlight the spiritual transformation of the client:

> It is not difficult to conclude that a spiritually transformed individual bears the stamp of self actualization. Decision making for such a person is clear and sometimes unconventional, and the person displays a love and compassion for mankind that breaks all barriers of race, culture, and creed. . . self-actualized persons have a kindred spirit with all human beings. They have a deep and gentle caring for all mankind and are therefore able to establish interpersonal relationships, both harmonious and profound.

The client enhances the self by fulfilling obligations to the self and to others. Personal integrity, in relationship to self and others, is not easily attained. There are always easier ways of doing things that will not place a heavy responsibility upon the self. The client often finds it easier to avoid doing something about a personal problem since an active involvement in its solution might mean that the client would have to change. The counselor finds it easier to tell the client what to do since such behavior seems more expedient than assisting the client to grapple with the time-consuming process of assuming self-responsibility.

Both clients and counselors often find it easier to avoid the self rather than confront the self. Such an avoidance often leads to an erosion of a sense of personal integrity and responsibility. Both the client and counselor, in their relationships both inside and outside of counseling, can avoid a sense of obligation to self and to other persons. It is this type of attitude, however, that leads the client and counselor toward behavior that is neither personally sustaining nor objectively helpful.

The counselor fulfills an obligation to clients by the quality of the counseling relationship. The counselor's personal obligation is to make a difference in the life of the client, to transform a caring attitude into counseling behaviors and responses that will enable the client to feel accepted, understood, and valued as a person. When existing in a qualitative counseling relationship, the client begins to assume an ever-increasing responsibility for personal behavior and the impact of that behavior upon others (Rogers, 1970).

Counseling relationships are not unselfish events—they are encounters that enhance the self of the giver, the self of the receiver, and the quality of the setting in which the giver and receiver live. In counseling, the selfish and unselfish fuse. The person helping another is helping the self.

The client evolves toward others in a sense of personal responsibility and ethical behavior. When the person, as either a client or as a counselor, is egocentric, we can expect a no-growth relationship for both the client and the counselor. In effective counseling, the client moves away from values that center exclusively on the self and moves toward values that include the self in relationship with others (May, 1969). Instead of merely saying, "This is good for me," the client begins to say, "This is good for me in my relationship with other people." The client moves from behavioral needs that merely enhance the self toward behavioral needs that enhance both the self and others.

The counselor's sense of responsibility evolves in much the same manner. Instead of engaging in counseling behavior that merely makes the counselor feel comfortable in counseling, the counselor moves toward counseling behavior that will be therapeutically helpful to the client. Such a counselor possesses a sense of responsibility that goes beyond personal needs. The counselor exists to help the client and translates this attitude into a relationship that is beneficial for the client, rather than just satisfying the counselor's needs. The counselor whose work is aimed at the well-being and development of the client will more easily resolve issues of personal responsibility and ethical behavior.

Responsible personal action occurs within the context of a respect for the dignity and worth of others. When the client begins to respect the dignity and worth of others, the client moves toward behavior that enhances and expands the self. When the mother expresses her respect for the dignity and worth of her adolescent daughter, it is within the context of such respect that the mother moves toward responsible personal behavior in her relationship with her daughter. When the adolescent daughter expresses her respect for the dignity and worth of her mother, she too becomes engaged in personally responsible behavior toward her mother. When either the mother or daughter loses a sense of the dignity and worth of the other, then a gap in their relationship becomes a chasm.

Counselors can also become so burned out in dealing with persons who possess problems that they can lose their sense of respect for their dignity and worth as persons. Kottler and Brown (1996:212) warn:

> Counseling is a very lonely profession. Much of the time is spent alone in your office, insulated from the rest of the world. You are cut off from all distractions, separated from those you care most about, and immersed totally in the world of other persons in great pain who demand your full attention. Furthermore , counseling work can become stale and predictable after a period of time. After seeing a hundred kids who won't go to class or a hundred men who won't express feelings to their partners or a hundred women who feel trapped in their lives, many of the issues seem the same.

Counselor burnout (Kottler, 1993; Wylie & Markowirtz, 1992) characterized by apathy, boredom, disillusionment, and negative feelings can compromise the counselor's person-centered beliefs and values and diminish regard for the client. Clients, instead of being treated as persons, become objects, and when a client becomes, consciously or unconsciously, an object, the counselor's sense of responsibility to that client is diminished. When this sense of responsibility is diminished, then there is a decrease in the effectiveness of counseling. Counselors who possess respect for the dignity and worth of persons translate that respect into counseling relationships in which the client feels fully prized, accepted, and understood (Frankl, 1963). To maintain respect for the dignity and worth of the client it is important that counselors avoid burnout by renewing their person-centered philosophical and attitudinal commitments, finding their own support systems, continuing their personal and professional development, and maintaining an appropriate balance between their personal lives and their calling (Corey & Corey, 1991; Kottler, 1995).

Love and peace are basic strivings and must be advanced during one's lifetime. Love and peace are abstract terms that are given lip service by various segments of our culture and this, in itself, is to be valued since we are at least talking about the meaning of such terms. The client who has experienced a successful counseling relationship is essentially a more loving person who attempts to bring to personal behavior, and the relationships with others, an increase in the personal expression of peace and love. This person senses the degree to which love is proportionately related to one's personal and psychological well-being and attempts to be more loving and acceptant in relationships with others (Fromm, 1956; Hammarskjold, 1969).

For the counselor, these same strivings are expressed in the quality of his or her counseling. The counselor's counseling model show how people can behave toward other people. The counselor's attitude toward clients embodies the characteristics of a person of love and peace. The counselor conceives counseling as a contribution to human evolvement. Humanity's journey toward the values of love and peace is a long one, and the counselor must possess a sense of urgency in helping persons move closer to these values as an outcome of the counselor's role.

The client transcends the self by moving toward a good beyond the self. A person realizes the raison d'etre of life when he or she moves from self-centered values and behaviors toward those that enrich the lives of others. The psychologically incapacitated person thinks and lives *only* for the self; the psychologically stable person is motivated toward the well-being of others. Living for the good beyond the self is an abstract concept, but responding to the needs of others enables us to translate an abstraction into concrete behavior.

For the client, an awareness of a good beyond the self is the energizing force that begins to move that client from selfish to more selfless behavior. To be aware of others, to be sensitive to their needs and interests, to be compassionate, to be willing to relate affectively, and to empathize with the human condition; all of these serve as evidences that the person can deflate one's ego needs and move toward a good, an attitude, that embraces others. If we look life squarely in the eye, we don't just see ourselves. We see ourselves in relationships with others; we see our lives linked to the lives of others; we see our behavior as it affects others. The client who transcends the self moves toward a good, a goal, in which the self enriches and expands the lives of others. The counselor who transcends the self moves toward the very same good.

The client is not determined by forces external to the self at all times the client possesses the capacity to choose freely. Counseling is an open relationship in which the client is free to move in any direction. This demands enormous faith and consistency on the part of the counselor—faith in the client's capacity to choose and consistency in holding to that faith regardless of the choices made by the client. The counselor conveys this faith in the client not only by what the counselor says but through the counselor's attitudes, which indicate to the client "you are the determiner of your destiny," "the directions for your life come from you," and "you can become more independent and self-sustaining." Through such attitudes the counselor communicates that the client *can* be more, rather than the feeling that the client *must* be more. Even though the potential for change exists, the client does not feel a compulsion to change. The client can choose to change or not to change, can choose to speak or not to speak, can choose to be defensive or not to be defensive, and can choose to be independent or dependent (Kostenbaum, 1974).

There is a world of external reality but it cannot be interpreted as being real apart from the client's definition of reality. Reality lies in each person's experience and perception of events and forces. In counseling, the client learns that instead of reacting to reality, he or she can influence reality in ways that enhance the self and others. The clients who made the following statements chose a new and inner reality, although their environmental influences remained unchanged:

> Now I'm not nervous. . . I used to be afraid. . . I thought everyone would laugh at me or make fun of me. . . now I'm not scared.
> I'm learning things about myself I never knew before. . . it's funny. . . I don't want to sound conceited. . . but I'm not as bad as I thought. . . you know the more I talk. . . ah. . . the more good I see in me.
> If I fight with my brother, well, I consider that natural. . . well, now I say to myself if Ma and Dad fight that's natural. . . it's not the fight but the way you look at it. . . I think. . . ah grownups are people, too. . . in other words. . . there must be times when they get mad. . . but the next time there's a fight at home. . . it won't bother me as much because I won't be the same. . . the way I think won't be the same.

As these client statements suggest, the capacity to choose is freely implemented in a counseling atmosphere that promotes it. This means that the counselor, rather than directing or manipulating, creates a relationship in which clients are first able to express their feelings about their needs and values. When clients sense that they can freely express themselves, they can also sense that they have the same freedom of choice in managing their lives.

The client can evolve toward the good. Counseling relationships reflect humanity's basic thrust to love, to grow, to share, and to nourish others. Although the wear and tear of life does blunt the tendency to cooperate and love, this caring motivation is rooted so deeply in human nature that it emerges as nourishing, and enhancing behavior in the most pedestrian activities of living as well as counseling.

Without each other, we cannot love, we cannot care, and we cannot be compassionate, empathic, accepting, and confronting. Giving and receiving help are nutrients that enable persons to function more fully and richly (Fabry, 1968). The rendering of assistance in counseling reflects the counselor's sense of social responsibility and is therapeutically reciprocal—for both the counselor and the client. Both grow and expand because they resonate to each other in time of trial, they touch each other's inner feelings, they share themselves, and they open themselves to their positive impulses. Moore (1994:30): captures this sharing and openess as a form of spiritual intimacy characterized by courage and pain :

> The idea of a soulful relationship is not a sentimental one, nor is it easy to put into practice. The courage to open one's soul to express itself or to receive another is infinitely more demanding than the effort we put into avoidance of intimacy. The stretching of the soul is like the painful opening of the body in birth.

In the encounter of the counseling relationship, hypocritical behavior is transcended. People trusting in their natural and intuitive feelings move out from behind their masks and expose their humanness in such ways as to seek "the greater good" for themselves and for others. Benjamin and Looby (1998: 93), in their examination of the spirituality inherent in person-centered counseling, comment:

> In that fragile moment, when the client becomes aware of his or her innermost self and shares this poignant revelation with the therapist, who conveys to the client unconditional acceptance, love, and nurturing, the client realizes perhaps for the first time the world is a *safe* place. The spiritual foundation for the client's new personal belief system has been rooted.

The person is a transcending being. Despite the powerful negative forces that operate to counter the natural thrust of the person to love and to cooperate, this tendency is so strong that it is never eliminated. It emerges in the form of human therapeutic experiences, at many different moments in the life of each person, and is expressed with particular clarity and meaning in the counseling relationship.

Openness to self and others is a requisite for developing the self. The counselor's role as a counselor and the client's role as a client are transcended by their humanness. The humanness of the counseling relationship implies that counselor and client must be prepared to reveal themselves—their strengths, liabilities, joys, sorrows, feelings, and values. Client openness and honesty is facilitated by counselor openness and honesty (Bugental, 1978).

It can be extremely difficult to live the flow of experience while counseling another person. Society teaches us to put on a facade, to pretend to be that which we are not. But counseling has no room for facades. People do not disclose themselves to people who play a role. The counselor facilitates personal revelation and growth in the client when the counselor is openly *being* the feelings and attitudes that are flowing within.

It requires courage to be real. Self-disclosure involves risk but so does personal growth. For the counselor who is willing to make the psychological investment necessary to close the gap between the role self and the real self, the risk of sacrificing the depersonalized professional mask is more than compensated for by the richness and fulfillment that comes with the liberation of the "essential" self.

Wrenn (1990:586) reminds us that who we are as a person is our most significant professional asset:

> Your personal influence, whether you are aware of it or not, whether you like it or not, is central to your effectiveness as a counseling psychologist or a counselor. It is easy to be seduced by technologies or other procedures that are exterior to your person because they are convenient in time and effort. Remember, however, that clients and colleagues read you as a person, not your skills or even your knowledge.

The transparent self of the counselor facilitates the client's unfolding of self and encourages the client to discover the meaning of personal experiences and existence. By becoming more human and transcending a role, the counselor nurtures openness and enables the client to recognize and activate personal human potentialities, to become psychologically stronger than the client was before counseling began. Disclosing one's self to others provides a therapeutic release, enables one to develop strong affiliations with others, and affirms the uniqueness and the fusion of our existences.

In an atmosphere that encourages openness of self, the client's processes of learning and discovery are enhanced. The client becomes more open to personal feelings, more open to the data of personal experiencing, more open to the stimuli of environment, more open to the points of view expressed by others, and more open to what is going on *now* internally. With openness to self and others, one's perceptual field expands, allowing new, varied, and rich data to come to light. Such openness and new data are necessary if one is to develop and change.

Periodically doubting one's basic beliefs can lead toward developing the self. Counseling, implicitly and explicitly, is an experience that expresses values. What an individual chooses to believe is an indicator of that person's values. What an individual chooses to share and exchange are reflections of what that person deeply cares about. The questions the person seeks to answer, the skills the person desires to acquire, the values the person weighs and ponders, and the ideas the person develops ultimately emanate from the deeply rooted first concerns inherent in the person's natural transcending tendencies—Who am I? What is my relationship to the world in which I live? These are deeply human questions that lie at the base of growth and change. They are questions that belong to all persons.

A person often must be alone in reflection, in contemplation, and in meditation to consider these questions, to reach into the inner recesses of a personal existence, and to identify the personally therapeutic experiences that can lead toward personal growth. These quiet times enable the person to engage in the struggle of moving toward an awareness of the relevancy and meaning of one's life and its relationship to others.

Such quiet times can be found within the process of counseling. Counseling provides opportunities to discover moral values for living. Moral values that have emerged from self-examination provide a coherent framework for interpreting experiences and events and requires reflection, honesty, courage, and a willingness to question and to doubt (Daniels & Horwitz, 1976). These qualities can emerge in a counseling atmosphere that encourages openness, accepts ambiguity, emphasizes the uniquely personal and subjective nature of understanding, promotes and facilitates the client's discovery of the personal meaning of ideas, and encourages the client to trust in the self as well as in external sources of beliefs and ideas. Through counseling, beliefs, values, and behavior can be freely scrutinized and questioned. From client scrutiny and questioning there can evolve a greater degree of self-knowledge, an expanded sense of self-determination, and an awareness that behavior is sometimes mysterious and requires continual examination (Moustakas, 1975).

Death is inevitable—it is the person's preparation for death that indicates the degree to which the self has been developed. The anxiety of fate and death is basic, universal, and inescapable. Fate and death are the way in which our self-affirmation is threatened by nonbeing. In anticipating one's own death, the person experiences existential anxieties when confronting one's finiteness (Kubler-Ross, 1975; Martin, 1975; Weisman, 1972). In dealing with this finiteness, the individual can give up and resign the self to being powerless and impotent, or the person can become neurotically active and manipulative to hide from the dread of powerlessness.

Some clients who enter counseling express the feeling that they have no control over their situations and problems. They seem to be helpless in handling their concerns. Other clients appear to control their anxieties by aggressively manipulating and exploiting people. In a facilitative counseling relationship, the client moves from resignation or neurotic activism to recognize the needs that each of us has for rootedness, relatedness, affiliation, and faith in our own being as a starting point in dealing with the problems of life.

Becoming more aware of the capacity to be in control of one's own behavior, the client discovers that experiences can be created that will nourish and expand the client's life and the lives of others. The client discovers an increasing pride and confidence in making personal choices, guiding one's own life. The client tends to value those objects, experiences and goals that contribute to personal development and to the development of others. In effective counseling, the client moves from valuing power, personal recognition, and superiority over other people to values which are beyond the self and ennoble the personhood of others. Death becomes more acceptable if the life that one has lived was in the service of the highest of human values. Selfish persons fear death more than selfless persons.

Life has direction and meaning, but the answer is not clear. Choices and actions emanate from the quest for personal values. The quest for values is a personal search for an answer to the most human of all questions—What is the meaning of my life? This is essentially a spiritual question, a question that humanity has sought to answer for centuries and a question that must be dealt with by every person (Hammarskjold, 1969). The meaning of life, from both a personal and universal perspective, has captured the attention, imagination, and thought of poets, philosophers, dramatists, and novelists. The meaning of one's life is a question that often permeates the counseling relationship—a question that deeply engages the counselor and the client.

The world of the client is composed of all things that have meaning for the client. The counselor cannot know beforehand what life means to a client. The counselor cannot find out about the client's world in a textbook. The only way to discover it is for the counselor to be totally open to what a client will reveal about the client's world. As the client unfolds a personal world, the client opens the self toward understanding that world and creating meaning and direction in his or her life.

The client's searching and processing of values in relation to the question—What is the meaning of my life?—is the essence of the client's movement in counseling. The process of counseling essentially involves the client's discovery of self and the purpose of one's life and behavior. As the client searches for the meaning of personal behavior, the client comes to grips with the values which influence that behavior. The client then begins to examine those values which have a positive or negative influence on the client's behavior.

Through this process the client comes to see life as a continuous process of becoming rather than a static state of being. Living becomes an adventure, tentative and risky, with meaning and direction created by, and coming from within, the client. In the process of becoming, the client's search for meaning through the counseling relationship evolves into a spiritual journey (Benjamin & Looby, 1998; Chang & Page,1991; Daniels, 1994; Grimm, 1994; Groh & Groh, 1990; Ingersoll, 1994; Kelly, 1995; Maher & Hunt, 1993; Van Kalmthout 1995; & Wilber, 1993). Counseling viewed as a spiritual journey requires that the counselor "cultivate a mind-set that is flexible enough to free spirituality from its religious confines and that has a distinct, individual meaning, relevant to the world views and philosophical orientation of each client being served. This diversity of definition implies flexibility and the creation of a climate that encourages inclusivity, not separateness" (Benjamin & Looby, 1998: 98).

Every aspect of living presupposes moral and human values. Counseling, as an aspect of living, is an expression of values and attitudes. The counselor expresses attitudes and values that mirror a continual examination of the self, life, and the unique counseling relationships in which the counselor participates. Values are part of functioning people, and developing a sensitivity to their existence and to their influence on behavior is a necessary investigation for the counselor who desires to become more effective (Macquarrie, 1970). Such an investigation will not only enable the counselor to develop a greater understanding of clients, but it will also enable the counselor to develop a keener sensitivity to his or her substance as a person and to ways in which his or her personal values can either inhibit or facilitate the personal growth of clients (Upham, 1973; Rokeach & Regan, 1980).

REFERENCES

Arbuckle, D. S. (1975). *Counseling and psychotherapy: An existential-humanistic view.* Boston: Allyn and Bacon, 392, 93.

Barnes, H. E. (1962). Motivation and freedom. *Rehabilitation Counseling Bulletin, 5,* 180-184.

Benjamin P., & Looby, J. (1998). Defining the nature of spirituality in the context of Maslow's and Rogers's theories. *Counseling and Values, 42,* 2, 92-100.

Boy, A. V., & Pine, G. J. (1968). *The counselor in the schools: A reconceptualization.* Boston: Houghton Mifflin.

Braaten, L. J. (1986). Thirty years with Rogers' necessary and sufficient conditions of therapeutic personality change: A personal evaluation. *Person-Centered Review, 1,* 1, 37-50.

Branden, N. (1971). *The disowned self.* Los Angeles: Nash, 171.

Bugental, J. F. T. (1978). *Psychotherapy as process: The fundamentals of an existential humanistic approach.* Reading, MA: Addison-Wesley, 126.

Chang, R., & Page, R.C. (1991). Characteristics of the self-actualized person: Visions from the East and West. *Counseling and Values, 36,* 2-9.

Coombs, A. (1986a). What makes a good helper? A person-centered approach. *Person-Centered Review, 1,* 1, 51-61.

Coombs, A. (1986b). Person-centered assumptions for counselor education. *Person-Centered Review, 1,* 1, 72-82.

Coombs, A. (1988). Some current issues for person-centered therapy. *Person-Centered Review, 3,* 3, 263- 276.

Corey, G., & Corey, M. S. (1991). *Helping the helper.* Pacific Grove, CA: Brooks/Cole.

Curran, C. A. (1976). *Counseling and psychotherapy: The pursuit of values.* Mission, KS: Sheed, Andrews, and McNeel.

Daniels, M. H. (1994). Spiritual, ethical, and religious values in counseling. *Counseling and Values. 38,*74-76.

Daniels, V., & Horowitz, L. (1976). *Being and caring.* Palo Alto, CA: Mayfield, 18.

deChardin, P. T. (1959). *The phenomenon of man.* New York: Harper and Row.

Egan, G. (1994). *The skilled helper* (5th ed.). Pacific Oaks, CA: Brooks/Cole.

Eysenck, H. J. (1972). *Psychology is about people.* New York: Library Press, 115-116.

Fabry, J. (1986). *The pursuit of meaning: Logotherapy applied to lip.* Boston: Beacon, 147.

Frankl, V. (1963). *The doctor and the soul.* New York: Knopf.

Frankl, V. (1970). *The will to meaning.* New York: New American Library, 6-62.

Fromm, E. (1956). *The art of loving.* New York: Harper and Row.

George, R. L., & Christiani, T. S. (eds.) (1995). *Counseling: Theory and practice* (4th ed.). Boston: Allyn and Bacon.

Glasser, W. (1965). *Reality therapy.* New York: Harper and Row.

Glasser, W. (1972). *The identity society.* New York: Harper and Row.

Grimm, D. W. (1994). Therapist spiritual and religious values in psychotherapy. *Counseling and Values , 38,* 154-164.

Graf, C. (1994). On genuiness and the person-centered approach: A reply to Quinn. *Journal of Humanistic Psychology, 34,* 2, 90-96.

Groh, C., & Groh, S. (1990). *The stormy search for the self.* Los Angeles: Tarcher.

Hammarskjold, D. (1969). Markings. New York: Knopf, 205.

Hart, T. J., & Tomlinson, T. M. (1970). *New directions in client-centered therapy.* Boston: Houghton Mifflin, 565.

Ingersoll, E. R. (1994). Spirituality, religion, and counseling: Dimensions and relationships. *Counseling and Values 38,* 98-111.

Kelly, E. W. (1995). *Spirituality and religion in counseling and psychotherapy: Diversity in theory and practice.* Alexandria, VA: American Counseling Association.

Kostenbaum, P. (1974). *Existential sexuality.* Englewood Cliffs, NJ: Prentice-Hall.

Kottler, J. A. (1993). *On being a therapist.* (rev. ed.). San Francisco: Jossey-Bass.

Kottler, J. A. (1995). *Growing a therapist.* SanFrancisco: Jossey-Bass.

Kottler, J. A., & Brown, R. W. (1996). *Introduction to therapeutic counseling* (3rd ed.). Pacific Grove, CA: Brooks/Cole.

Kubler-Ross, E. (1975). *Death: The final stage of growth.* Englewood Cliffs, NJ: Prentice-Hall.

Macquarrie, J. (1970). *Three issues in ethics.* New York: Harper and Row.

Maher, M., & Hunt, T. (1993). Spirituality reconsidered. *Counseling and Values, 38,* 21-28.

Martin, D. (1975). An existential approach to death. *Journal of Thanatology, 3.*

May, R. (1969). *Love and will.* New York: Norton.

Mearns, D. (1994). *Developing person-centered counseling.* London: Sage.

Mearns, D., & Thorne, B. (1988). *Person-centered counseling in action.* Beverly Hills, CA: Sage.

Moore, T. (1994). *Soul mates: Honoring the mysteries of love and relationships.* New York: Harper Collins.

Mowrer, O. H. (1964). *The new group therapy.* New York: Van Nostrand.

Nacmias, E. (1990). The spiritual: A state of awareness in person-centered therapy. *Renaissance, 7,* 1, 2.

Quinn, R. H. (1993). Confronting Carl Rogers: A developmental-interactional approach to person-centered therapy. *Journal of Humanistic Psychology, 33,* 1, 6-23.

Rogers, C. R. (1964). Toward a modern approach to values: The valuing process in the mature person. *Journal of Abnormal and Social Psychology, 68.*

Rogers, C. R. (1970). On encounter groups. New York: Harper and Row.

Rogers, C. R. (1995). What understanding and acceptance mean to me. *Journal of Humanistic Psychology, 35,* 4, 7-22.

Rogers, C. R., & Stevens, D. (1975). *Person to person.* New York: Pocket Books, 47.

Rokeach, M., & Regan, J. F. (1980). The role of values in the counseling situation. *Personnel and Guidance Journal, 58,* 576-682.

Tillich, P. (1952). *The courage to be.* New Haven, CT: Yale University Press.

Upham, F. (1973). *Ego analysis in the helping professions.* New York: Family Service Association of America, 78.

Van Kaam, A. (1966). *The art of existential counseling.* Wilkes-Barre, PA: Dimension.

Van Kalmthout, M. A. (1995). The religious dimension of Rogers's work. *Journal of Humanistic Psychology, 35,* 4, 23-29.

Weisman, A. D. (1972). On dying and denying. New York: Behavioral Publishers.

Wilber, K. (1993). The great chain of being. *Journal of Humanistic Psychology, 33,* 3, 52-65.

Wrenn, C. G. (1973). *The world of the contemporary counselor.* Boston: Houghton Mifflin, 7.

Wrenn, C. G. (1990). From counselor toward becoming a person. *Journal of Counseling and Development, 68,* 5, 586.

Wylie, M. S., & Markowitz, L. M. (1992). Walking the wire. *Family Therapy Networker,* 19-30.

Chapter 5

THE COUNSELOR'S ROLE

In order for a counseling theory to meet the requirements of being legitimately labeled as a theory, it must possess and promulgate a concept of the counselor's role (Stefflre & Grant, 1972: 4-7). Person-centered counseling has described the role of the counselor as the counselor counsels—within the counseling process. Person-centered counseling theory, however, has neglected to identify the role of the counselor outside of the counseling relationship. In fact, no theory of counseling has done this in *explicit* terms, although all theories of counseling, including the person-centered view, imply what the counselor's role should be outside of counseling. Our purpose in this chapter is to clarify this issue by developing a generic and eclectic concept of the counselor's role which accommodates the implicit requirements of the different theories of counseling.

The counselor's role emerges from a theoretical foundation that is substantive and has credibility in the arena of practice. We test theory by investigating the successful implementation of that theory, and when we apply theory, we must also consider the counselor's role since it is a natural extension of a theoretical viewpoint. This is the essential difference between professional and nonprofessional viewpoints regarding the counselor's role. A professional viewpoint is an applied extension of theory; a nonprofessional viewpoint of the counselor's role is not grounded in any theory.

When conceptualizing a counselor's role, one needs to substantiate that role in terms of a counseling theory that serves as the basis for the counselor's specific functions (Boy & Pine, 1980). A concept regarding what a counselor should or should not do is meaningless unless there is a rationale for the role concept. When discussing foreign policy, one often hears someone say, "The United States should . . .," and what follows is a particular opinionized statement. When considering what the United States should do, one cannot separate such a statement from a democratic theory of government. A statement becomes credible because it is an extension of a particular theory of democracy. When someone states that "The United States should. . .," and then is unable to handle the questions, "Why? "What is the rationale for your position? How is your viewpoint consistent with the principles of democracy?" we then are justified in questioning the validity of what that person thinks the United States should do regarding its foreign policy.

Sometimes there is a tendency to hide behind the word *professional*, the feeling being that as long as we use the word, all that we do suddenly becomes purified and acceptable. A degradation occurs when one proceeds to use the term *professional* as a protective adjective to give apparent sanction to *any* and *all* functions of the counselor.

The counselor's role concept is an extension of a counseling theory which in turn depends upon the counselor's concept of behavior as expressed within a personality theory. The counselor's role concept is also a reflection of what the counselor is as a person: the counselor's values, life style, human experiences, and inner philosophy. When we begin to look at the counselor as a person, we come to grips with the extent to which the counselor's personhood influences what the counselor does or does not do on the job (Hart & Tomlinson, 1970; Rogers, 1942, 1961). It would be naive to think that all a counselor needs to do, in order to function professionally, is to read a policy statement regarding the counselor's role. If the attainment of professionalism were this simple, any profession could achieve credibility simply by producing policy statements. The counselor's role cannot be clarified through the distribution of policy statements. It becomes clarified when the counselor examines which functions serve the needs of clients and which serve the needs of the counselor or the organization which employs the counselor (Boy, 1984).

FACTORS INFLUENCING THE ROLE OF THE COUNSELOR

The counselor's role is not created in a vacuum. It is developed as an outgrowth of influences that affect the counselor. Some of these influences are positive and result in the counselor, or group of counselors, developing a role description truly aimed at meeting the needs of clients. Other influences are negative in that they result in role descriptions that involve the counselor in a potpourri of activities that circumvent the needs of clients. These influences affect how the counselor conceives and executes a role description, and it is the purpose of this section to identify such influences and the degree to which they prompt the counselor to include therapeutic counseling as the top priority in a role description. Person-centered counselors typically identify therapeutic counseling as the most important function of the counselor's role (Boy & Pine, 1979; Boy, 1984).

The degree to which a counselor develops a role focused on counseling and related therapeutic activities is proportionately related to the influence of the following factors. Factors influencing the counselor in a positive manner yield a role description that is therapeutically inclined. Factors negatively influencing the counselor result in a role description that is not therapeutically inclined.

Community Expectations

Some community expectations can have a positive influence upon the role of the counselor. In communities where the counselor is perceived as someone to whom personally troubled persons can turn, the counselor is encouraged to develop a role that emphasizes his or her commitment to counseling.

When a community senses the need and importance of counseling in the lives of people, it furnishes the counselor with the needed support, which prompts the counselor to move toward a role in which counseling is the core of a counselor's responsibility.

When the community expectation is that the counselor will counsel, then the counselor feels comfortable in fulfilling community expectations by devoting the major portion of each working day to counseling, and the community's recognition of the importance of counseling becomes spelled out in the counselor's role description.

Some other communities expect the counselor to function as a clerk who pays careful and detailed attention to tabulating the behavior of clients. Such a community expectation can prompt the counselor to develop a role in which his or her clerical activities are given prominence. Counseling would be given a low level priority in this counselor's role because of the community's expectation.

Institutional Policies

Some institutional policies have a positive influence upon the role of a counselor, especially in those institutions that recognize the need and importance of counseling. When the counselor is bolstered by such an institutional policy, the counselor is encouraged to feature the importance of counseling in a role description.

When institutional policy is sensitive to the personal and human needs of clients, the counselor is prompted to acknowledge this sensitivity by giving counseling the highest priority in a role description. The counselor is motivated to engage in counseling because institutional policy encourages such an involvement.

Other institutional policies have a negative influence upon the counseling dimensions of a counselor's role. Some institutions desire that the counselor administer institutional policy and therefore cast the counselor into the role of an administrator rather than allowing him or her to engage in counseling. Such institutional policies are designed more to preserve the institution as an institution rather than to serve the human needs of clients (Hurst, Moore, Davidshofer, & Delworth, 1976). Faced with the need to administer institutional policies as a primary function, the counselor features such administrative activities in a role description while relegating counseling to a secondary level of importance (George & Christiani, 1986).

Administrative Behavior

Some administrators can have a positive influence upon the counselor's interest in counseling. Such administrators perceive the counselor as a colleague and have no need to slant the role of the counselor toward the administrator's needs and interests. They acknowledge the counselor's judgment that counseling will best serve clients, and they give the counselor the support that is necessary for the counselor to emphasize counseling as the primary role responsibility. Some administrators desire to facilitate the use of existing skills among staff members, and therefore create an administrative environment that encourages staff utilization of their specialized skills. These administrators further realize that services will be more efficiently delivered if the administrative atmosphere is supportive and encouraging (Bogue & Saunders, 1976; Boy & Pine, 1971; Flowers & Hughes, 1978). In such a reinforcing administrative environment, the counselor is encouraged to feature counseling as the core dimension of his or her role.

Other administrative behavior can deflect the counselor away from primarily engaging in counseling. Some administrators desire to make use of the counselor as a loose-ends coordinator or junior executive. They are so overwhelmed by their administrative responsibilities that they seek relief from these responsibilities and enlist the aid of the counselor in the performance of these responsibilities. Once committed to their performance of administrative functions, the counselor has difficulty in finding the time to engage in counseling.

Counselor's Formal Preparation

Some counselors are graduates of programs that emphasize the need and importance of counseling. Such counselors have intellectually and attitudinally committed themselves to the importance of counseling and identify it as the most important aspect of their roles.

Such counselors realize that when all the different kinds of human problems are examined, counseling emerges as one of the most objective processes for helping clients with these problems. Since counseling produces results, such counselors become committed to providing clients with counseling relationships. They invest themselves essentially because they are products of preparation programs that give primacy to the importance of counseling as the core dimension of the counselor's role.

Other counselors are products of preparation programs that have prepared the counselor to do everything but counsel. Such programs have constructed courses and learning experiences in which prospective counselors primarily learn how to assess, count, diagnose, manage, evaluate, measure, and administer. Products of such programs do not identify with the importance of counseling but instead identify with activities more characteristic of the work of psychometricians, researchers, or administrators.

Attitudes of Colleague Counselors

Some colleague counselors furnish the counselor with the peer support necessary to give counseling major consideration in the role of the counselor. They are counselors who have seen the depths of human turmoil and have concluded that the most effective way to alleviate that turmoil is to assist clients through counseling. They viscerally understand how the process of counseling furnishes clients with the psychological strength to change behavior. They construct a role description that emphasizes the counselor's obligation to counseling. Such colleague counselors compose the support system that encourages the counselor to list counseling at the top of a list of role priorities.

Other colleague counselors may inhibit counselor attempts to give priority to counseling having developed a comfortable work existence for themselves and not wanting that existence disturbed (Sweeney & Witmer, 1977). They identify more with paperwork than the psychological needs of clients and always manage to create a mountain of paper behind which they can hide. They desire to support and maintain the status quo because such an attitude is a better guarantee that they will have a job tomorrow. Looking busy is more important than being busy.

Such counselors resent the counselor who is committed to counseling. They seem not interested in becoming involved with clients or their problems. It is much easier to shuffle paper than to attend to the more fundamental human needs of clients. The existence of such colleagues makes it difficult, but not impossible, for the counselor to give role priority to counseling.

The Counselor's Self-Concept

The counselor's self-concept often influences the degree to which the counselor includes counseling in a role description. The counselor who conceives the self to be a giving self, a person-centered self, a self that desires to be of service to clients in the improvement of behavior, gives high priority to counseling. Such a counselor realizes that the more willing the counselor is to affectively extend the self toward the client, the more positive will be the outcomes of counseling (Hulnick, 1977). The giving aspect of the counselor's self-concept will directly influence the counselor's featuring of counseling in a role description. The selfless counselor, the giving counselor, the counselor who exists for the client's existential and behavioral development, desires to translate this inclination into counseling relationships. These inclinations become realized when the counselor develops a role that emphasizes the importance of counseling.

Other counselors possess inclinations that conceptualize the counselor as expert, more knowledgeable, and better able to discover answers to problems than clients themselves. Such counselors want to do things to and for clients rather than helping clients to do for themselves. Such counselors focus their work day on a myriad of "doing" activities rather than on counseling. They typically don't have the metabolism or patience to sit with clients during the counseling process.

The Counselor's Theoretical Inclinations

A counselor's theory of counseling is essentially an expression of the counselor's self-concept. The counselor who knows the self and recognizes certain caring needs will be inclined toward a theory of counseling that fulfills the self and those needs. Certain theories of counseling are focused on the basic human needs of clients and emphasize counseling as a caring process. Person-centered counseling is explicitly one of these theories. Such theories accommodate the counselor as a counselor, rather than defining the counselor as an information dispenser, psychometrist, advisor, or environmental engineer. Counseling is central to such theories and those counselors who identify with such theories typically emphasize counseling in their role descriptions. They see counseling as the primary mode for assisting clients, and they express this commitment in their role descriptions.

The Counselor's Career Goals

Some counselors seem themselves as counselors for the lifetime of their careers. In their early professional development, they make an intellectual and visceral commitment to serving human needs through the process of counseling. They stay with that commitment throughout their professional careers because they realize that counseling affords them a unique opportunity to help the human condition to improve. Their values commit them toward clients whom they wish to serve through counseling. They are professionally fulfilled when they make a contribution through counseling. They desire to serve clients and they express that desire through the counseling dimension of the counselor's role. They never waiver in their commitment to function as professional counselors. They see counseling as a noble, person-centered, and continuing professional commitment.

Other counselors have their eye on administration. They prefer to feature role functions which give them experience in administration. They tend to do little counseling. It is unrelated to their future career goals.

The Needs of Clients

Counselors who engage in counseling do so because the needs of their clients are best met through this process. They realize that as organizations and agencies do a variety of things to help clients, there must also exist a counselor who has the time, energy, skills, and inclination to attend to the counseling needs of clients. They further realize that behavioral change will occur basically when the client is exposed to a series of steady, sustained, and continual counseling sessions. A client needs to be attended to as a person; to be in an association with a counselor who possesses and expresses attitudes of caring, understanding, empathy, acceptance, positive regard, authenticity, and concreteness. It is this kind of relationship that best meets the needs of the client and induces behavioral change. A client exposed to such counselor attitudes is able to move toward behavioral change. Such a counselor will feature counseling as a role priority because it has a direct impact on the human and behavioral needs of clients.

Other counselors conceive client needs in a far more superficial way and are therefore not inclined to give counseling a high priority. Such counselors appear to want to isolate themselves from the legitimate counseling needs of clients. Their role descriptions appear to be self-serving rather than serving the needs of clients.

Many current counselors are much like Shakespeare's *Hamlet.* They have reached a point where they must decide whether they are "To be. . . or not to be" when considering the issue of giving top emphasis to counseling in their role descriptions. But unlike Hamlet, counselors cannot mull over the question too long. If they procrastinate, they will find that pervasive and negative influences have gained in strength and the future of the counseling pro-

fession will be a shell of what it might have been. Other helping professionals will identify a host of activities to help clients and if counseling is included, they could identify it as the least important of these activities. The importance of the counseling process will endure only if it is conceived to be
important by counselors themselves.

CONSULTATION

Gunnings (1971) asserts that the counselor must be willing to confront systems that have dehumanized the person and oppressed minorities. Osipow
(1971) states that counselors are obligated to foster institutional changes so
that these institutions will more accurately meet human needs. Morrill and
Hurst (1971) show that counselors can best meet human needs by becoming
involved in preventive and developmental outreach programs. Ivey (1973)
argues that unless the counselor gives greater priority to consultation, the
human condition for all persons will never be significantly improved. While
counselors counsel, some organizations are grinding on and engaging in
behaviors that tend to produce negative psychological consequences for persons.

Lewis and Lewis (1977:156-157) emphasize that social action should be
part of *every* counselor's role because:

1. Negative aspects of the community environment may be detrimental to the
growth and development of individuals.
2. Positive aspects of the community environment can support individual
growth and development.
3. Counselors are helpless in their attempts to serve individuals if environmental factors do not change to keep pace with individual change.
4. Self-determination itself is not only a political goal, but a mental health goal.
5. Counselors, working alone, and individual citizens, working alone, are both
powerless to make the community responsive to the needs of community
members. (pp. 156-157)

Kurpius (1978b:335) points out the following in presenting a rationale for
consultation:

Persons functioning as consultants do not model authority and control. Rather,
their newly developing image and related functions are quite the opposite—
they model helping behaviors that are nonjudgmental and noncompetitive.
Such behaviors reinforce openness and collaboration that create mutually beneficial work situations and work outcomes. These persons are being recognized
as the long needed "new professional" in the work force.

Price (1972:365) develops a community perspective in evaluating psychological dysfunction and focuses on understanding the stressful and hostile social and environmental influences that contribute to the development of problems among individuals:

> Wholesale use of traditional psychotherapy is inappropriate in that not everyone experiencing some emotional discomfort requires the intensive intervention of individual or even group psychotherapy. For many, educational experiences in stress management, relaxation techniques, career planning, or interpersonal communications among many others may be of the most benefit and a wiser use of our limited professional resources.

In terms of consulting in a school setting, Wigtil and Kelsey (1978:416) go on to state that: "No longer is it appropriate or even ethical to only adjust the students to the system, it is also important that counselors influence the adjusting of the learning environment to the students".

For the person-centered counselor, the consultative contributions are essentially an extension of the human attitudes that characterize person-centered counseling (Boy & Pine, 1981). That is, the person-centered counselor defines the consultative aspect of the counselor's role as a reflection of the fundamental attitudes and processes of person-centered counseling rather than being the application of mechanical procedures which are far removed from the person-centered viewpoint.

Person-centered counselors have traditionally emphasized the primacy of counseling as the most essential and effective contribution toward improving the human condition. Counseling has been seen as the one and, sometimes, only activity in which the person-centered counselor engages. We also recognize that person-centered counseling has been generally remiss in failing to more explicitly conceive the counselor as also being a consultant, social activist, advocate, and change agent. It is logical that the counselor's role also emphasizes the importance of consultative activities that serve to improve not only the human condition of individual clients but the humanness of organizations established to serve those clients. Kurpius (1978a:320) has noted: "Consultation is one process for synthesizing environmental and human adjustments, and although consultation is not a panacea for all ills, it does provide an alternate form for influencing change."

The person-centered counselor's role more accurately serves human needs when it gives priority to both counseling and consultation. The impact of the person-centered counselor's role becomes enlarged when it includes both (Boy & Pine, 1981).

CONCLUSION

Today's person-centered counselor is at the proverbial crossroads. One road may be traveled by making concessions which are contradictory to the philosophic and applied dimensions of the person-centered view. Taking this road will provide greater organizational acceptance if one is willing to give up the expression of fundamental professional values through one's role. It is a road usually paved with easy advancement opportunities if one conforms to established procedures. The other road requires maintaining a commitment to what you affectively and cognitively believe at the deepest levels of your professional feelings and thoughts. This road is far more difficult to travel because it requires the courage to question procedures which may not be in the best interest of a person-centered process which as a long-established record of producing positive results. It is a road less frequently traveled; but if person-centeredness is a deeply rooted human, intellectual, and professional commitment, one cannot avoid traveling this other road. Maintaining a role commitment to the person-centered view has never been easy for its practitioners, but maintaining the commitment energizes the counselor to continue to work toward what is institutionally required to more effectively apply person-centered counseling and consultation.

REFERENCES

Bogue. E. G., & Saunders, R. L. (1976). *The educational manager: Artist and practitioner.* New York: Worthington Jones, 4-5.

Boy, A. V. (1984). Are counselors counseling? *Arizona Counseling Journal, 9,* 26-30.

Boy, A. V., & Pine, G. J. (1971). *Expanding the self: Personal growth for teachers.* Dubuque, IA: Wm. C. Brown, 45-46.

Boy, A. V., & Pine, G. J. (1979). Needed: A rededication to the counselor's primary commitment. *The Personnel and Guidance Journal, 51,* 527-528.

Boy. A. V., & Pine, G. J. (1980). Avoiding counselor burnout through role renewal. *The Personnel and Guidance Journal, S9,* 161-163.

Boy, A. V., & Pine, G. J. (1981). The client-centered counselor as a consultant. *Pennsylvania Journal of Counseling, 1,* 3-4.

Flowers, V. S., & Hughes, C. L. (1978). Choosing a leadership style. *Personnel, 55,* 51-59.

George, R. L., & Christiani, T. S. (1986). *Counseling: Theory and Practice* (2nd ed.). Englewood Cliffs, NJ: Prentice-Hall.

Gunnings, T. S. (1971). Preparing the new counselor. *The Counseling Psychologist, 2.*

Hart, J. T., & Tomlinson, T. M. (1970). *New directions in client-centered therapy.* Boston: Houghton Mifflin, 74, 120.

Hulnick, H. R. (1977). Counselor: Know thyself. *Counselor Education and Supervision, 17*, 69-72.

Hurst, J. C., Moore, M., Davidshofer, C., & Delworth, U. (1976). Agency directionality and staff individuality. *The Personnel and Guidance Journal, 54*, 313-317.

Ivey, A. E. (1973). Counseling–Innocent profession or fiddling while Rome burns? *The Counseling Psychologist, 4*, 111 - 115.

Kurpius, D. (1978). Introduction to the special issue. *The Personnel and Guidance Journal, 56*, 320 (a).

Kurpius, D. (1978). Consultation theory and process: An integrated model. *The Personnel and Guidance Journal, 56*, 335-338 (b).

Lewis, M., & Lewis, J. (1977). *Community counseling: A human services approach.* New York: Wiley, 156-157.

Morrill, W. H., & Hurst, J. C. (1971). A preventive and developmental role for the college counselor. *The Counseling Psychologist, 2.*

Osipow, S. H. (1971). Challenges to counseling psychology for the 1970s and 80s. *The Counseling Psychologist, 2.*

Price, R. H. (1972). *Abnormal psychology: Perspectives in conflict.* New York: Holt, Rinehart and Winston.

Rogers, C. R. (1942). *Counseling and psychotherapy.* Boston: Houghton Mifflin, 11, 29.

Rogers, C. R. (1961). *On becoming a person.* Boston: Houghton Mifflin, 55.

Stefflre, B., & Grant, W. (1972). *Theories of counseling* (2nd ed.). New York: McGraw-Hill.

Sweeney, T. J. & Witmer, J. M. (1977). Who says you're a counselor? *The Personnel and Guidance Journal, 55*, 594.

Wigtil, J. V., & Kelsey, R. C. (1978). Team building as a consulting intervention for influencing learning environments. *The Personnel and Guidance Journal, 56*, 412-416.

Wubbolding, R. E. (1978). The counselor educator and local professional associations. *Counselor Education and Supervision, 18.*

Chapter 6

THE COUNSELING RELATIONSHIP

Person-centered counseling holds the relationship to be central, real, and an end in itself for fostering growth. Indeed, much of the research on the relationship was initiated and developed by the client-centered therapy tradition. Carl Rogers (1957) theoretical propositions spawned nearly two decades of further theory and research on the relationship. Peaking in the seventies the research on the concept of the relationship seemed to diminish until Gelso and Carter (1985) made a significant contribution to the professional literature in a two-part article written to restimulate research and theory on the relationship. They provide an enlightening and challenging context for the ideas we present in this chapter.

Gelso and Carter suggest that in counseling the relationship usually emerges silently and imperceptibly. They define the relationship as "the feelings and attitudes that counseling participants have toward one another, and the manner in which these are expressed" (1985:157). Further on the authors note the paradox that the people who focus the most intensely on relationship issues—the humanistically- oriented theoreticians—have devoted, at best, little attention to the analysis of the different components or parts of the therapy relationship. Drawing upon the work of Greenson (1967), the authors propose three components of a therapeutic relationship: the working alliance, the transference configuration, and the real relationship.

Gelso and Carter (1985:164-190) offer five propositions about each of the three components within and across theoretical orientations. The component of the working alliance (characterized by mutual liking, trust, and respect) involve the following five propositions:

1. Regardless of the duration of counseling or therapy, it is important that the alliance be established relatively early if the treatment is to be successful.
2. Within and between different kinds of genres of counseling, the strength of the working alliance that is required for successful outcome varies according to the difficulty of the demands of the treatment .

114

3. In terms of the working alliance, the bonding aspect develops most slowly, whereas if therapy is to proceed effectively there must be at least general agreement early in the work about the goals appropriate for treatment and the tasks that are necessary to attain these goals .

4. In line with Greenson's (1967) conceptualization, the importance of the working alliance waxes and wanes during the various phases of intervention.

5. Clients vary in their ability to form alliances, and therapists, too, vary in their ability both to form and cultivate working alliances .

The component of the transference configuration entails the following five propositions:

1. To varying degrees, transference occurs in counseling of every theoretical orientation, and it plays an important role in both process and outcome.

2. The course of transference is predictable in nonanalytic as well as analytic counseling, but the course will differ for successful and unsuccessful cases.

3. How transference reactions are dealt with by the counselor has consequences for both the process and outcome of counseling .

4. Just as in the case of transference, counselor counter transference occurs in counseling of every theoretical orientation .

5. It is important that the counselor strive to understand his or her counter transference experience, as this can be a useful guide to detecting clients' subtle but important issues and to responding effectively to clients .

The third component, the real relationship, can be summarized by examining the following propositions:

1. It is important (to process and outcome) that a positive real relationship exist from very early in counseling .

2. Whereas the importance of the real relationship depends upon the therapist's theoretical orientation in the therapist's eyes, theoretical orientation is beside the point in the client's eyes .

3. Although individual counselors and theoretical orientations vary in the extent to which they cultivate and do their work through and with the real relationship, all relationships include this component, and counselors of every orientation must attend to the real relationship .

4. The real relationship increases and deepens across the duration of therapy

5. Although we talk about "the real relationship" in a way that suggests it is an equal and reciprocal relationship, expectations and actualities of the real relationship are probably different for the two participants .

Urging that attention be focused on these major components, regardless of one's theoretical orientation, Gelso and Clark encourage therapists to focus on the components central to their orientation. Stimulated by Gelso and Clark's work, we delineate in this chapter the components of an effective person-centered counseling relationship and indicate how the totality and interaction of these components define the person-centered relationship. We view these elements as essential in both Phase One and Two of our person-centered eclectic approach.

We believe an effective person-centered counseling relationship is characterized as:

A *face-to-face* relationship
A relationship in which the *client is voluntarily involved*
A relationship possessing *sensitive communication*
A relationship possessing *genuine acceptance* of the client by the counselor
A relationship in which the *counselor empathically focuses* on the needs and
    feelings of the client
A relationship that is *liberating*
An open-ended relationship in which *outcomes essentially emerge from the
    client*, not from the counselor
A relationship in which the client's desire for *confidentiality* is respected
A relationship that calls for *acquired attitudes and skills* on the part of the
    counselor
A relationship based upon a substantive rationale reflecting *philosophical
    and psychological principles* emanating from theoretical and empirical
    considerations of the person, human behavior, and society
A relationship in which the counselor exhibits a *concept of the person*
A relationship in which *being precedes becoming*
A relationship *of interacting and interdependent* core conditions.

FACE-TO-FACE PRESENCE

In a world that is becoming more technological, some are encouraging counselors to make more use of technology in their counseling (Stewart, Winborn, Johnson, Burks, & Engelkes, 1978; Walz, 1984). From our viewpoint, the necessary face-to-face presence of counseling precludes the notion of counseling conducted via telephone, television, letters of correspondence, computers, and other nonpersonal modes of communication. In the past, some writers have indicated that counseling can occur between two individuals through the mails, for example (Jones, 1963: 216). Although one could consider some letters as highly personal and emotionally evocative, a telephone conversation as cathartic and helpful in immediate crisis situations such as the threat of suicide, and television and computers as vehicles of communication that have the potential for accommodating some of the numerous and varied needs of humans, counseling, according to our definition, occurs only in a face-to-face relationship. The physical presence of two people, counselor and client, provides an emotional contiguity that does not exist in a person-thing-person medium of communication. A telephone call cannot accommodate the nuances and subtleties of communication represented in body language, facial expression, physical gesture, and the messages of the eyes. A visual image on a television screen cannot open a door, embrace, or project the emotional warmth of a fully-dimensioned person. Counseling is a human relationship involving the physical presence of persons who freely share themselves in ways not found in a face-to-image or face-to-voice communication. In counseling, the client's world is being elucidated by the counselor's *being* there in an atmosphere of *openness*. Counseling takes place in the light of **dasein**–the "being there" of two persons in an existential encounter.

The quality of **dasein**–is exquisitely and elegantly captured by Moustakas (1986) who writes that the ideal counseling relationship is characterized by three distinctive features: **being in, being for,** and **being with. Being in** refers to the counselor's empathy for the client, the counselor's ability to crawl under the skin of the client and to see, feel, think, and experience the world of the client in the here and now, and to communicate that empathy so the client knows that in this moment he or she is understood. **Being for** refers to the counselor's unconditional acceptance of the client so that the client sees in the counselor a caring person who is present for the client. **Being with** refers to the separateness of the counselor and the client suggesting that while the counselor is empathically resonating with the client the counselor is a congruent person who expresses genuiness and authenticity. We believe these qualities of being, which characterize the ideal counseling relationship according to Moustakas, can only be found when two people are in face to face presence with each other.

VOLUNTARY INVOLVEMENT

The counseling process begins when the client becomes voluntarily involved (Rogers, 1970). In seeking help the client takes an independent and responsible step of much significance. The client has arrived at the point where a problem has become discomforting enough to prompt the client to do something about it.

Client-initiated counseling has a more human foundation than one into which the client has been forced. It is very doubtful that a counselor can develop a person-centered concept of a desirable human image among clients who are required to participate in counseling.

Unfortunately, in all too many situations, counselors are directed by administrative fiat to see certain clients. Some counselors try to work around this by saying to clients that they are not being required to engage in counseling, they are being invited. But counselors are only deluding themselves to think that clients perceive a required association with a counselor as anything but a compelled relationship.

Client initiation of counseling is an essential ingredient for a meaningful relationship from our point of view. Beck (1965:1) has pointed this out to counselors in discussing the implications of the view of existential philosopher, Sartre:

> . . . it must be remembered that the whole act of counseling is voluntary because of the twin ideals of freedom and dignity assigned to the individual. The last thing an existentialist counselor would want to do is to give a person a chance to evade his own responsibility for choice and action, a chance to hide behind "authority" or the "collective demands of society." This would be a negation of what existentialism stands for. In that one structures the counseling situation toward a counselor's choice, to that degree does he infringe upon the freedom and commitment of the client.

Clients will become voluntarily involved in counseling when the counselor motivates them to seek help. Well developed orientation procedures delineating the role of the counselor, the purposes of counseling, and the counseling experience are necessary for developing a positive image of the counselor and the counseling process. Such orientation procedures have influenced clients to think well of counselors and counseling and to become voluntarily involved in the counseling process.

Of course, the most valuable way of helping persons to freely choose counseling for themselves is through qualitative counseling relationships. The counselor who can assist clients can expect them to return for further counseling assistance; those clients who have a good reaction to counseling will transmit this feeling to peers within an institution or within a community.

The number of client requests for counseling provides a good measure of the quality of a counseling service. If counseling is not helpful and not characterized by warmth, trust, and acceptance, the number of voluntary requests for counseling will be small, indicating the poor quality of the program.

In the case of referred clients, we feel that if the counselor indicates the source of referral and the reason why the referral was made, and clarifies the relationship by indicating what the client may expect from counseling, then the client may decide if counseling is to occur. The client will usually react by relating to the counselor and freely choosing to enter the relationship.

When a counselor respects human rights that counselor respects the client's freedom of choice regarding whether or not to enter a counseling relationship.

SENSITIVE AND EMPATHIC COMMUNICATION

Communication between counselor and client is expressed via affective, cognitive, verbal, and nonverbal modes. Effective counseling requires multiple modes of communication and is encouraged and facilitated by a nonthreatening atmosphere. Effective communication occurs when the counselor receives what the client wants to communicate and the client receives what the counselor wants to communicate.

In order to respond to a client, the counselor must be reasonably free from the influence of personal needs and anxieties which distort perception. The counselor needs to develop an affective sensitivity that is keenly attuned to the nonverbal and subtle cues conveyed through tone of voice, posture, bodily movement, a way of breathing, physical mannerisms, expression of the eyes—in other words, the subterranean signals that constitute the subliminal "language" of counseling. Counselor sensitivity to the complementary combination of verbal and nonverbal, cognitive and affective codifications opens up possibilities of communication that otherwise would be closed. Such awareness and sensitivity enable the counselor to directly experience the client, to receive and transmit intuitively. Although the person-centered viewpoint requires that the counselor be sensitive to what the client says and how it is said, it further asks the counselor *to assimilate what the client is feeling and experiencing as the client is speaking.*

The person-centered counselor is open to experience. The counselor's perceptual field is capable of change and adjustment, and it is not necessary for the counselor to distort perceptions to fit a previously formed concept. Openness to experience is contingent upon the counselor's freedom from threat, which in turn is an expression of the counselor's positive feelings about the self. The more positive the self of the counselor, the more positively he or she relates to clients. The more acceptant the counselor is of the self, the more acceptant he or she is of others. The client who is accepted and who experiences a relationship in which openness is prized becomes more open. The client's perceptual field widens. To hear the client, the counselor must become immersed in the client's flow of experience. Truly hearing the client's inner voice requires that the counselor hear the client's feelings.

GENUINE ACCEPTANCE

When a person is not required to defend the self, when that person can be what he or she is, there is an opportunity for behavior to change. The client who is free to be unique, to be different, and to hold different values, is also free to look at the self. Acceptance of the client means giving the client the opportunity of holding and expressing personal meanings without attack or moralization; the ability to see things in the client's own way (Gendlin, 1970; Kottler & Brown, 1996).

When the client experiences acceptance of the self, the individual also feels safe to explore personal meanings. *The client feels accepted when he or she experiences genuine acceptance.* If the client does not feel that "it's all right to be myself here," or if difference is not valued, the client becomes defensive. The defensive client feels compelled to defend perceptions and consequently narrows these perceptions because of the threat represented in a counselor moralization, condemnation, or attack. A partial view of the self by a client results in superficial communication with a counselor. On the other hand, the client who is accepted, who feels that "it's all right to be me, I can say what I like, I can be negative, I can be positive, I can be confused, I can talk, I can be silent, no one is going to judge me or preach to me, I can be what I feel" will freely and openly relate to the counselor.

Acceptance means that there are no reservations, conditions, evaluations, and judgments of the client's feelings, but rather a total positive regard for the client as a person of value. The client is valued and accepted as a person regardless of the negative feelings expressed. It is not acceptance up to this or that point and no further, but acceptance even though the client possesses values, attitudes, and feelings different from those of the counselor. Acceptance of the client is not dependent upon the client's meeting certain moral or ethical criteria. It is complete and unconditional.

To unconditionally accept another person is not easy. Accepting another person's behavioral and value differences, and the whole range and variety of behaviors, attitudes, beliefs, and values which clients bring to counseling requires counselor self-acceptance. Rogers (1995:19) in writing about the interrelationship between counselor self-acceptance and unconditional acceptance of the client says:

> It is only when I can be myself, when I can accept myself, that it is possible for me to understand and accept others. There are plenty of times and plenty of relationships in which I do not achieve this, and then it seems to me life in these relationships is superficial. My relationship with these individuals is not particularly helpful. I tend to make these people dependent on me or hostile to me. I do not like the results which ensue when I fail to profit from the learn-

ing I have mentioned. On the other hand, in the rather rare experiences. . . when I am able to accept myself as I am, and to be that self; when I am truly understanding of the way life seems to this other person, and when I can accept him as a separate individual who is not necessarily like me in attitudes, feeling, or beliefs, then the relationship seems exceptionally profitable; and both the other person and I gain from it in deep and significant ways.

FOCUS

The more the counselor empathically focuses on the needs and feelings of the client, the more the counselor understands the existential character of person- centered counseling. Existentialism requires that the counselor help the client to learn that his or her feelings and experiences are of value and relevance. It means giving to the client the feeling that he or she can trust the self and draw from within the self in order to discover new meanings. Empathetically focusing on the client's needs and feelings enables the client to become more aware of internal strengths. The counselor who centers on the needs and feelings of the client, freely and without reservation, says, in effect, "You are the more important person in this relationship." In this kind of atmosphere the client begins to feel that the most meaningful learning is the learning that comes from within; that out of the client's values, attitudes, feelings, and experiences emerge the best possible answers and guidelines for personal behavior. When the client experiences the empathic understanding of the counselor, the client begins to realize that those inner meanings can lead to more personally satisfying, appropriate, and self-enhancing behavior (Aspy, 1975; Patterson, 1986; Rogers, 1975).

The counselor who concentrates on the client's problem is not necessarily concentrating on the client. Person-centered counselors work with persons not problems. Mearns (1997:132) argues:

> The person-centered approach demands that the counselor grounds her working in the individuality of the client in front of her rather than designing that working aound a specific 'problem' or stereotype of a client group. For example, the person-centered counselor would seek to work with the person who was depressed rather than to work with the problem of depression. Similarly, the person-centered counselor would be seeking to meet and work with the individual client who happened to be gay rather than working with the client in a special way because he was gay.

A problem is an abstraction. It can be diagnosed and dissected; it can be explored and discussed; it can be written up in a case study; and it can be worked on coldly and scientifically. But to focus on a problem is to attend to a fragment of the person. Counseling, from a person-centered viewpoint, is not concerned with fragments. Needs and feelings must be considered in terms of the total person, the client as a being. Disproportionate attention to a problem usually means too much attention to superficials. The client can confront the personal meaning of behavior and move in the direction of becoming more fully functioning only when he or she feels that the counselor's primary commitment is to the client as a person and not with the client's problem. The central focus in person-centered counseling is the client as a person while other theories emphasize what they consider to be the most effective treatment modes for certain diagnosed problems. These are two very different ways of looking at clients and the process of helping them.

LIBERATING QUALITY

To be liberating requires emotional security and self-acceptance on the part of the counselor. If a client begins to express bitter invectives against a group, an institution, or an ideal with which the counselor strongly identifies, it requires an emotionally secure counselor to accept such expressions and feelings without moralizing and condemning. The counselor's beliefs and values will be constantly tested by clients who hold different views. But when the counselor truly believes that counseling exists for the liberation of the client, the counselor will not feel compelled to defend personal beliefs and values. If the client is to grow and understand the psychological meanings of certain experiences, the client must feel free enough to reveal the internal self without fear of contradiction or interference from the counselor. Most clients who enter counseling have been conditioned by society to hide their real selves. They have been taught to conceal their more authentic inner feelings in their relationships with others. The emergence of the authentic self, the evolvement of self-understanding, and the exploration of the internal world of the client come about when the client feels free to hold certain values, to accept them, to change them, or to reject them, and when the client experiences a freedom to remove the protective layers that cover inner feelings. Person-centered counseling requires the counselor to facilitate this process for the client.

OUTCOMES EMERGE FROM THE CLIENT

A person defines the self from the choices and actions he or she takes. Although a person lives in a physically determined world governed by physical laws, the individual still has the awesome power of choosing a life to live. An existential dimension of person-centered counseling is the recognition of the client's capacity to make choices and to take action on the basis of these choices (Kemp, 1971, pp. 20, 28). Counseling is a process and relationship in which the individual is free to become more free. It is *a relationship that facilitates growth and change in the client, which enables the client to become more freely and fully functioning.*

Clients must possess the freedom and right to make choices and decisions. This demands enormous faith and consistency on the part of the counselor—faith in the client's capacity to choose, and consistency in holding to that faith regardless of the choices the client makes. No client is incapable of making choices, although some may feel that they cannot. Often individuals have been directed and controlled to such an extent that they feel others should make choices for them. They fear becoming involved in self-determination since it is often an untried behavior. The counselor who is empathic and accepting of this attitude and enables the individual *to be* will facilitate the client's becoming more open to personal experience and perceiving the self with more confidence. The client who has been accepted and understood, and who experiences the deep faith of the counselor, will begin to see that if decisions are to be meaningful, they must be personally conceived, owned, and executed.

CONFIDENTIALITY

Effective counseling cannot occur unless the confidentiality of the relationship is assured. If a client cannot feel secure in revealing the self to the counselor, it is highly doubtful that counseling will be helpful and facilitating. Self-revelation and exploration take place only in an atmosphere of trust (Pietrofesa, Leonard, & Van Hoose, 1978; Pietrofesa, Hoffman, & Splete, 1984).

The client enters the counseling relationship more openly when it is known that the counselor will hold in confidence what is said. It is essential that the client feel completely secure about the confidential nature of the relationship; otherwise, he or she is uncomfortable and conceals the self.

Too many clients have bared their souls to counselors in what appears to be a confidential relationship only to find out later that what they revealed in a "moment of trust" was communicated to others. In some settings the counselor is perceived as the last person to be trusted.

Maintaining client confidences is not always easy. The ethics of counseling provide that, in those situations where information received in confidence indicates that the client may do serious harm to the self or to others, intervention by the counselor may be necessary. If the counselor feels that a confidence must be broken, the counselor should certainly do some soul-searching to find out if the break is necessary, and if it is being done for the good of some organization or group or because of the counselor's insecurity, ignorance, or ineptitude (Kottler & Brown, 1985).

No universal standard regarding the maintenance of client confidences can be clearly determined. Each counselor must translate general standards into a personal standard. The secure and competent counselor who has been able to translate the philosophical foundations of counseling into the practicality of daily work, is aware not only of the depth of the obligation to the client in matters of confidence but of the many uncomfortable moments that will be experienced in maintaining this ethical standard.

ACQUIRED ATTITUDES AND SKILLS

In the past, the counselor was essentially a dispenser of advice and information who in many cases was insensitive to the larger dimensions of the counseling role and function. Today's counselor must be highly knowledgeable in both the art and science of counseling. Today's counselor can no longer be just technically proficient. Regardless of the setting in which counselors work, they must be more sensitive to the potential contribution of their counseling to humanity; their functioning must be based on a broader perspective of the person and the counseling process. They must become involved in contributing to an improvement in the human condition by becoming more knowledgeable regarding the counseling relationship and its potential for assisting persons to improve their psychological stability.

Associations concerned with the professionalism of counseling support and affirm the concept of a quality educational program that is the *beginning* level of preparation for a counselor. This means that there is a specific body of knowledge that the counselor must have; knowledge that must continually be expanded, refined, and modified.

PHILOSOPHICAL AND PSYCHOLOGICAL PRINCIPLES

Professionalism is composed of counseling competency, ethical behavior, and an attitude that reflects one's philosophical, theoretical, and empirical views of the person, human behavior, and the counselor's role (Bergin, 1970). At its roots, counseling is a process expressing the counselor's philosophy of life. This means that each counselor must answer basic questions regarding the nature of human nature before effective counseling can occur.

The professional counselor has formulated a well thought-out rationale that guides professional behavior. The policy statements of the counseling profession leave no doubt about the need for a firm theoretical and philosophical foundation for counseling. A counselor cannot select appropriate role functions without considering human needs and the most effective counseling process for meeting these needs. The counselor cannot achieve the status of a professional without a consideration of these needs.

Beck (1965:1) believes it is imperative for counselors to consider the philosophy on which they base their functioning: "No field of endeavor which touches human lives can afford to leave its philosophical presuppositions unexamined".

One of the primary responsibilities of the professional is to examine and understand the basic purposes of professional activity. Arbuckle (1975) sees counseling as the expression of human values and human attitudes, a process in which the counselor develops a philosophical concept of the person, human nature, and the purpose of life. For Arbuckle, the first question that should be examined by the counselor is the question of *why* we do what we do, rather than *how* we do it.

The professional counselor has a philosophical and theoretical rationale that gives insight to the what and how of counseling. Out of a rationale for counseling emerges a consistent identity which translates itself into a professional role. Nietzche has said, "He who has a *why* to live can bear with almost any *how*." The counselor who has a "why" for counseling can more easily develop the "hows." The professional counselor does not have to search for methods of facing unusual situations, new experiences, and different clients. The professional counselor's "why" for counseling serves to clarify the "how." A counselor who does not begin to examine the "why" of personal and professional behavior will find it difficult to attain an integrated personal and professional life–the goal of a person-centered counselor.

A CONCEPT OF THE PERSON

We view the person as being free. The person may act or refuse to act, change or not change; as a free existent, the individual is nothing definite or finished, but is constantly coming to be. *Becoming is* more characteristic of the person than mere *being*. As a free existent, the person is responsible for personal human acts, which mirror the self and are expressed in a highly personal way (Patterson, 1986).

The person may be described as a responsible being, capable of self-direction, self-regulation, and self-understanding, and a being in the process of becoming. The person is a very complex being in whom many complicated elements fuse to form an interacting whole. Because the person is unique among all creatures and infinitely complex in derivations and being, the person can never *be fully* understood by the self and certainly not by anyone else. This uniqueness and complexity preclude any accurate diagnosis or statement of human needs and problems by others. This view makes the client the expert in self-diagnosis and in the identification of one's own human needs, problems, and the processes required to deal with them. The person-centered counselor assists the client to solve the client's own problems through the client's own resources.

The goals of person-centered counseling are to help the person to become more self-aware and self-actuated, to move forward in a positive and constructive way, to preserve and nourish personal uniqueness; to release within the person the positive forces for growth that the person possesses; and to facilitate self-clarification and self-understanding so that the client may discover the purpose of one's existence and the meaning of one's behavior.

This can be accomplished if the counselor can create a relationship in which the counselor is understanding, acceptant, empathic, permissive, concrete, and genuine, and if the counselor can consistently demonstrate a respect for personhood. When it is accomplished, then both the counselor and the helping process are person-centered.

BEING PRECEDES BECOMING

Before the client can *become*, the client must have the right to be. A client moves toward more personally satisfying behavior only when current behavior is examined and judged to be restrictive, inadequate, or harmful. A certain behavior is rejected only after it has been allowed to exist and only after it has been perceived as being damaging to the self (Combs, 1971; Kemp, 1971: 6). A client is motivated to change behavior when self-defeating behaviors are recognized and replaced with those that enhance the self.

For the self of the client to be freed for growth, however, it must first be accepted as it is. Acceptance of the client means an acceptance of the client's values and attitudes as an integral part of the client's behavior. The counselor does not have to accept the client's values and attitudes as the counselor's own, but he or she must be willing for the counselee to hold different values and attitudes–for an individual is only free to change values and attitudes when there is freedom to first hold them; and when the client feels that personal values and attitudes are not condemned, judged, or labeled as "bad," the client can then allow them to be discussed and evaluated. Behavioral change occurs when such dialogue and evaluation produce the desire to reject certain values and replace them with new and more self-enhancing values.

INTERACTING AND INTERDEPENDENT CORE CONDITIONS

It should be clear that the counseling relationship we describe in this chapter reflects the basic core conditions of *empathy, genuineness, or congruence,* and *unconditional positive regard.* These core conditions were developed, articulated, and constantly reiterated by Rogers throughout his career (Rogers, 1951, 1961, 1974, 1979, 1980). Nacmias (1990) has often used the metaphor of the loving situation when speaking about the core conditions. He says:

> I say that the first (congruence) concerns the loving person (the therapist). the second (unconditional positive regard) the beloved person (the client) and, finally, the third (empathy) is the quality of the relationship that links the two, namely love in action.

Mearns and Thorne (1988:19) report that a student, after assessing person-centered counseling wrote:

> Really, when you get down to basics, person-centered counseling is very simple. It's all about loving. It's about being free to treat other people in a loving way. It's trying to put loving into helping.

What constitutes the loving situation in counseling is the totality of the core conditions. Braaten (1986) emphasizes that the core conditions represent facets of a whole and it is the gestalt of the conditions that represents the therapist's contribution in therapy. He writes (1986:47):

A few examples will illustrate that these conditions do not operate independently but are parts of a whole having a range for autonomous expression. An overly obsessive-compulsive client will not tolerate a therapist who is perfectly empathic. A client who struggles to overcome unhealthy symbiosis may be threatened if the therapist is too warm and caring. A client who is attempting a more mature individuation may be overwhelmed if the therapist is uncritically genuine and self- disclosing. A client in an acute schizophrenic panic may have to be hospitalized for a while before the usual therapist conditions will . take effect.

Mearns and Thorne (1988:92-95) indicate that the core conditions often exist in combination, e.g., unconditional positive regard and congruence where the existence of one facilitates the development of the other: when the counselor accepts the client then it is easier for the counselor to trust the client and consequently feel free to be fully congruent. Another example might be the relationship between congruence and empathy where congruence allows the counselor to be an accurate rather than a shadowy and distorting reflector to the client.

We can best summarize this chapter on the relationship drawing from the words of Mearns and Thorne (1988: 15):

> The core conditions are simple enough to state, but for a counselor to develop and maintain such attitudes involves a lifetime's work and demands a commitment which has profound implications not only for the counselor's professional activity but for his/her life as a whole.... The words can trip off the tongue but their significance is little short of awe-inspiring.

REFERENCES

Arbuckle, D. S. (1975). *Counseling and psychotherapy: An existential-humanistic view.* Boston: Allyn and Bacon.

Aspy, D. N. (1975). Empathy: Let's get the hell on with it. *The Counseling Psychologist, 5.* 10-14.

Beck, C. E. (1965). *Philosophical foundations of guidance.* Englewood Cliffs, NJ: Prentice-Hall.

Bergin, A. E. (1970). Psychology as a science of inner experience. In J. T. Hart & T. M. Tomlinson (Eds.). *New directions in client-centered therapy.* Boston: Houghton-Mifflin, 61-69.

Braaten, L. J. (1986). Thirty years with Rogers' necessary and sufficient conditions of therapeutic personality change: A personal evaluation. *Person-Centered Review, 1,* 1, 37-50.

Combs, C. (1971). The treatise on existential counseling by C. G. Kemp. *The Counseling Psychologist. 2,* 43.

Gelso, C. J., & Carter, J. A. (1985). The relationship in counseling and psychotherapy: Components, consequences, and theoretical antecedents. *The Counseling Psychologist, 13,* 2, 155-244.

Gendlin, E. T. (1970). Existentialism and experiential psychotherapy. In J. T. Hart & T. M. Tomlinson (Eds.). *New directions in client-centered therapy.* Boston: Houghton Mifflin, 73.

Greenson, R. R. (1967). The Technique and practice of psychoanalysis (Vol. 1.) New York: International Universities Press.

Jones, A. J. (1963). *Principles of guidance* (5th ed.). New York: McGraw-Hill.

Kemp, C. G. (1971). Existential counseling. *The Counseling Psychologist, 2,* 2-30.

Kottler, J. A., & Brown, R. W. (1996). *Introduction to therapeutic counseling (3rd ed.)* Pacific Grove, CA: Brooks/Cole.

Lister, J. L. (1967). Theory aversion in counselor education. *Counselor Education and Supervision,* 6, 92.

Mearns, D., & Thorne, B. (1988). *Person-Centered Counseling In Action.* Beverly Hills, CA: Sage.

Mearns, D. (1997). *Person Centered Counseling Training.* London: Sage.

Moustakas, C. (1986). Being in, being for, and being with. *Humanistic Psychologist, 14,* 2, 100-104.

Nacmias, E. (1990). The spiritual: A state of awareness in person-centered therapy. *Renaissance, 7,* 1, 2.

Patterson, C. H. (1986). *Theories of counseling and psychotherapy* (Fourth Edition). New York: Harper and Row.

Pietrofesa, J J., Hoffman, A., & Splete, H. (1984). *Counseling: An introduction.* Boston: Houghton Mifflin.

Pietrofesa, J. J., Leonard, G. E., & Van Hoose, W. (1978). *The authentic counselor* (Second Edition). Chicago: Rand McNally, 117-178.

Rogers, C. R. (1951, renewed 1979). *Client-centered therapy.* Boston: Houghton Mifflin, 483-522.

Rogers, C R. (1961). *On becoming a person.* Boston: Houghton Mifflin.

Rogers, C. R. (1970). A conversation with Carl Rogers. In J. T. Hart & T. N. Tomlinson (Eds.). *New directions in client-centered therapy.* Boston: Hougton Mifflin, 532.

Rogers, C. R., & Wood, J. (1974). Client-centered theory: Carl Rogers. In A. Burton (Ed.), *Operational theories of personality.* New York: Bruner/Mazel.

Rogers, C. R. (1975). Empathic: An unappreciated way of being. *The Counseling Psychologist 5,* 2-10.

Rogers, C. R. (1977). *On personal power.* New York: Delacorte.

Rogers, C. R. (1980). *A way of being.* Boston: Houghton Mifflin.

Rogers, C. R. (1986). A comment from Carl Rogers. *Person-Centered Review.* 1, 3-5.

Stewart, N. K., Winborn, B. B., Johnson, R. G., Burks, H. M., & Engelkes, J. R. (1978). *Systematic counseling.* Englewood Cliffs, NJ: Prentice-Hall, 43-44.

Walz, G. R. (1984). The role of the counselor with computers. *Journal of Counseling and Development ,* 6. 135-138.

Chapter 7

CARL ROGERS' INFLUENCE ON THE BIRTH OF MY CHILDREN*

BEATE HOFMEISTER

I was interviewed by Carl Rogers in July 1983. A transcript of that audio-tape session is followed by comments of both the client and the therapist. A medical case history about the author's infertility adds factual evidence to the persona consequences that followed the interview. My experience has led me to conclude that the quality of a short (25-minute) interview can provide enduring effects for the mental, emotional, and perhaps even the physical, disability of a client.

This *Interview* by Carl Rogers (CR), therapist, and Beate Hofmeister (BH), client, took place in July 1983. The interview took place at a cross-cultural communication workshop in Geneva, Switzerland to demonstrate Carl Rogers' work to the participants. The workshop's topic was "Cross-Cultural Communication and the Resolution of Social Tension." During the time of the conference a new phase of international disarmament talks were being conducted in Geneva, but that ended without positive results. Carl Rogers and I were surrounded by a semicircle of 120 participants during a large group meeting.

CR: Beate, I appreciate your being here [background noises!.... Shut out the people, and shut out the microphone, and shut out the damn machines and I guess I will be quiet for a moment [one minute silence]. And now I think I can be with you [shuffling of feet, but more silence] and I'd be very glad to hear whatever you want to talk about.

BH: Yeah, I want to talk about things that are related to our workshops topic. And to me something personally very touching is the state—yeah, the state of the world—you could call it. I live in an area in Germany where the woods are about to die, the water is being contaminated, there are six atom-

*Beate Hofmeister, "Carl Rogers' Influence on the Birth of My Children," *Person-Centered Review*, Vol. 2, No. 3, August 1987, pp. 315-328. Copyright 1988 by Sage Publications, Inc. Reprinted by permission of Sage Publications, Inc.

ic reactors in our. . . we have a big arsenal of chemical weapons there, and—I moved out of the city in order to stay at least mentally healthy. And it ended up having phantom-fighters going over the house every day. And this really scares me very much.

CR: You sound very frightened and almost despaired. You are just continually in danger of technology, and arms.

BH: Yeah. Yeah, I feel that all of my personal life—I can manage those things. Like—I will find a way on my own. But with these fears I really, I really don't know what I can do about it. I feel it is completely out of my control and it's like a feeling—the end may come, come to pieces tomorrow or so—just by accident.

CR: So it is both a feeling of hopelessness and a feeling that ah—we might all be destroyed tomorrow.

BH: Yeah. And what am I doing, I am striving for things that I think are important to me, but also I feel: Isn't it—you know—completely—I don't know what! To strive for things while the world—maybe comes apart, may be vaporized tomorrow—just by an accident.

CR: Does it make any sense to try to do constructive things when we may all be blown up?

BH: Yeah. [pause, more slowly] Yeah—and—it makes me feel—feel suicidal. It seems so stupid to care for life in a situation like that one.

CR: You ask yourself: Is it really worth living under such a—such a terrible situation? It really does make you contemplate suicide.

BH: Yes. I really want to live and I want to build things, I want to do things, and here I am—I mean—tending my dog, because I don't want to have any children, to raise in a world like this—I mean. [pause] It's...

CR: Your own desire seems so reasonable and normal and yet you feel you can't have children in this terrible world. And you are cut off from any of the constructive outcomes that you really would like.

BH: Yeah—I'm doing them, but—I need so much energy doing them. Just to get me going again and—yeah—it seems so—the little personal world seems so—yeah, I don't know—out of perspective!— in view of those bigger political issues, when they arise.

CR: I'm concerned because there are two things that I want to do: I want to ask someone to let me know when 25 minutes has gone by. You will be a timekeeper? [audience: Yes!] And I also want to take off my jacket. I didn't know it would be so warm. Can you hold this for me? [Gives away the microphone to take off his jacket] I'm a little sorry for the interruption, but I do realize: Personally you are working toward constructive things, but it's like having to. . . tread water or something, to get there, so many obstacles, so much—so much potential difficulty in a way.

BH: You-know, I think I am strong and I can do things, but this completely weakens me. I don't know how. [short pause]

CR: You are a strong person, but in this situation all your strength is sapped away.

BH: Yeah, I don't see anything I can **really** do about it. I mean, if I go to a politician–I don't have any trust in changing them. It's just so enormous that while trying to change it–I don't know–I mean while driving here I had an accident, just becauase I was inattentive for part of a second and this might happen to the next atomic reactor or to one of those jet- people flying there, being just inattentive–and being human in a way.

CR: Hhm, hhm. You were human enough to let your attention stray for a minute and an accident happened. And it might happen to one of them.

BH: Yeah. Yeah.

CR: With much more disastrous results.

BH: Yeah. Yeah. Spoil, spoil the world–and I have tried ways of coming at it. I went to meditation–workshops and came to face with my own aggressions. But I really don't, don't have an answer and I feel completely [searching for words] ah hhm, I don't know what.

CR: What the hell can I do? I feel completely blocked, so to speak.

BH: Yeah. Yeah.

CR: Paralyzed.

BH: Just paralyzed.

Both: Paralyzed.

BH: And I turn around and get–do jokes, you know, just kind of get myself up again, and–but really deep down, very often I kind of do things not to **feel**, to feel these very underlying fears.

CR: So that you could lighten the surface sometimes, but down. . .

BH: Yeah.

CR: deep there are the same feelings of apprehension and hopelessness.

BH: [Silently] Yeah. [Very loud and fast:] Sometimes I think: Shouldn't I live just on a one-to- the-next-minute basis, and not plan anything, just take life from one minute, but I could not live like that. Yeah, I don't have that outlook!

CR: Hhm.

BH: I have it in my career, I–yeah. And I feel so much in need–of emotional support and–I feel there is a need that nobody could fill. You could fill it by abolishing all those arms, but what happens is that they are putting more and more arms into Germany.

CR: So you feel your needs are not unreasonable or impossible. They could be met. But here it is against the context of more and more arms, and more and more destructiveness all around you.

BH: I, I, I think–I don't feel ah hhm an ill person or anything, but I feel I–I'm just not made up to, to, to get along with these, with the emotional side of it. I can understand it intellectually and I can find intellectual solutions, but–I don't think–that will get me anywhere.

CR: It sounds to me as though you are saying: I am a healthy person, but I am in a sick situation.

BH: Yeah. Yeah, very sick, sick situation. The other day I heard Karl Popper giving a lecture and saying: "We are the only generation who in the whole university–in the whole universe–who can blow, blow this beautiful planet to pieces" and that really–that's very–very touching to me.

CR: It almost brings tears to your eyes, doesn't it? Thinking of the fact. that we might destroy this beautiful, wonderful universe. We are the first generation who can do it.

BH: [Crying:] I mean–just by chance! And–I don't see a way of getting away from that. Stopping it! [Pause]

CR: It just fills you with tears to think of the tragedy of the–and how little you do about it.

BH: [Crying] I really–I just, just have to try to be strong. . . [crying]. .. destroy me. [Crying]

CR: Saying: I can try to be strong, but to what, to what purpose?

BH: I'm not strong enough to–for that! I'm not strong! [Crying]

CR: You are a strong person, but not strong enough to live in that situation!

BH: . . . Yeah. . . life seems to get so absurd, if I can't...[not understandable, said crying]

CR: If what?

BH: If I get into contact with these feelings, life just starts being absurd! [Crying]

CR: Hhm.

BH: I'm not sure whether I am just cynical working with people and giving, giving hope to them and saying: Oh, you can change your life for the better, when really,–yeah, when really I see that I, I can't change it.

CR: When you are in your work trying to give hope to people and yet, within yourself you feel: Is there hope?

BH: I feel that I don't really hope, I don't have much hope for–for the-world!–Yeah! And I try to, I know in my family there are some people who are busy in government things and trying to free prisoners from, from the East by buying them. And–I think, you know–it's kind of–it's trying, but it's not changing anything.

CR: People you know, and perhaps you too, are making efforts, but will it change anything significant at all?

BH: Yeah, and I try to, try to make them bring others here to this workshop, because I, yeah! I had hoped of. . . [crying]. . . just meeting someone–changing a little bit and. . . [crying]. . . nobody seems to be interested in those human questions. They are just talking and talking [in tears] on an intellectual level, which I'm sure won't change anything.

CR: What you want is for people to be in touch with their feelings about it, not just talk, talk, talk about it!—And you have, had hopes that perhaps here you might find something in the way of at least steps toward change!

BH: Yeah, if not steps toward change at least solitary or—you know, I mean—even being afraid together.

CR: Hhm, hhm.

BH: Yeah, it also scares me that I find people here are always talking on these intellectual levels and I can tune into that and talk about very elaborate things, but I don't see it will change this situation at all! [In tears]

CR: You feel that it might be better even if we were all afraid together.

BH: Yeah.

CR: At least that would be in touch with the feelings not just the intellect.

BH: Yeah! I think that would at least be some support for, for a situation as helpless as that [crying]. Yeah!

CR: Just to know that others are as despairing and afraid as you are would be a support, somehow!

BH: Yeah! [Pause]

CR: You would not feel so alone!

BH: Yeah!—I feel getting in touch with things again! If I think about these things, I get sort of—reality is so absurd that I, I really have to see that I get in touch with reality again. I will touch things, or at home I grab my cat or something—

CR: Hhm. Hhm.

BH: I mean just to keep me, to keep me sane.

CR: Hhm. Hhm. Somehow have to keep your feet on the ground somehow, or touching something that's real. And I guess the thing that most likely would be. . . is to touch something that is real in other people, too.

BH: Yeah. Yeah, Yeah! Get into touch with people and—I think. Maybe it's a—a naive solution—but I, I really, I would deeply believe people get into touch again [crying] and. . . with these really abstract things that—maybe we can make it stop then [in tears].

CR: You do have a belief that if people could really be in touch with each other genuinely on a deep level, that might accomplish something.

BH: Yeah! Yeah! I mean we'll have conflict and everything, but if we are in touch we can work it through! [Tears]

CR: It wouldn't be smooth but it would be real.

BH: Yeah, yeah! And—yeah, the most frightening thing—I think—is the bomber pilot driving there and dropping all these bombs, destroying everything without seeing or being in touch with it.

CR: Hhm, hhm.

BH: Or just pushing a button and killing millions of people.

CR: Hhm, hhm.

BH: . . . where you don't even have to look at what you do [crying].

CR: They are all so separated from the consequences of their actions that this makes it incredibly impersonal!

BH: Yeah, I think the only way to stop it is really to [sighing] to get personal balance again! Like if I moved to a village in order to avoid this, this faraway thing and in this community if I go away my neighbor says "Hello" and if I come back he will take me into his arms—now he is a completely uneducated man, I'm quite sure he is almost illiterate, but—I think he knows more about the world than all these politicians!

CR: One thing that comes through in almost everything you say is how much you dislike the abstract, the intellectual. . . so distant from the realness of people.

BH: Yeah. From, from, yeah from, life!

CR: Yeah, from life!

BH: I mean, life really is very simple!

CR: That's why you spoke on the simplicity of your neighbor: Just being real! And in touch with you.

BH: Yeah, and give more worth to—I think we devaluate those things! We devaluate love, we devaluate—being in doubt or just being together! Even here—I mean the people who come here are a rather entitled or privileged group, but even here we go again into trying to be intellectual, or trying to show how, how intelligent we are, or whatever, and—I really think—yeah—we are so used to, to, to go away from those...

CR: So even here you are disappointed in the—in the intellectual quality, the abstract quality of the fact that people are up in their heads.

BH: Yeah. I don't want to evaluate intellectual things. They are very—I, I appreciate them, but if they stop us, if they are between getting into contact, then I really resent them! And, yeah—I feel on a political level this is what brought us the atomic bomb and what brings usually these stupid talks about "Abrusting"—about dearming—while everybody takes money to, to buy all the arms they can produce!

CR: It is just an absurdly contradictory situation, in which we—people say one thing and do the complete opposite.

BH: I feel I can—I can't say anything else about it—and I feel very—shaken and torn—to try to stay, not to break down.

CR: You. . . I'm sort of at the end of my rope, sort of the end of my rope and I don't see how I can go further and—I feel if I went further I might just break up, crack up!

BH: Yeah. Yeah, I'm also afraid that it might happen here and I, I don't want that to happen.

CR: You are really afraid personally, that might happen to you if you delve anymore deeply into these feelings.

BH: Yeah. I'm very, very scared of it!

CR: Your feeling of fear is just deep, and real, and very present for you!

BH: Yeah. I've, I've had very deep, deep fears that blocked me for a while in other things, I'm–I still have, get fears in other parts of my life where I feel, I can go to people who support me and I can go at those fears and–I don't always find a solution, but I won't block me and I can go on, and usually my life widens, I feel more alive, or–the older I get, the younger I feel! [Laughs]

CR: Sharing your fears. . . it does not block you from expressing, makes you feel younger? Better?

BH: Yeah, makes the world alive!

CR: Hhm.

BH: And–if I concentrate on this other side–it really is a feeling of the world coming to an end. And–in driving here we stopped by a town and saw the lake and the mountains and it was very, very–you know–just so beautiful and there was water just next to my feet and birds being there. It was just being in harmony with. . .

CR: Hhm, hhm.

BH: Yeah, with life and with nature. And then these thoughts came, you know, the next second, I mean [crying] just glow out! Just could glow and this is it!

CR: There you could feel this appreciation of how beautiful our world is, and how marvelous it is.

BH: Yes!

CR: And then the thought comes: Yes, but it might be vaporized any moment.

BH: Yes. Yes.

CR: And it's the thoughts that are very. . .

BH: [Cries] I can't say anything! [Very silently] - [Pause] I really want to, I really want to live, and I think I really, I have a very–I really

CR: It's just a plea: I, I love life, I want to live. I want to be alive!

BH: [Crying] Yeah. Yeah. [Stammering] I'm so afraid that it could be taken away at any minute.

CR: Life is so rich, and so full, and so marvelous, and yet, there is always that fear hanging over you.

BH: Yeah! It is good that you are there! It is good that you are there!

CR: You really appreciate being with me and my being with you.'

BH: Yeah. Yeah.

CR: I appreciate being with you!

BH: I can't say anything else.

CR: You've said all you can say. So here you would like to stop?

BH: Yeah.

Comments *(immediately following the interview)*

BH: I appreciated the opportunity of talking to you, because I know that you are a person who can be very close to somebody without grabbing at a person. And I really don't want to be grabbed, but just have somebody to be close to. It does not take away the problems but I feel, I'm being understood and that probably is enough for the next two days, or maybe longer than that–I don't know. It makes it more reachable.

CR: This was a very moving interview for me, because I feel, Beate is speaking for so many others and–it was very touching! And–was moved by her statement that "even if we were just afraid together" that might be of some help. Just being human with each other, sharing our feelings, somehow takes away the edge of the despair. And–I certainly didn't plan to, and I'm sure you didn't either, to discover some easy or quick solution, but I do feel, that to me it seemed like a good relationship, and open relationship. I gradually felt more and more at ease in moving around in your world and sensing what your world is like. I guess somehow–one thing that–also was very moving to me–because I have six grandchildren and three great-grandchildren–was when you said that you have to take care of your dog, because you didn't feel you could bring children into a world like this. That was very, very moving.

BH: We had lots of problems with terrorism in Germany. When I got into touch with my feelings, I could understand why people become terrorists. Sometimes I am very angry too.

CR: It has a lot of meaning to me, Beate, that your situation is so, so awful, that you came to really understand the feelings of the terrorists: destroy!

BH: Yeah, change, change things, in such an absurd forceful situation, change it by force. I mean it would not be my solution. I, I, I think life is it, but also I could understand how somebody gets to such despaired conclusion.

CR: You would not do it, but it did become understandable. Also she [Beate] spoke not only of the indifference of people, but of the fact that they are afraid to face their own feelings. Their own feelings are so awful that it is easier to . . . [unintelligible] it on entirely, I think that is a very real part of the situation.

BH: Also I can't grasp: Like in my family–Germans started two wars and–which I don't understand! In my family all the men in two generations have been killed. My father was the only survivor. And in my generation– my age group two people have killed themselves. So this is really something I don't understand, and I don't understand how a country like my country, ,goes on, or how a country like the U.S. is going on–and not stopping it, having lived–I mean–if war had been away–but I mean we all still see them. I've had clients who were severely crippled from the Vietnam War. And nobody stops! I can't grasp that.

CR: It seems incredible to you that we could go through that experience time and again.

BH: [Shortly after the workshop] For me the answer to all this was: In such a crazy and dangerous situation the only thing that you can do is live, to do it, try to feel how it is to live. And that's all.

The following comments were made by Carl Rogers during the Conference on the Evolution of Psychotherapy in 1985 in Phoenix, Arizona.

I held an interview with a woman in West Germany, a demonstration. I thought, "I can't be of any help to this woman." What she was describing was the fact that she lived in an area, which, first of all, was polluted by chemical plants, so she had moved away from the city. Now she found that she was in the midst of a whole lot of missile emplacements, and now the United States was going to plant more missiles right in her backyard practically, and she felt utterly hopeless. She felt sure that at any moment she might be incinerated. Her life was just one desperate hopelessness. She said she would permit herself to have a dog, because she could tolerate that. She certainly would not permit herself to have a baby because the future was too black. I didn't know how to—I was thinking during the interview: "There is not one thing I can do about the problems she is talking about, except to understand." And so I understood as deeply as possible—as deeply as I was capable—her despair, her hopelessness, the impossibility of her situation. After the interview she said she thought it was helpful, although I wasn't sure why.

A number of months later, nearly a year later, she wrote me to say, that it had been a remarkably helpful interview, that somehow she has never been able to get out completely her feelings. People were so struck by the desperate quality of her situation, that they could not permit it to all come out. "If the world is not quite as bad as you think it is, oh—you ought to listen to my situation, I'm in a worse situation," there were all kinds of helpful comments, but never an understanding that went deep enough to permit her to find any sort of creative solution. She said after that interview she was able to become reconciled to the fact that all right, her situation was very bad. She was fortunate in the fact that if war came, she would almost certainly be among the first to be destroyed. She was somewhat thankful for that.

She also began to realize that there were things she could do. She joined the peace movement, she became active in that she went on with the different creative things that she was doing with her life. And at the end of the letter she said, "And now I am having a baby." And last year I saw her. She is now having her second child; she has really found very creative solutions to a really desperate life situation. So that I feel: Yes, therapy does provide the nurturing situation in which creativity can emerge.

The comments below were made by Carl Rogers during the Cross Cultural Communication Workshop, Szeged, Hungary, 1986.

We had an interview several years ago. I remember that as a very difficult interview for me, because she brought up things that I had not thought of a client bringing up. So I ask myself, "Can I be prepared for the unknown, for the unexpected, for something I didn't have any idea might come up? And can I be free of making judgments, can I hear whatever comes out and accept it as it is without making a judgment about it? And can I begin to catch the real flavor of what it is like to be my client at this moment? And can I accept the fact that almost certainly in the beginning I will make mistakes?" I will not understand quite correctly. Because I like to be able to accept the fact that I may make mistakes and then correct myself to get in real tune with the client. And not to be critical with myself if I do have a little difficulty in understanding just the exact meaning. And I guess the main thing I ask myself is, "Can I let myself go and really let myself enter into this other person's world, just as this world exists for him or her?" And then one other thing occurs to me: This is only going to be a very brief interview of 15 minutes. "Can I be prepared for the fact that perhaps not much will happen, and also be prepared for the fact that sometimes in 15 minutes very significant things happen. In other words, I just want to be the maximum of flexibility and openness to whatever comes forth."

Medical History of My Infertility and Personal Consequences That Followed the Interview

At age 14 I had begun to menstruate, but never was able to reach a periodical cycle. During my teens I found it quite comfortable that I did not bleed. I traveled around the world for six weeks to three months each year during that time and attributed the irregularities to that and also to my youth. At age 19 I became sexually active and began to take the pill for birth control. For the next 12 years without intermission I used a low-hormone pill. During these years my husband and I did not want children of our own and were agreed that in the world as we experienced it, we would adopt children if we felt the wish to educate and live with children.

When we moved to the countryside our life situation and attitude changed in a way that we both hoped to have children. For the next three years my reproductive functions could not be stimulated and finally my gynecologist referred me to a university where hormone treatment was suggested for my infertility. I took the medication at home and was informed about the necessary medical compliance, which meant to have sex according to a schedule. As a result, a multiple pregnancy was to be expected. I did not want to give birth to five children at once and I could not imagine being involved sexually without being emotionally ready. I felt that there is no use in forcing my body into something she does not want to do naturally. (I prefer to refer to my body as "she" because "it" reduces the awareness of my femininity.) My husband supported me and was content to live without children as we had done for the last 14 years.

Philosophically, I thought that not anything that can be done has to be done, and that I would have to dispense with my hope for gestation. I felt quite alone in the sadness and mourning for my unborn child or children. At the same time, I did want to understand the meaning of what my body wanted to teach me. I understood that I had to get into better contact with it and started my own program, which included concentration, relaxation, and meditation and some of the methods outlined by Simonton, using imagery of my body and its functions. I did not do this to become fertile, but to learn more about myself. Two times each day for about 15 minutes I would take time for myself, lie down and do the exercise I had prescribed for myself in my mind. After a while I could locate my inner organs and became aware of the fact that blood pressure and temperature were too low in my inner sexual organs. I enjoyed influencing these parts and felt fresh, active, and healthy any time I had been through my be-good-to-yourself time. I am quite aware of the fact that there was no scientific medical explanation for this or the following, but that did not bother me at all.

At the time of the interview with Carl this had all happened. I felt in good contact with my body, she had become my friend. In the interview with Carl I felt deeply understood, but I would not have dreamed that it might have any influence on my physical condition. Intellectually I was very astonished that there might be any connections between my infertility and my desperation about the world situation and my fear of the future. After the workshop I wanted to understand more fully and mentally what had happened in that short period of having another person be with me. I listened to the audiotape, tried to analyze it, and found some concluding sentences that were important: A new generation, with our support, can change the world. We will change the world by investing ourselves in this new generation. I will do for life what I can in my personal life. This will influence others. Very slowly the future did not seem so black. I felt supported in knowing that there is a network of persons who do want constructive changes and work for them. I do not attribute it to chance that my daughter was born 11 months after the interview. Since there was no menstruation, the time of her conception remains unknown.

(I was surprised and happy when I—in addition to my subjective feeling—received proof of my pregnancy.) The pregnancy and birth all were quite natural. I was very astonished when, after her birth, some of the participants of the Geneva workshop asked me whether I attributed her birth to that interview. Not knowing the specific background they must have had an intuitive understanding of the impact of that interaction. I am also very thankful that 18 months after my daughter's birth I bore a son. I hope I will be blessed with a third child. They are my hope and my investment in the future.

CONCLUSIONS

A short 25-minute interview that provided the person-centered conditions for growth had an enduring effect on my outlook for the future and the accompanying cognitions. I knew about all the behavioral methods and techniques to change the perception of a depressive (which I don't consider myself to be). My cognitions began to change when I felt fully understood and accepted my reality. Emotionally the despair is gone today. I enjoy the growth of my children and my growing with them. I hope those dark sides of living in the 1980s can be changed toward a more constructive way of being more human, more natural, more earthy. I just do the best I can.

There is no external proof that my theory is right, that this interview helped me to overcome my infertility or changed my physical disability, but also is not refutable. I thank Carl for my babies.

Chapter 8

PERSON-CENTERED GROUP COUNSELING

The characteristics of person-centered group counseling that set it apart from other forms of group counseling revolve around its emphasis on philosophy, natural goals, definitions, the complexity of the process, the counselor as a person, the mode of communication, confrontation, and voluntarism.

PHILOSOPHY

Person-centered group counseling finds its philosophic nourishment from the insights of Carl Rogers, and others, regarding the nature of the person, how and why the person perceives and behaves and under what circumstances, and the degree to which a person's self-concept influences perceptions and behavior. This is a rich philosophical heritage and the person-centered group counselor attempts to put it into practice, both professionally and personally.

In translating the basic philosophical constructs of person-centered counseling into the group setting, the Rogerian counselor is still person-centered. This essentially means that the person-centered group counselor focuses on the intrapersonal and interpersonal needs of group members and places those needs ahead of the counselor's needs. Although person-centered counselors are now generally liberated from the constraint of not merely reflecting the feelings of clients, this liberation should not translate itself into an experience in which the counselor's needs to be emotionally open and honest bring about domination of the individual or group experience so that the client's needs are pushed into the background and the counselor's needs are brought to the foreground of the helping process. Our experience indicates that some person-centered counselors have used the group experience to push into the foreground certain personal concerns that the process model of the theory prevented them from introducing in the past.

142

Rogers (1971:278) expresses this concern when he indicates that:

> If I am currently distressed by something in my own life, I am willing to express this in the group. I do have some sort of professional conscience about this, however, because if I am being paid to be a facilitator, and if my problem is severe, I feel that I should work it out in a staff group or with some therapist rather than taking the time of the group.

Kopp (1976:5) clearly illustrates the concern we have that some counselors may use the individual or group process in purely selfish terms: "One of the luxuries of being a psychotherapist is that it helps to keep you honest. It's a bit like remaining in treatment all our life."

We agree that the counseling profession offers a counselor a vehicle for being psychologically stable and that a competent and sensitive counselor should be continually involved in examining personal goals, motives, and values; but this is quite different from the deliberate use of the counseling relationship for selfish reasons. Gendlin (1970) presents a balanced view that enables the counselor to be both an experiencing participant in the process of counseling while also being attentive to the needs of clients: "Therapy must be experiential. . . experiencing is a moving, directly felt process. Interpersonal relationships carry the experiencing process forward, as the therapist expresses his own actual reactions. . . at the same time gives room, attention, and reference to the client's felt reactions" (p. 93).

If a counselor is philosophically person-centered, then that counselor must give way to the needs of the group when his or her personal needs are in conflict with, or interfere with, the needs of the group.

NATURAL GOALS

The goals of person-centered group counseling revolve around the needs of group members, and these goals can never be specifically identified until the counselor has met with a group and goals evolve from within the group through the process of verbal interaction. There are, however, certain general goals that characterize person-centered group counseling. These goals provide the counselor with a framework for applying person-centered counseling.

Rogers (1967:178) indicates that the group experience is aimed at returning to participants an ownership of self and that the process is naturalistic. That is, participants, by their very nature, will move toward goals that express their humanness and that this movement is a very natural process:

Group members show a natural and spontaneous capacity for dealing in a helpful, facilitative, and therapeutic fashion with the pain and suffering of others .

. . . He (a group member) knew intuitively how to be understanding and acceptant.

. . . This kind of ability (to be understanding and acceptant) shows up so commonly in groups that it has led me to feel that the ability to be healing or therapeutic is far more common in human life than we might suppose.

and

. . . Psychotherapy is releasing an already existing capacity in a potentially competent individual (Rogers, 1959: 221)

Coulson (1970:6-11) reinforces the goal of allowing human nature to take its course in the following statements:

. . . the critical group event is simply the process of time passing and our staying together.

. . . The sole necessary and sufficient condition for an encounter group is that there be an occasion for it .

. . . The encounter will happen if you give people sufficient time together without a distracting task and put someone with them as a leader who will not do traditional leader things—who knows enough, that is, not to get people organized, not to tell them how to encounter, or to set up an agenda.

Martin (1972) has said that if the client is enabled to have the self emerge in a natural way, then the client will: ". . . come as close to the truth that he can stand to come and he will do so repeatedly."

Meador (1975) indicates that group-centered counseling is a natural experience for the client that is facilitated by the attitude of the counselor: ". . . the growthful potential of any individual will tend to be released in a relationship in which the helping person is experiencing and communicating realness, caring, and a deeply sensitive nonjudgmental understanding."

Rogers (1967) further believes that counseling should not only be a natural experience for the client, but that the development of a more enlightened theory of person-centered group counseling can be served by naturalistic observation: "I am not aiming at a high level theory of group process but rather at a naturalistic observation out of which, I hope, true theory can be built."

DEFINING THE PROCESS

We prefer to call the application of the person-centered view "person-centered group counseling" because such a titling indicates that the group procedures used flow from a particular and unified theory. Rogers (1970:4-5) prefers to call the process a basic encounter, although he admits that the process is similar to those encounter processes labeled as "T-groups" and "sensitivity training."

T-group: originally tended to emphasize human relations skills but has become much broader in approach.

Encounter group (or basic encounter group): tends to emphasize personal growth and the development and improvement of interpersonal communication and relationships through an experiential process.

Sensitivity training group: may resemble either T-group or encounter group.

Person-centered group counseling is also preferred by us since it gives the process an identity that is separate from those groups with which Rogers (1970: 4-5) does not have a theoretical or process congruence: sensory awareness groups, body awareness groups, body movement groups, creativity workshops, organizational development groups, team-building groups, Gestalt groups, and Synanon or "game" groups.

Rogers (1970:33) defines the basic encounter with an illustration taken from the process:

A man tells, through his tears, of the tragic loss of his child, a grief which he is experiencing for the first time, not holding back his feelings in any way. Another man says to him, also with tears in his eyes, "I've never before felt a real physical hurt in me from the pain of another. I feel completely with you." This is a basic encounter .

Bebout (1974:372) gives a more formal definition to the basic encounter: "Encounter happens psychologically without physical touching—it is mental contact, lasting or momentary. It requires two or more people being equally and emotionally open, direct, expressive, and personal in communicating with each other."

Although Rogers (1970) identifies the basic encounter group as being different from a Gestalt group and indicates the difference by stating that in a Gestalt group the "therapist focuses on one individual at a time, but from a diagnostic and therapeutic point of view" (p. 5), Hansen, Warner, and Smith (1976), in their identification of the different theories of group work, lump both approaches together in a chapter entitled "Self Theory and Gestalt

Encounter Groups." On the other hand, Gazda (1975), in his presentation of eleven different theories of group work, retains a traditional labeling of the Rogerian basic encounter group when he calls it "client-centered" group counseling.

Both Rogers and Bebout, in the preceding definitions, indicate that the basic encounter is an event within the process of group interaction. Both definitions imply that groups meet until, at some time, the basic encounter takes place between and among participants. We believe that the basic encounter is a desired and necessary experience within the process of group work but, once again, we prefer to label the process as "person-centered group counseling" because such a labeling captures the meaning and range of the entire process rather than a specific event (the basic encounter) within it.

Coulson (1970:6-16) believes that a basic encounter group takes place informally and develops whenever time is available and persons gather in an unstructured way. He goes on to further clarify his definition of the basic encounter group:

> An encounter group is what happens when you have a lot of time to spend with people and no agenda.
> . . . if there is to be room for feelings in our communal lives, as I think there must be if we are to grow, an uncluttered special occasion is necessary. But no more than this is necessary. A basic encounter group is simply such a special occasion.
> Though one hears it is so, an encounter group is not really defined as "where one vents his emotions." It is rather where, because there is nothing else to do, one moves eventually toward talking about what is hard to say.

From Coulson's definitions we see that a basic encounter can occur almost anywhere and under any circumstances as long as persons have the time to come together in a group, have no agenda, and are willing to share feelings that are typically difficult to share in other settings.

Both Rogers and Coulson desire to have the basic encounter concept applied in a variety of settings in order to liberate persons from feelings that have typically hampered their lives. In fact, Rogers (1970: 135-148) visualizes the basic encounter concept being applicable in industry, government, race relations, families, educational institutions, a process that can bridge the generation gap, and a process that can contribute to world peace by easing international tensions. By labeling the process as "basic encounter," the implication is that they hope to free it from the formal field of counseling and psychotherapy and make it more available to the average person in a world that is becoming more impersonal and insensitive. We fully support the intentionality of the basic encounter, but we also desire to have professional counselors and psychotherapists exposed to the broader dimensions of person-centered group counseling and apply them to improving the group process. Further, by identifying the process as being "person-centered counseling," there is a formal attachment to the past and current literature and research of person-centered counseling. We do not wish to see the philosophy, process, and research of person-centered counseling lost or forgotten. Therefore, we see "person-centered group counseling" as a better assurance that this relationship will be preserved. Those who have misinterpreted and misused the basic encounter concept, and Rogers has identified them (1970:158), have partly done so because of an ignorance regarding the undergirding attitudinal and process principles fundamental to the person-centered viewpoint. We wish to keep a spotlight on those principles and feel that this can best be done by the linking label of "person-centered group counseling."

Rogers, with every fiber of his being, was committed to the process of basic encounter as a way of saving humanity from interpersonal isolation and oblivion in a world that is rapidly becoming more technological (Landreth, 1984:32). The deep level of Rogers' commitment is seen in the following statement regarding basic encounter which he made while being interviewed (Evans, 1975:32):

> . . . it's one of the most significant social inventions of this century because it is a way of eliminating alienation and loneliness, of getting people into better communication with one another, of helping them develop fresh insights into themselves, and helping them get feedback from others so that they perceive how they are being received by others.

Since the mid 1970s, Rogers was committed to promulgating the potential of the basic encounter group as a vehicle for the peaceful settlement of the tensions that now plague our planet and may lead to its destruction (Rogers & Ryback, 1984).

COMPLEXITY OF PROCESS

Person-centered group counseling, because of the unstructured nature of the process, presents the counselor with a complexity that is not evident in the more structured and counselor-centered process models. In the person-centered process, with its focus on the natural emergence of the self to each of the group participants, the counselor is required to be more sensitive, more involved, and generally more attentive to the natural emergence of attitudes and behaviors among group members. In politics, an autocratic leader generally has the process of government under tight control and is less confused regarding what should be done and when it should be done. A democratic leader, in politics, has the process of government under a loose control, governs by consensus and is often more tentative regarding what should be done and when it should be done.

Because of the democratic nature of person-centered group counseling, its process can become quite complex and can only be made clear by a counselor with the capacity to deeply grasp what is occurring and make sense out of a sometimes confusing and simultaneous current of intrapersonal and interpersonal reactions and exchanges. Kottler and Brown (1996:203) note that "group situations contain a virtual overload of stimuli to attend to." To attend to the simultaneously interacting complexities and behaviors inherent in group counseling requires a wide variety of group leadership skills (Corey, 1995): active listening, clarifying, summarizing, questioning, confronting, reflecting feelings, supporting, empathizing, facilitating, intiating, evaluating, providing feedback, disclosing oneself, modeling, linking, protecting, and suggesting. One principal means for developing group facilitation skills, significant insights into the group process, and counselor empathy and cross cultural sensitivity is through group supervision with counselors engaged in group counseling (Corey, 1995; McAuliffe, 1992 Newman, Friesen, & Grigg, 1991; Newman & Lovell, 1993; Parker, 1991; Shalit, 1990; Skovholt & Ronnesstad, 1992). Regardless of how acquired, the application of group leadership skills involves artistic, nuanced, and deeply perceptive attention and sensitivity, here and now listening, and empathic responsiveness.

If Rollo May's (1967) observation regarding what the counselor is required to do in individual counseling were applied in person-centered group counseling, we can envision the complexity of the counselor's task when the counselor attempts to absorb all of the following from all members of the group:

> ... the counselor is sensitive to all the little expressions of character, such as tone of voice, posture, facial expression, even dress and the apparently accidental movements of the body. Nothing, not even the smallest movement or change in expression, is meaningless or accidental and the only question is the counselor's ability to perceive these expressions and sense something in their meaning.

Lakin (1972:61) indicates that when any group counselor is both a participant and observer, the complexity of the process is compounded. He states that the group counselor must learn: ". . . how to remain rational and intellectually alert while fully immersed in an emotionally involving experience; or put another way, how to be both participant and observer."

Ohlsen (1974:144) observes that the counselor's responsibilities in the process of group counseling are more demanding than in individual counseling:

> The counselor's responsibilities to his clients in individual counseling and group counseling are similar, but his responsibilities are more demanding in the latter. While trying to detect and reflect the speaker's feelings, encouraging him to act, and reinforcing his desired behaviors, the counselor also must note how the speaker's behavior is influencing others and how the behavior of others is influencing the speaker.

Beck (1974:144) confirms the complexity of the process of person-centered group counseling by indicating that the counselor's nervous system becomes overloaded: "There is too much going on at one time, in terms of the simultaneous behaviors of the various members, their interactions with each other and the therapist's own reactions, for him to be able to sort out all that is important on the spot. You might say that the nervous system becomes overloaded."

The counselor who utilizes a structured approach will find it easier to keep the group process under control since such a process is not characterized by the same depth, range, and complexity as is the person-centered group process. *A structured process may, indeed,* be good for the well-being of the counselor, but the more important consideration should be its short- and long-range benefits for participants. Does it do more for the group counselor than it does for participants?

Because the process of person-centered group counseling is unstructured and evolves in a spontaneous and natural manner, it is therefore more complex and requires a high level of psychological stability and process sensitivity on the part of the counselor.

STAGES OF GROUP COUNSELING

Drawing upon the work of Corey (1995) and Gladding (1995), Kottler and Brown (1996) delineate three stages of group counseling with each stage characterized by a specific group focus and agenda besides the individual goals of each member:

1. *The beginning stage* is defined by the processes of making introductions, establishing ground rules, determining purposes, building trust and levels of comfort. Issues of inclusion are paramount in this stage.
2. *The working or middle stage* emerges when members begin focusing on and exploring specific issues, disclosing their feelings and personal

material, and confronting inconsistencies. Issues of control, affection, and cohesion are predominant.

3. *The final or closing stage* involves effective group termination and occurs when group members resolve unfinished issues within the group, assess what they have learned, discuss plans for change, deal with ending issues, and say good-by.

Throughout these three stages of group counseling the person-centered counselor must be simultaneously sensitive to the processing issues of the group while attending to each individual's concerns and issues. To facilitate individual and group development in person-centered group counseling through these stages requires more than skills and techniques—it calls upon the very being and personhood of the counselor.

THE COUNSELOR AS A PERSON

A person-centered approach to group counseling puts far greater emphasis on the facilitative quality of the counselor *as a person* rather than emphasizing the counselor's knowledge and use of specific and predesigned procedures. It views the counselor's presence as the basic catalyst that prompts group participants to make progress. Other theories of group counseling emphasize the counselor's use of strategies, gimmicks, and techniques, and assume that the counselor's presence is therapeutically less important than his or her knowledge of such specific and predesigned procedures. For example, Gross (1977:316) recommends that analytic and evaluative procedures should characterize part of the group counselor's behavior. The use of such techniques, however, would be far removed from the counselor's facilitative role in person-centered group counseling. As Rogers (1971: 278) has indicated, an effective facilitator avoids such interpretive comments since they can never be anything but high-level guesses. The person-centered view has always emphasized that effective individual or group counseling comes from counselors who possess psychological stability and are able to translate this stability into facilitative attitudes that are beneficial to the group.

A person-centered group counselor's presence finds its expression not in leading a group but in the creation of a facilitative climate in which the group can lead itself. Hobbs (1951: 292) identified this important quality some time ago, and more recently, Bebout (1974:414) emphasized its importance when he stated that the essential difference between Rogerian group counseling and other approaches revolves around the counselor's ability to influence the development of a self-actualizing process for the group. He goes on to indicate that other approaches do not do this. Instead they may: ". . . rely on the leader's charisma or expertise, on methods or exercises, or they may discredit or distrust entirely the value of group self direction."

Upham (1973:78) goes a bit further when he indicates that some practitioners serve their own needs rather than the needs of clients: "The practitioner may also push the client towards change in ways that meet the practitioner's needs and not those of the client."

Hansen, Warner, and Smith (1976) also note the importance of the counselor as a person in group counseling. They indicate that the counselor must possess the psychological stability to model behaviors that are facilitative to group members and that they can use in their intrapersonal and interpersonal exchanges.

Hobbs (1964:158) indicates the tremendous importance of the counselor's personhood when he identifies the following attitudes that should characterize the person-centered group counselor:

> Of primary importance is one's own personal philosophy, one's attitudes toward people. More and more, techniques seem less and less important. Techniques come later; they grow out of and are demanded by one's orientation to human relationships in therapy. To be effective in therapy, it is believed, requires a deep and abiding confidence in the ability of most people to be responsible for their own lives. It requires some humility about how much a person can do for others, aside from making it possible for them to realize themselves. It requires putting aside tendencies to evaluate what is good and right for other people. It requires a respect for their integrity as individuals, for their right to the strength-giving act of making a living and by their own choices. And it requires, perhaps above all, a confidence in the tremendous capacities of individuals to make choices that are both maturely satisfying to them and ultimately satisfactory to society.

Kell and Mueller (1966:78) argue that the counselor's personhood might be the only *reliable* source for affecting change in clients:

> The counselor, as in any other occupation, has primarily himself to bring to the helping relationship. He may learn of technical aids such as tests; he may learn interviewing techniques; he may read widely and copiously about people; he may search desperately for a philosophy or an orientation; he may even attempt to copy the behaviors of those who are regarded as experts. Yet, ultimately, what he brings to his encounters with clients is himself.

Coulson (1970:10) states that a counselor errs in attempting to manufacture manipulative techniques with a group:

> The leader of an encounter group errs if he tries to *make* the group happen. He errs in missing the opportunity to find out what people *really* are like when they are not being manipulated. He errs in taking away from the members the rare opportunity to be what they want to be, without performance expectations. He errs also because *it simply isn't necessary* to manufacture the events of encounter.

Coulson (1970:13) goes on to indicate that the group counselor's personhood had better be integrated, whole, and real when he identified the process model that the person-centered group counselor should utilize if group members are to be brought into contact with their feelings: "If you want people to talk about their feelings, then talk about your feelings." The person-centered group counselor needs to be attitudinally a selfless person in order to engage in the quality of listening identified by Rogers (1970:47):

> I listen carefully, accurately, and sensitively as I am able to each individual who expresses himself, whether the utterance is superficial or significant, I listen. To me the individual who speaks is worthwhile, worth understanding; consequently, he is worthwhile for having expressed something. Colleagues say that in this sense I *validate* the person.

Rogers (1971: 276, 277, 279) also calls attention to the importance of the counselor's personhood when identifying elements that should characterize person-centered group counseling. These elements are not manufactured techniques; they cannot be contrived. They emerge from the positive attitudinal components of the counselor as a person: acceptance of the group and acceptance of the individual within the group. A counselor who is less than humanly sensitive will have difficulty expressing these attitudes to a group if they are not values embedded in the counselor's personhood.

Rogers (1970) goes on to identify nonfacilitative attitudes and approaches on the part of a group counselor that will interfere with, and hamper, the process and progress of the group experience for participants:

1. Exploitation
2. Manipulation
3. The counselor who is a dramatist
4. Dogmatism
5. Self-centeredness—focusing on the counselor's problems
6. Interpretation
7. Exercises or activities—the counselors who says, "now we will all. . . "
8. The counselor who withholds himself from emotional participation in the group—holding himself aloof as an expert (pp. 66-67).

Kottler (1994:302-304) identifies several unethical behaviors which often emerge in group counseling:

1. Promising groups members there will be no pressure for members to participate when we know there are constant subtle, unconscious, and overt pressures placed on goup members reluctant to participate.
2. Promising group members "that their group is a safe place in which to disclose personal secrets, explore sensitive areas, and take risks" when we cannot "guarantee that other members will not: (a) act insensitively, manipulatively, or abusively; (b) violate confidentiality by telling others what was disclosed; or (c) pollute the therapeutic experience by being obnoxious, obstructive, or excessively self-centered."
3. Promising confidentiality in the group when we know "confidentiality is more difficult to mandate and virtually impossible to enforce because group members are not bound to ethical codes or to the leader's promises."
4. Inappropriate counselor self-disclosure. "The use of self-disclosure is probably the single most abused therapeutic intervention. Group leaders who like to hear themselves talk; who, because of ego deficiencies, attempt to impress clients with their prowess; or who use group time to meet their own needs are acting unethically."

The ethical hazards of group counseling are succinctly summed up by Kottler (1994:303):

The reality of group practice is that confidentiality cannot be enforced; individual privacy is diluted; participants feel coercion and pressure to conform; verbal abuse is likely; and the leader has less control over proceedings, and clients receive less attention and close monitoring than is true in individual treatment. (Roback, Ochoa, Bloch, and Purdon, 1992; Van Hoose and Kottler, 1985)

The counselor who subconsciously feels that the group experience exists more for the counselor, or the enhancement of a theory, than for the group, will find it easier to engage in the preceding attitudes and manipulative techniques. It is not easy to be person-centered. It requires the counselor to confront the self and deeply examine attitudes and behaviors and weigh the degree to which they facilitate the group process and the degree to which they are self-serving. Such introspection requires the courage to face one's attitudes, motives, values, and goals before the counselor can move toward selfless behaviors that are truly person-centered.

If the group counselor's personhood is intact, and if the facilitative dimensions of that personhood can be communicated to group members, then Rogers (1970: 15-37) indicates that the counselor will set in motion a series of positive experiences for group members. They will begin the group experience by milling around, resisting personal expression or exploration; they will start by describing past feelings, expressing negative feelings, and will move toward the expression of immediate interpersonal feelings in the group. A healing capacity will begin to emerge and represent the beginning of change; facades will be cracked. The individual will receive feedback and be confronted, the members will engage in helping relationships with each other outside of the group sessions, the basic encounter will occur, positive feelings and closeness will be expressed, and behavioral changes will occur within the group.

In identifying the goals of the therapist-leader, Beck (1974: 427-430) links these goals to the personhood of the counselor in that these goals are expressions of that personhood and contribute to the establishment of a person-centered climate:

1. The facilitation of individuals (or group members) to take responsibility for themselves in whatever way is realistically possible at any particular time.
2. Problems and conflicts can be clarified and solved via a process of self-understanding and the development of an empathic understanding of others.
3. The recognition of the client as the client is, a recognition of the client's reality as the client sees it.
4. Attempts to offer an attitude which is nonjudgmental in order to facilitate exploratory and self- reflective behavior in the client.
5. Recognize the significance of maintaining as high a degree as possible of clarity about his/her own views, feelings, and reactions while he/she is in the therapeutic relationship.

In a study that investigated the relationship between counselor and participant behaviors in the group counseling process, O'Hare (1979:4) found that counselor behaviors such as empathy, congruence, and positive regard will elicit self-exploration behaviors among group members.

The client's self-exploration in a group, according to Meador (1975:176) occurs in proportion to the possession and demonstration of three attitudes that flow from the counselor as a person: "He tries to experience and communicate his own reality, the process of his inner self as that moves and changes in the group; a caring for the persons in the group marked by a respect for their uniqueness; and a deeply sensitive nonjudgmental understanding.

As a person, the person-centered group counselor possesses a seriousness of purpose. When group members allow a counselor to enter their internal world of feelings, this opportunity carries with it a grave sense of responsibility. Meador (1975:193) puts it aptly when he says:

> . . . underlying the motives of the therapist is a kind of seriousness about what is going on in a group. There is often hilarity, boredom, chit-chat, but the unfolding process of human change has an awesomeness that he cannot take

lightly. When a therapist calls himself into seriousness, realness, caring, and understanding naturally follow.

Whether involved in individual or group counseling, the person-centered view emphasizes the quality of the counselor's personhood as the basic influence for facilitating attitudinal and behavioral changes among clients.

MODE OF COMMUNICATION

In person-centered group counseling, the mode of communication among group members is essentially verbal, but the approach does not exclude other modes of communication when they emerge from group members in a natural and spontaneous way. Other concepts of group counseling identify exercises, gimmicks, and games that the counselor imposes on group members without their consent, or if the consent is given, it is given with a feeling that the counselor knows best. Such manipulative techniques are not only an infringement on the rights of group participants, but they are often used by counselors who are unsure regarding their ability to communicate feelings at the verbal level, don't trust the ability of group members to communicate feelings verbally, and desire to quicken the process.

Some group counselors take it for granted that such manipulative techniques are a part of the group counseling process. Ohlsen (1977:137-142) identifies the following: magic shop, intimacy exercise, pairing, approach-avoidance exercises, relaxation exercises, fiddler game, self-appraisal exercises, autobiographies, and autobiographies of the future.

Coulson (1970:12), who feels that an effective basic group encounter occurs in a natural and spontaneous process that is free from manipulative techniques, has this to say regarding the issue:

> To my mind, there's nothing wrong with exercises, with activities, with structure as such; it is what we do with them that hurts. Better ambiguity than what we are tempted to do with structure, which is to let it substitute for *ourselves.*
>
> . . . They (personal values) can't be "tricked" out any sooner than they will come out, given time and the absence of distracting agendas, tasks, games, and discussion topics. And if the values *are* tricked out, then they will disappear again very quickly once the trickster is gone.
>
> . . . I walked in on a student encounter group recently just in time to hear one young man say to another, "I wanted to get to know you better, that's why I suggested the backrub." (!) Our culture desperately needs ways you can get to know people like the cop on the street corner. And it won't be through asking him to take his shirt off or offering to pass him around in a circle.

A statement by Carl Rogers (1979), included in a brochure describing a summer basic encounter institute of the La Jolla Program in California, a program in which participants experience the basic encounter process, clarified his position regarding the issue: "It does not greatly stress the 'exercises' which have become such a large bag of tricks for many group leaders."

CONFRONTATION

Confrontation, within the process of person-centered group counseling, is used with a sense of responsibility that respects the dignity and integrity of the person being confronted. Confrontation is not the primary emphasis of a person-centered group counselor as it is with counselors who use other approaches. It is part of the process of person-centered group counseling but in no way is the whole process. In person-centered group counseling, confrontation is generally a reactive response rather than a proactive response. Confrontation emerges in a natural and spontaneous manner and is not pre-planned as an expected part of person-centered group counseling.

Some (Hansen, Warner, & Smith, 1976:144) imply that confrontation has become the major new process dimension of person-centered group counseling and depict Carl Rogers as being more willing to engage in more active and confrontative interaction with group members. Their observation is linked to an inaccurate past image of the Rogerian counselor as being passive, stoic, and generally sitting on a nondirective backside. Carkhuff and Berenson (1977:75) perpetuated this wooden image when they indicated that the lack of confrontative behavior has been a: ". . . rather precise reflection of a polite middle class, and will function most effectively with persons who share the attitudes, the values, and the potential of this polite middle class."

In our opinion, person-centered counselors have been confrontive. Indeed as Mearns (1994:93) argues:

> Person-centered counseling is full of confrontation, with the client being challenged to juxtapose one perspective against another; or a present response contrasted with his longstanding view of himself. These confrontations are offered in the context of a person-centered way of being: in other words , they are founded on the sincere respect which the counselor feels toward the client, they reflect the counselor's struggle to understand the client and they are communicated in a way which keeps the client at the centre of his locus of evaluation.

Those who are sensitive to the depth and power of an accurate reflection of a client's feelings realize the confrontative potential of such an empathic reflection (Tscheulin, 1990). Those who misunderstand the meaning of an empathic reflection of feeling, and instead interpret it as a repetition of what a client has said rather than a response to the feelings behind the words, will have trouble understanding the confrontative elements that have always been a part of the person-centered process.

Person-centered counselors have always had a commitment to being genuine and congruent. In its earliest applications the authors feel that person-centered counselors did engage in confrontation because the attitudes of genuineness and congruence required them to do so. Today's person-centered counselor engages in confrontation both indirectly and directly. Indirect confrontation is engaged in through reflections of feelings that possess a confrontative element:.

> You find it difficult to be honest even though you realize that your dishonesty is making you lose respect for yourself.
> Being yourself with your family is almost impossible because you fear risking yourself. It takes a lot of courage for you to be you.
> You have such a craving for food that you'll almost eat anything, anytime... even though you realize that such eating habits are producing disastrous results.

Directive confrontation is engaged in through self-disclosing statements when the person-centered counselor is feeling ingenuine or incongruent:

> I don't feel close to you at all. I feel that you're avoiding being truly honest with me.
> I don't feel any sense of commitment on your part. Your words sound reasonable but I don't get any feeling that you're willing to follow through on your words.
> I couldn't feel very comfortable doing that. It may make sense to you, but to me it would be an infringement upon the rights of others.

Rogers (1970:52 clearly demonstrates a person-centered attitude toward the issue of confrontation: "I endeavor to voice any *persisting* feelings which I am experiencing toward an individual or toward the group, in any significant or continuing relationship."

In the preceding, Rogers indicates that he is willing to express "any *persisting* feelings." Too many counselors express momentary or fleeting feelings without regard to whether or not these feelings are persistent. They, so to speak, "shoot from the hip" with their confrontations. The person-centered counselor, instead, uses confrontation when *persisting* feelings indicate that the confrontation would be useful for the client, the group, the therapeutic atmosphere of the group, or the counselor's sense of genuineness and congruence (Landreth, 1984).

The person-centered counselor uses confrontation in a professionally responsible manner. Rogers (1970:55) says: "To attack a person's defenses seems to me judgmental. If a person seems distressed by my confrontation or that of others, I am very willing to help him 'get off the hook' if he so desires".

Although Rogers is willing to engage in confrontation, he also indicates that there is a more primary way of communicating with group members (Rogers, 1970): ". . . the meaning these experiences have for him now and the feelings they arouse in him. It is to these meanings and feelings that I try to respond" (p. 47).

Bauer (1966:51) has indicated that with certain clients, confrontation should be avoided: ". . . only the experienced psychotherapist fully appreciates the fact that insight can sometimes be dangerous and a goal in therapy may be to prevent certain insights from ever becoming apparent".

Malouf (1968:343) expressed the same concern when he stated: ". . . one should be extremely cautious in using direct feedback with highly sensitive or disturbed individuals" .

Carkhuff and Berenson (1977:29) admonish that the counselor might fulfill a neurotic need through confrontation: ". . . the necessity of the therapist expressing himself at all times is not supported. Again, genuineness must not be confused with free license for the therapist to do what he will in therapy, especially to express hostility. Therapy is not for the therapist".

O'Hare (1979:7) concludes that the process of confrontation must be well placed and well timed and should not be used indiscriminately: "This study suggests that such confrontation may be inhibitive, perhaps delayed until the later sessions of an ongoing counseling group when sufficient trust and group cohesiveness have developed".

Confrontation does have therapeutic value when used responsibly. It enables the counselor to penetrate meanings and feelings that might not otherwise become exposed. Carkhuff and Berenson (1977:179) articulated its value when they said: "Confrontation precipitates crisis; but crises are viewed as the fabric of growth in that they challenge us to mobilize our resources and invoke new responses. Growth is a series of endless self-confrontations. The therapist who serves as an authentic model of confrontation offers the client a meaningful example of effective living".

Egan (1973:132) suggests that counselors attempt to develop a balanced and integrated relationship between confrontation and support: "Confrontation without support is disastrous; support without confrontation is anemic".

Moustakas (1972:21) provides insight into the experiencing and process dimensions of confrontation:

. . . the direct challenge of facing a conflict, the willingness to experience fear, anger, sorrow, pain, intensely and deeply, when these feelings are caused by a sense of urgency, loss or disillusionment. The confrontation shakes up the individual, puts him in a turbulent state, and forces him to use new energies and resources to come to terms with his life–to find a way to himself .

Egan (1970) offers guidelines for making confrontation a constructive experience in the group process:
1. Confrontation should be done to demonstrate one's concern for another.
2. Confrontation should be a way of becoming involved with another person.
3. Confrontation should address itself primarily to another's behavior and only tangentially to that person's motivation.
4. Each person should be willing to confront himself or herself honestly in the group.

Perhaps, the place of confrontation in the person-centered counseling relationship, whether it be individual or group counseling, is best defined by Mearns (1994:95):

If confrontation is seen in terms of helping the client to hold a mirror to himself in ways which are least likely to encourage defensive reactions, then there is considerble confrontation, in many different forms within person-centered counseling. However, if confrontation, is seen as an aggressive way of forcing the counselor's views onto the client then person-centered counseling will have no truck with it.

VOLUNTARISM

A fundamental issue in counseling today is the voluntary use of a counseling service by clients rather than continuing the emphasis on the required counseling of referred clients. If a counseling program is to be respectful of human rights, the determination as to whether to make use of a counseling service should be left to the discretion of the person. If the person feels the need of counseling, he or she should be able to initiate and develop a relationship with a counselor.

To many counselors, allowing the person to decide whether to make use of a counseling service poses a real threat, especially among those counselors whose employment can only continue on the basis of counselor-initiated contacts with clients. The person-centered counselor would not hesitate to allow clients the right to determine whether or not they will make use of a counseling service. A counseling program will attract voluntary self-referrals in proportion to the quality of the counseling rendered.

Kneller (1964:100), from an existential viewpoint, had this to say regarding the issue of voluntarism and its relationship to group membership

> The doctrine of sociality teaches that the individual will lose his loneliness if he is taught the right way to belong to and behave in the group. But even in the group, say the existentialists, the individual does not escape his loneliness. In fact, he may become "homeless," because he has abandoned his real home, which is his own authentic self. The fact of being known under some socially approved category does not of itself allay anxiety. Not that the existentialist would prevent the individual from joining the group. The opportunity should always be afforded. But acceptance of the opportunity should never result from social pressure; rather, it should spring from one's own uninhibited will. By extension, one should always be afforded the opportunity to be different, even to be eccentric, not for the sake of eccentricity but because all human beings are intrinsically different. A genuine group or society is thus made up of individuals who have made their own decision to join.

In an important publication, the American Psychological Association established "Guidelines for Psychologists Conducting Growth Groups" participation: "Entering into a growth group experience should be on a voluntary basis; any form of coercion to participate is to be avoided."

REFERENCES

Bauer, F. C. (1966). Guidance and psychiatry. In T. C. Hennessey (Ed.), *The inter disciplinary roots of guidance.* New York: Fordham University Press, 51.

Bebout, J. (1974). It takes one to know one: Existential-Rogerian concepts in encounter groups. In D. A. Wexler & L. N. Rice (Eds.), *Innovations in client-centered therapy.* New York: John Wiley, 367-420.

Beck, A. P. (1974). Phases in the development of structure in therapy and encounter groups. In D A. Wexler, & L. N. Rice (Eds.), *Innovations in client-centered therapy.* New York: John Wiley, 421-464.

Carkhuff, R. R., & Berenson, B. G. (1977). *Beyond counseling and therapy* (2nd ed.). New York: Holt, Rinehart and Winston.

Corey, G. (1995). *Theory and practice of group counseling* (4th ed.). Pacific Grove, CA: Brooks/Cole.

Coulson, W. (1970). Inside a basic encounter group. *The Counseling Psychologist. 2,* 6-22.

Egan, G. (1970). *Encounter: Group processes for interpersonal growth.* Belmont, CA: Wadsworth.

Egan, G. (1973). *Face to face.* Monterey, CA: Brooks/Cole.

Evans, R. J. (1975). *Carl Rogers: The man and his ideas.* New York: Dutton.

Gazda, G. M. (Ed.). (1975). *Basic approaches to group psychotherapy and group counseling.* Springfield, IL: Charles C Thomas.

Gendlin, E. T. (1970). Existentialism and experiential psychotherapy. In J. T. Hart & T. M. Tomlinson (Eds.), *New directions in client-centered therapy.* Boston: Houghton Mifflin.

Gladding, S. T. (1995). *Group work: A counseling speciality* (2nd ed.). Englewood Cliffs, NJ: Merrill.

Gross, D. R. (1977). *Group counseling in counseling: Theory, process and practice.* Belmont, CA: Wadsworth.

Guidelines for psychologists conducting growth groups. (1973). *The American Psychologist, 28,* 933.

Hansen, J., Warner, R., & Smith, E. (1976). *Group counseling: Theory and process.* Chicago: Rand McNally.

Hobbs, N. (1951). Group-centered psychotherapy. In C. R. Rogers, *Client-centered therapy.* Boston: Houghton Mifflin.

Hobbs, N. (1964). In G. C. Kemp (Ed.), *Perspectives on the group process.* Boston: Houghton Mifflin.

Kell, B. L., & Mueller, W. J. (1966). *Impact and change: A study of counseling relationships.* New York: Appleton-Century-Crofts.

Kneller, G. F. (1964). *Existentialism and education.* New York: Philosophical Library.

Kottler, J. A. (1994). *Advanced group leadership.* Pacific Grove, CA: Brooks/Cole.

Kopp, S. B. (1976). *If you meet the Buddha on the road, kill him.* New York: Bantam.

Kottler, J., & Brown, R. (1996). *Introduction to therapeutic counseling* (3rd ed.). Pacific Grove, CA: Brooks/Cole.

Lakin, M. (1972). *Impersonal encounter: Theory and practice in sensitivity training.* New York: McGraw-Hill, 107.

Landreth, G. L. (1984). Encountering Carl Rogers: His views on facilitating groups. *The Personnel and Guidance Journal, 62,* 323-326.

Malouf, P. J. (1968). Direct feedback: Helpful or disruptive in group counseling? *The School Counselor, 15..*

Martin, D. (1972). *Learning-based client-centered therapy.* Monterey, CA: Brooks/Cole.

May, R. (1967). *The art of counseling.* Nashville, TN: Abingdon.

McAuliffe, G. J. (1992). A case presentation approach to group supervision for community college counselors. *Counselor Education and Supervision, 31,*163-174.

Meador, B. D. (1975). Client-centered group therapy. In G. M. Gazda (Ed.), *Basic approaches to group psychotherapy and group counseling.* Springfield, IL: Charles C. Thomas, 175-195.

Mearns, D. (1994). *Developing Person-Centered Counseling.* London: Sage.

Moustakas, C. (1972). *Loneliness and love.* Englewood Cliffs, NJ: Prentice-Hall.

Newman, J. A., Friesen, J. D., & Grigg, D. N. (1991). The supervision of experiential systemic therapy for individuals, couples, and families. *The Clincal Counsellor, 1,*2, 12-20.

Newman, J. A., & Lovell, M. (1993). A description of a supervisory group for group counselors. *Counselor Education and Supervision, 33,* 22-31.

O'Hare, C. (1979). Counseling group process: Relationship between counselor and client behaviors in the helping process. *The Journal for Specialists in Group Work.*

Ohlsen, M. M. (1974). *Guidance services in the modern school.* New York: Harcourt, Brace and Jovanovich.

Ohlsen, M. M. (1977). *Group counseling* (Second Edition). New York: Holt, Rinehart and Winston.

Parker, R. J. (1991). What is really the problem? A simulation to train beginning consultants. *Counselor Education and Supervision , 31,* 81-89.

Roback, H. B., Ochoa, E., Bloch, F., & Purdon, S. (1992). Guarding confidentiality in clinical groups: The therapist's dilemma. *International Journal of Group Psychotherapy, 42,* 81-103.

Rogers, C. R. (1967). The process of the basic encounter group. In J. F. T. Bugental, (Ed.), *Challenges in humanistic psychology.* New York: McGraw-Hill, 172, 178.

Rogers, C. R. (1970). *Carl Rogers on encounter groups.* New York: Harper and Row.

Rogers, C. R. (1971). Carl Rogers describes his way of facilitating encounter groups. *American Journal of Nursing, 71,* 275-279.

Rogers, C. R. (1979). In brochure, *The La Jolla Program.* La Jolla, CA: Center for Studies of the Person.

Rogers, C. R., & Ryback, D. (1984). One alternative to nuclear planetary suicide. In Levant, R. I., & Shlien, J. M. (Eds.), *Client-centered therapy and the person-centered approach: New directions in theory, research, and practice.* New York: Praeger, 400-422.

Shalit, E. (1990). Experiential supervision as an adjunct to regular supervision of psychotherapy. *Clincal Supervisor, 8,* 1, 109-130.

Skovholt, T. M., & Ronnestad, M. H. (1992). Themes in therapist and counselor development. *Journal of Counseling and Development, 70,* 4, 505-515.

Tscheulin, D. (1990). Confrontation and non-confrontation as differential techniques in differential client-centered therapy. In G. Lietaer, J. Roumbats, & R. Van Balen (Eds.). *Client-centered and experiential psychotherapy in the nineties* (327-336). Leuven: Leuven University Press.

Upham, F. (1973). *Ego analysis in the helping professions.* New York: Family Service Association of America.

Van Hoose, W. H., & Kottler, J.A. (1985). *Ethical and legal issues in counseling and psychotherapy* (2nd ed.). San Francisco: Jossey Bass.

Chapter 9

PERSON-CENTERED PLAY THERAPY

This chapter has been developed to inform the reader regarding how person-centered counseling can be applied to children. Since play is the natural language of the child, person-centered counseling uses the format and stimulus of play therapy to apply the fundamentals of person-centered counseling. When person-centered counseling becomes applied to the process of helping children, its attitudinal and communicative fundamentals remain intact. What changes is the format and stimulus for interacting with the child client. Play therapy provides the counselor with the best format and stimulus for eliciting and absorbing the feelings that influence the thinking and behavior of children. We include this chapter because of our interest in providing children with an opportunity to do something about emerging problems while these problems are in their early and formative stages. Attending to them early can do much to diminish their impact during later stages of the child's life. Many of the problems faced by adolescents and adults today would be less incapacitating if counseling and its play therapy application were available in the childhood stages of the problem's development. If applied then, there is the strong possibility that the problem would be less severe, less burdensome, and even not part of a person's adolescent and adult years. The strength of helping children through counseling and play therapy is its potential to prevent problems from taking root during the psychologically formative periods of one's life.

Caplan and Caplan (1973) offer a historically enduring perspective on the extraordinary power of play in the child's psychological development. They cite some exceptional and unique features of play which we paraphrase as follows:

Play is a voluntary activity. It is intensely personal. Self-powered, it embodies a high degree of motivation and achievement. Play is an autonomous pursuit through which one assimilates the outside world to support one's ego.

Play offers freedom of action. Play is always free in the sense that each act can be performed for its own sake and for its immediate results. During play, one can carry on trial and error activities without fear of ridicule or failing.

Play provides an imaginary world one can master. Play is a voluntary system that admits both reality and fantasy. The one who plays is in full control. In the world of play one can reduce one's world to a manageable size so that it can be manipulated to suit personal whims.

Play has elements of adventure in it. It has uncertainty and challenge which can prompt one to be exploratory. In play, the ordinary laws of life do not count since play is larger than life.

Play provides a base for language building. The earliest years are nonverbal. Words come from a foundation of play experiences, from encounters with people, objects, and events which make up our world. Play nourishes reflective thinking, associative memory, and the naming and labeling necessary for the eventual mastery of reading.

Play has unique powers for building interpersonal relations. Play provides contacts with others while letting us engage in natural behaviors. Much of play aids our psychosocial development by helping us to define ourselves and fit that definition into a social context.

Play offers opportunities for mastery of the physical self. One can learn body control through active physical play. Physical play helps us to improve our laterality, directionality, and coordination.

Play furthers concentration. One's power of concentration in the here-and-now world is improved through play. That improved ability to concentrate can be generalized to activities outside of play.

Play is a way to learn about ourselves. Play helps us to learn how we'll respond to a certain set of circumstances. Connections are made between stimuli and responses during play and we can see equivalent stimuli outside of play which generate similar responses. We begin to see a unity to how we respond to certain stimuli both in play and outside of play.

Play is a way of learning about roles. In early play, children imitate the behavior, attitudes, and language of the important adults in their lives. Play may be considered a rehearsal for adult roles and anticipatory to adult life. Adults learn about the similarities and differences in role expectations in play and outside of play.

Play is always a dynamic way of learning. The layers of meaning implanted by play often include conscious organization of the environment, explorations of physical and social relationships, and deep levels of fantasy. One's perceptions of reality often evolve out of play requiring fantasy.

Play refines one's judgments. Play is often an accepted vehicle for expressing one's feelings and thoughts. Through play one analyzes which feelings and thoughts can be expressed and accepted by others and which cannot.

Play is vitalizing. Play has important neurophysiological effects on us. Play is a diversion from routines, demands, and pursuits. For a period of time, play permits one to reverse one's behavior and do the opposite of what one has been doing. Play is essential in order to bring renewed vigor to the formal and required activities of our lives. Play enables us to engage in natural and spontaneous behaviors so necessary to freeing us from the pressures of life.

PLAY AND COGNITIVE DEVELOPMENT

According to Piaget (1951), play is an indispensable step in the child's cognitive development. Play is the bridge between sensory-motor experience and the emergence of representative or symbolic thought. In his study of play, Piaget concluded that there are three main categories of play: practice games, symbolic games, and games with rules.

Practice games appear first and are an outgrowth of the imitative activities which are characteristic of the sensory-motor period of development. Such games may lead to improved motor performance or to destructive performance (e.g., knocking over blocks). They may develop into constructive games like building or weaving which are viewed by Piaget as a bridge between play and work.

Symbolic games imply representation of an absent object and are both initiative and imaginative (Piaget, 1951). Insofar as these games symbolize the child's own feelings, interest, and activities, they help the child to express the self creatively and to develop a rich and satisfying fantasy life. Between the ages of two and four symbolic play is at its peak. One type of symbolic play identified by Piaget is compensatory play which involves doing in make-believe what is forbidden in reality. Closely related to compensatory play is play in which emotion is acted out in gradual degrees, so that it becomes bearable. Often children will use play to act out unpleasant scenes of actions. In reliving them by transposing them symbolically, they reduce some of the unpleasantness and make the situations more tolerable. The function of symbolic play is seen in the "make-believe" games of children from two to four. According to Piaget (1951:134), symbolic play frees "the ego from the demands of accommodation".

Games with rules. After the age of four or five, symbolic play becomes increasingly social, according to Piaget. Symbolic games lessen as socialization progresses. Around the age of seven or eight there is a definite decline in symbolic play coinciding with increased interest in school and in socialized activities. The child becomes involved in games with rules which are essentially social, leading to increased adaptation. Piaget believes that since these games persist even among adults, they may provide the explanation of what happens to children's play; that it dies out in later years in favor of socialized games through which the child develops social skills and attitudes (Pulaski, 1971). The child is required to share, to cooperate, and to assume different rules and consequently learns the first lessons of mutuality in social relations and begins to build more complex relationship skills.

THE PSYCHOSOCIAL VALUE OF PLAY

Play is the child's natural medium of expression (Axline, 1969). "In his talk and his toys are his words" (Ginott, 1961) and this form of communication gives the adult a tool with which to understand and relate to the child with confidence and warmth (Schiffer, 1969; Moustakas, 1973; Orlick, 1983; Rubin & Tregay, 1986). Indeed, Allen (1942) was one of the first to observe that it would be difficult to establish a relationship with a child without play activity. Axline's (1964) book, *Dibs: In Search of Self,* provides a historically renowned example of play as an accepting, reflecting, clarifying, and communicating relationship with a child.

Amster (1943:63-67) was one of the first to identify the enduring values and benefits coming from play:

1. Play can be used for diagnostic understanding of the child. . . We can observe the child's capacity to relate to the self and others, the child's distractibility, rigidity, areas of preoccupation, areas of inhibition, aggression, perception of people, wishes, and the child's self-perception. In the child's play, the child's behavior, ideas, feelings, and expressions help our understanding of the child's problem and how the child sees it.

2. Play can be used to establish a working relationship. This use of play is helpful with the young child who lacks the adult's facility for verbal self-expression and with the older child who shows resistance or inability to articulate.

3. Play can be used to break through a child's way of playing and the child's defenses against anxiety. This is helpful as an additional way of treating distortions in a child's way of playing.

4. Play can be used to help a child verbalize certain conscious material and associated feelings. This use is helpful when a child hesitates to discuss certain material.

5. Play can be used to help a child act out unconscious material and to relieve the accompanying tension. This cathartic use of play deals with symbolic material which may have deep significance to the child. The child

counselor must be aware of how much release in play the particular child can tolerate.

6. Play can be used to develop a child's play interests which the child can carry over into daily life and which will strengthen the child for the future. This use of play has particular importance because of the correlation between the play and work capacities of an individual .

Erickson (1964:10-11) points out the psychological value of play when he says that "the child's play is the infantile form of the human ability to deal with experiences by creating model situations and to master reality by experimenting and planning. . . To 'play it out' in play is the most natural self-healing measure childhood affords."

Nelson (1968) argued that many of the elements and principles of play therapy are appropriate to helping all children with their psychosocial development. He cites the work of Moustakas (1959) and Axline (1969) on play therapy with "normal" children as supporting the concept of helping all children through play activities.

Meeks (1968) believed that any process of helping through play should not be diagnostic but should be compatible with child-centered goals since child-centered play therapy offers (1) a most favorable condition for children to experience growth, (2) allows the child to face feelings through a natural medium of expression, and (3) by facing feelings, it assists the child to control them or abandon them. Through play the child is able to realize the power possessed by the self, can be an individual, think, make decisions, and become more mature. In presenting a theoretical basis for the use of play to help children, Nelson (1968) points out that play provides a vehicle for the individual to explore thoughts and feelings and evoke self-enhancing courses of action, behavioral patterns, or attitudes. This process may take place on a nonverbal as well as on a verbal level. The historically established function of play is to facilitate psychosocial self-exploration and clarification and is consistent with the contemporary goals of child-centered counseling.

GENERAL CHARACTERISTICS OF PLAY THERAPY

Although there is a variety of approaches used in play therapy, there are certain general basic characteristics (Ellis, 1973:120-127.) First, play therapy involves the use of play media ranging from unstructured materials such as sand and clay to more structured toys such as dolls and play houses. Second, through the use of play materials, and through talking, the child expresses feelings and experiences. Third, as a result, the child experiences a solution to a problem, a reduction in tension, or a release of emotion.

What magic function does play possess that enables it to work so well as a therapeutic tool? Through play, the child expresses forbidden physical impulses in a symbolic way, releases anxiety and hostility, tells stories about traumatic situations thus relieving tension, and symbolically manipulates toys in such a way as to test out possible solutions to problems. And finally, through play the child externalizes or projects painful feelings of shame and inferiority, bridges the gap between dreams and reality, and even assumes a role different from the child's normal life role (Landreth & Verhalen, 1982).

BRIEF HISTORY OF PLAY THERAPY

The beginnings of play therapy emanated from a Freudian or psychoanalytical attempt to deal with children and their emotional concerns. One of the primary goals of Freudian therapy was to bring repressed and denied experiences into conscious awareness. This was usually accomplished through free association which worked well with adults but not as well with children who would refuse to free associate. Viewing this as a significant problem, Anna Freud modified the classical psychoanalytic approach by indicating that children do not generally have transference problems and could therefore interact with an adult therapist. To reach a child, she would often play with the child. Such play, however, was considered preliminary to the real work of psychoanalysis and not central to it.

Independently of Anna Freud, Melanie Klein began developing her own techniques with children, which also evolved from the theories of Freud. She assumed that a child's play activities were as motivationally determined as free association in adults, and could thus be interpreted to the child. The term used to describe this process was "play analysis" and it became one of the first approaches which provided interpretations of children's behavior.

Soon after Klein and Freud, Jesse Taft began applying Otto Rank's theories to play therapy, bringing about some important changes in the goals and procedures of therapy with children. Rank's focus was on "relationship therapy"—the relationship between therapist and client was seen as growth producing in its own right, and the emotional problems, as they existed in the immediate present, were more important than the past experiences of the client. From these influences emerged "nondirective" play therapy which reflects the Freudian concepts of permissiveness and catharsis, repression, play as natural language of the child, the meaningfulness of apparently unmotivated behavior, the Rankian emphases on unexpressed feelings rather than on content, and on the diminution of the authoritative position of the therapist.

These were the early thoughts and ideas of play therapy. These thoughts and ideas began to take on more breadth and depth, research regarding their effectiveness was started, and the following formal approaches to play therapy emerged.

APPROACHES TO PLAY THERAPY

Psychoanalytic

The psychoanalytic approach uses interpretations of the child's behavior in the play therapy sessions. Interpretation consists of making connections for the child where the child sees none. Sometimes these connections are between a defense and a feeling or between a fantasy and a feeling (Ellis, 1973). The psychoanalyst hopes, through interpretation, to help the child achieve some insights into the child's behavior and problems. In the process of achieving this the therapist tries to make the unconscious conscious to the child for the purpose of enabling the child to recognize personal feelings and defenses and deal with them directly (Levy, 1978). Psychoanalysts work on the child's past in order to provide a cleared and improved ground for future development. Psychoanalysts are convinced that their treatment process is essential for alleviating certain kinds of symptoms, such as acute anxiety, and a sense of helplessness and inadequacy.

Release Therapy

Release therapy is an approach developed by Levy (1939) as a particularly useful way of relieving severe anxiety, fear reactions, or night terrors precipitated by traumatic experiences (surgical operations, accidents, divorce of parents). In this approach, the therapist supplies the child with dolls and other play media and depicts a ploy concerned with what the therapist feels is the child's major problem, e.g., separation from mother. This approach is advocated by Levy as most appropriate for children under ten who present a recently acquired symptom generated by a specific event in the form of a frightening experience. Levy (1939) argued that it was important for the appropriate use of this approach "that the child is suffering from something that happened in the past and not from a difficult situation going on at the time of treatment" (p. 916).

Existential Approach: Relationship Therapy

Moustakas (1959, 1973, 1977, 1997) borrows a phrase from Otto Rank and entitles his form of play therapy, "relationship therapy." Moustakas characterizes play therapy as a unique growth experience created by one person seeking and needing help and another person who accepts the responsibility of offering it.

A sense of relatedness of one person to another is an essential requirement of individual growth. For children, as well as adults, this involves an internal struggle. But the struggle must take place within a relationship where the child eventually feels free to face the self, where the child's human capacity is recognized and respected, and where the child is accepted and loved. The child will then be able to become more and more individualized. The focus lies in the *present* living experience—the existential moment. The child is able to see the therapist as a new reality in the present world, and from this relationship, the child reclaims the powers of the child's individual nature and affirms the real self. The helping relationship is one in which the adult maintains a deep concern for the psychological growth of the child, is sensitive to the child's individuality, and possesses the ability to explore the child's psychosocial experiences with the child.

Three basic attitudes which Moustakas feels should be conveyed to the child are faith, acceptance, and respect.

Moustakas feels that a child who has *faith* knows:

1. Personal growth.
2. What can be done, when an adult says to the child, "That's up to you," or "You're the best judge of that."
3. What will be done in the future, when an adult says to the child, "It is important that you do what you want."

In the matter of *acceptance*, there must be a commitment on the part of the counselor to accept the child's feelings, the child's personal meanings and perceptions. A statement on the part of the counselor such as, "Mmm," "I see," "That's the way you feel," "You're really afraid of him," "It can be anything you want it to be," conveys acceptance of the child's viewpoint.

In the matter of *respect*, the counselor has concern for the individual child as a person and wants the child to be self-helping. One does not probe or otherwise violate the child's privacy. One empathically follows the child in play.

Moustakas outlines stages of the play therapy process as follows:

1. The child starts with undifferentiated behavior that is hostile, anxious, and/or regressive.
2. The clarification state in which the child's actions become more specific.

3. Stages of ambivalence by the child about the child's traditional or characteristic actions.
4. Undifferential positiveness on the part of the child (anger mixed with positiveness).
5. Modified and moderated reactions by the child.

Person-Centered Approach

According to Axline (1969), there is a powerful force within each individual which constantly strives for complete self-realization. This may be characterized as a drive toward maturity, independence, or self-direction; and it needs good "growing ground" to develop. For the child, Axline views the "growing ground" to be the playground.

The playroom atmosphere grants the child permission to be open and honest in the process of play. The child is accepted completely, without diagnosis, evaluation, or pressure to change. The counselor recognizes and clarifies the expressed emotions or feelings of the child through a reflection of the feelings behind the child's words. This offers the child an opportunity to learn to know the self, and to chart a course for attitudinal and behavioral change. All suggestions, restraints, and criticisms are absent from the counselor's behavior, and are replaced by a complete acceptance of the child and a permissiveness for the child to feel, think, behave, and play in a personally honest manner.

In a child's playing out of feelings—tension, anxiety, etc.—the child brings these to the surface, gets them into the open, faces them, and learns to control them or abandon them. When the child has finally achieved an emotional catharsis, the child begins to realize that one can be an individual—to think, make decisions, become psychosocially more mature, and in so doing, realize "selfhood."

Building on the work of Axline, Ginott, and Moustakas, Garry Landreth (1991, 1993) has made a major contribution to the person-centered literature through his formulation of child-centered play therapy. In child-centered play therapy the relationship is the key to growth. Landreth (1991:60) in describing child-centered play therapy says:

> Child-centered play therapy is both a basic philosophy of the innate human capacity of the child to strive toward growth and maturity and an attitude of deep and abiding belief in the child's ability to be constructively self-directing. It is based on an understanding of the observable natural forward movement of the human organism through developmental stages of growth which are normally progressive and always toward greater maturity. This tendency is innate and is not externally motivated or taught. Children are naturally curious,

delight in mastery and accomplishment, and energetically live life in their continual pursuit of discovery of their world and themselves in relation to the world.

The focus of child-centered play therapy is on the child rather than the problem, the present rather than the past, feelings rather than thoughts or acts, understanding rather than explaining, accepting rather than correcting, the child's direction rather than the therapist's instruction, and the child's insight rather than the therapist's knowledge. The objectives of child-centered play therapy are to help the child to develop a more positive self-concept, assume greater responsibility, become more self-directing, become more self-accepting, become more self-reliant, develop and internal source of evaluation, and become more trusting of self. In child-centered therapy the child is viewed as behaving as an organized whole, motivated to enhance the self, goal-directed, valuing, being the best determiner of a personal reality, best able to perceive the self, and interested in maintaining the self. Throughout the relationship, the therapist unconditionally accepts the child, empathically listens and reflects feelings, and is congruently genuine with the child.

GROUP PLAY THERAPY

Ginott's (1961) main emphasis is on group psychotherapy with children—working with children in groups within the playroom setting. Ginott indicates that in group play therapy the presence of other children seems to diminish tension and stimulate activity and participation. The group induces spontaneity in children. They begin to relate to the group's therapist and trust that person more readily than in individual relationships outside the group. This observation is confirmed by Schiffer (1969).

Ginott feels that the medium which is best suited for the psychological growth of children is play. In therapy, this "is equivalent to freedom to act and react, suppress and express, suspect and respect." The *group* setting further provides a tangible *social* setting for the discovery of new and more satisfying ways of relating to peers. For the aim of play therapy is to help children develop behaviors which are consistent with society's standards (Bleck & Bleck, 1982).

Group play therapy is generally accepted as a better method to use when the child's problems are primarily social (Schiffer, 1969; Bleck & Bleck, 1982). On the other hand, individual therapy is deemed more useful for individualized emotional problems. The only difficulty with this approach may be the fact that individualized emotional problems are often expressed socially. There are times when a combination of individual and group therapy is useful. For example, individual therapy may be given for the first session and group therapy for subsequent sessions. Some therapists will have individual therapy with a child and then encourage the child to invite friends to a group therapy session. Such a group may be even more valuable for therapy than a group chosen by the therapist because often the child will invite withdrawn youngsters who are not particularly troublesome and hence unlikely to be referred for therapy by adults.

There are a number of other distinct advantages in the group approach. For one thing, *there is the sharing of a problem* and the realization that a particular problem is not unique. This factor makes the problem seem less "earth-shaking" to the child. Also, *there is the interplay of personalities* which adds a new dimension to therapy. In a group play session one may find significant emotional fluctuation from person to person ranging all the way from smiles to tears. In addition, as a result of the rapt attention which members show toward the activities of their peers, the group may notice one child forging ahead at a particular task and try doing the same. This results in a positive reinforcement for certain activities. Sometimes in group play it is not even necessary for other group members to "try out" a particular behavior because they can vicariously experience it by watching it being expressed by one of their play therapy peers (Bleck & Bleck, 1982).

INDIVIDUAL PLAY THERAPY

Individual play therapy becomes enhanced when it includes the following eight principles derived from Axline's (1969) historic work.

1. The helper must develop a warm, friendly relationship with the child, in which good rapport is established as soon as possible.
2. The helper accepts the child as the child is.
3. The helper establishes a feeling of permissiveness in the relationship so that the child feels free to express feelings.
4. The helper is alert to recognize the *feelings* the child is expressing and reflects those feelings back to the child so that the child gains insight into the meaning of such feelings and their relationship to behavior.
5. The helper maintains a deep respect for the child's ability to solve problems. The responsibility to make choices and to institute change is the child's.
6. The helper does not attempt to direct the child's actions or conversations. The child leads the way; the helper follows.
7. The helper does not attempt to hurry the play process along. It is a gradual process and is recognized as such.

8. The helper establishes only those limitations that are necessary to anchor the helping process to the world of reality and to help the child develop a sense of responsibility in the relationship.

When using individual play, the helper must become sensitive to the pitfall of functioning as a "playmate." Helping children through play requires empathic personal and professional qualities. It is not meant to be a maudlin, sugar-coated, or sentimental approach to working with children. Play is used to facilitate communication, self-awareness, and to put the child in contact with the reality of the child's behavior. To help the child move in these directions, the helper must be genuine, empathically understanding, warm in a nonpossessive way, concrete, and possess skills in reflecting and clarifying feelings (Moustakas, 1973).

In the play therapy relationship, the child learns that one can do anything that one likes in the room—that it is a time in which there is an absence of pressure—that this is the child's room and the child's hour. The helper accepts the child as the child is at the moment and does not try to mold the child toward socially approved behavior. The child is not forced or manipulated to play with certain toys and is freely permitted to remain silent and inactive if the child chooses. The helper accepts the meaning of the child's symbols at the child's level and works at the child's level of communication even when the meaning appears obvious. The helper, by being accepting, observing, and understanding, learns something of how life is going for the child—from the way the child handles materials we learn something about the child's level of maturity—from verbalizations made while the child is at play we learn something about the child's feelings about the self and others.

The helper makes no interpretation of the child's behavior or selection of play materials. The child is not reduced to an object to be analyzed. In using play media the helper works with the child's current behavior. There is no reliance on historical or case history information about the child. This here-and-now view stresses the importance of seeing the child's world in the present. The child in play shows personalized ways of seeing, choosing, and acting at this moment in time. No matter what the child has endured in the past, a positive, facilitating *present* experience contributes to the child's psychosocial stability. Providing positive, present experience does not depend on knowing the child's past experiences or on the subjective and sometimes biased interpretations of the meanings of those experiences contained in the case history.

Catharsis and insight, which occur for the child during the process of play, are not by themselves therapeutically curative. Catharsis in children usually involves mobility and acting out. Acting out has no curative effect beyond pleasure and release and it does not usually lead to self-evaluation, awareness of motivation, and attempts to change behavior. This is particularly true in young children for whom acting out becomes just fun. Insight also has its limitations. For children, there is no direct relationship between insight and behavioral change. Often insight is a result rather than a cause, attained by children who have grown emotionally ready through the play process to become acquainted with denied elements of their experiences.

Beyond catharsis and insight the use of play gives the child an opportunity to try out new behavior in the safety of an accepting and permissive atmosphere created by the counselor. By providing the child with the opportunity to be, the child is encouraged to experiment with new roles and behaviors and to vicariously experience the kind of psychosocial behaviors that the child would like to move toward and own.

SELECTION OF PLAY MATERIALS

Nearly any toy, as Nelson (1968) points out, has expressive possibilities in the eyes of the child, but he suggests three key criteria for selection of play materials for use with children: (1) select materials that may be used in a variety of ways such as clay, paints, and pipe cleaners; (2) select materials that promote communication such as toy telephones; and (3) select materials (punching bag, hand puppets) that encourage the expression and release of aggressive feelings. Generally, the more unstructured and flexible the toys, the more readily the child can express his or her imagination and feelings through them.

Ginott (1961) indicates that there are five major criteria for selecting and rejecting materials for play therapy, stating that a play therapy toy should: (1) facilitate the establishment of contact with the child by the helper; (2) evoke and encourage catharsis; (3) aid in developing insight; (4) furnish opportunities for reality testing; and (5) provide a vehicle for sublimation.

The toys used with children should be within each child's realm of play. If exposed to toys that are too old for the child, the child won't be able to express true emotions through them. By using toys the child is used to playing with, the child will feel free to be imaginative and reveal psychosocial needs and feelings (Moustakas, 1973).

Beiser (1955) studied the free choice of a selected group of toys of 100 children, 79 boys and 21 girls, ranging from two to twelve years of age, who had been referred to the Chicago Institute for Juvenile Research. Each toy was tabulated according to the total number of children who played with it (popularity), a ratio of popularity and total dynamic interpretations stemming from play with a toy (communication value), frequency with which the toy stimulated fantasy on the child's part (fantasy stimulation), the breadth and number of dynamic interpretations that could be made from a child's play with an individual toy (dynamic spread), and a combined total ranking of toys. In terms of highest combined total rankings, toys were listed in the following order: (1) doll family, (2) soldiers, (3) guns, (4) clay, (5) paper and crayons, (6) animals, (7) planes, (8) Nok-Out Bench, and (9) trucks. The lowest Combined Total ranking toys were: (1) pencil, (2) paste, (3) scissors, and (4) ball.

The particular toy used by a child should not be an issue. It is more important that it is something which will motivate the child to see the toy as having meaning, see it as something which can be incorporated into play, and see it as a vehicle through which feelings can be expressed. Helping the child to select facilitative toys is an important early step in the play therapy process.

Landreth (1991:115-116) suggests several general guidelines for selecting materials. Materials should be durable and communicate a message of "be yourself in playing" rather than "be careful," provide children with a variety of choice in medium of expression, not be complex, be appropriately manageable, and not require the therapist's help to manipulate. He offers the following questions as important evaluative criteria for selecting play materials. Do the materials:

1. Facilitate a range of creative expression?
2. Facilitate a wide range of emotional expression?
3. Engage children's interests?
4. Facilitate expressive and exploratory play?
5. Allow exploration and aggression without verbalization?
6. Allow success without prescribed structure?
7. Allow for noncommittal play?
8. Have sturdy construction for active use?

PLAY MATERIALS

The following play materials have been used with varying degrees of success by Dorfman (1951), Ginott (1961), Axline (1969), Moustakas (1959, 1973, 1997), Krall (1989), Landreth (1991), and O'Dessie (1997).

Doll Family/Doll House–A spacious doll house appropriately furnished and peopled with dolls depicting male and female, children and babies. The treatment accorded by the child to a parent and sibling dolls can give the counselor an understanding of the child's perceptions of self and others within the family context. The sleeping patterns in the doll house may be of some interest (Ginott, 1961) as well as the targets of anger and affection. In some studies, it has been found that the child most often selects the doll family as play material. There are some who feel that through the use of dolls, the child is best able to express feelings. It should be borne in mind that all acting-out with dolls or puppets is not significant. It is only significant when the child uses these media to express a variety of feelings or to work through feelings that are troublesome.

Toy Animals–Some children find it difficult to express aggressive feelings against people even through the make-believe world of dolls. They do, however, find they can express aggressive feelings in safety against "bad" animals. It should also be pointed out that toy animals can elicit feelings of affection and love.

Blocks–Blocks satisfy children's need for risk and adventure and may also serve as a substitute object for hostility. Blocks enable children to build and destroy without dire consequences and are very amenable to a rapid rebuilding. The child can destroy a block building over and over again and learn in the process that one's aggression is not catastrophic.

Water–Water play can involve pouring water, blowing bubbles, squeezing sponges, washing, soaking, and rinsing anything that can be immersed. Water, according to Ginott (1961), is perhaps the most effective of all playroom materials. It does not require any special skills so every child can play with it with success. It enables even the meekest of children to experience a sense of accomplishment. The materials make too little demand and offer so little resistance that every child can manipulate them. It allows for cleansing or it can become, in the child's imagination, an agent for messing. Water play is limited only by the child's imagination. Materials for water play are inexpensive, readily available, and a delight for children.

Sand Box–Sand is another excellent medium for the child's aggressive play. It can be thrown about with comparative safety–dolls and other toys can be buried in it–it can be "snow," "water," or a "burying ground." It can also elicit creative impulses and provide excellent opportunities for the use of the child's imagination.

Easel and Finger Paints–These offer a suitable outlet for the satisfaction of the child's needs to mess. They are nonthreatening media which allow children to translate feelings into color and movement. Even for the over-controlled and inhibited child, the contact with soft, colorful, mercurial-like substances encourages spontaneity and a free flow of fantasy.

Clay–Clay allows for success at any level of a child's development and skill. It provides an outlet for both creative and destructive urges. It lends itself to random manipulation; it requires no intermediary; it can be used by aggressive children to punch and pound; it gives a sense of accomplishment in the child's mastery of pliable material.

Aggressive Toys–These should be chosen with care to avoid physical harm to the child. Punching bags and pounding boards provide harmless outlets for expressing hostility. Noise making toys such as drums and xylophones can also be used by children for a nondestructive expression of hostility.

Puppets–Many children find that they can use the anonymity of puppets to express their feelings in safety. Puppets are a delight to work with and can be manipulated by the child to express a wide range of psychosocial needs and feelings.

Many other toys can be used to enhance the psychosocial development of the child (Caney, 1972). It should be noted that almost every toy which can evoke a negative response can also produce a positive response. This was brought about in a graduate course when students who were experientially learning about play began to talk about their personal reactions to the spring back punching bag. During the time the graduate students played with the materials, nearly all of them had a chance at the punching bag and expressed delight in hitting the bag as hard as they could. However, a few students stated that when they approached the punching bag, rather than hit it, they hugged it. What emerged in the ensuing discussion was that toys and other play materials are neutral objects and whatever feeling is expressed with a toy is a reflection of the person using it rather than the toy itself. It is not surprising then, when a child picks up a toy gun, looks at it momentarily, and then puts it aside saying, "I wish people would stop hurting each other." For the child the toy gun may bring forth a feeling of sadness rather than aggression. It is wise to put aside stereotyped images about the emotional valences of toys and to encourage the child to share perceptions and feelings as these are evoked by the toy or medium used in play.

THE PLAYROOM

The necessity of having a special room set aside and furnished for helping children through play is questioned by Axline (1969) who believes there are many possibilities for using the medium of play within limited budget and space appropriations. A small rug, an easel, and a toy box located in a corner of a room would constitute an adequate play media environment. In the toy box would be a doll family, a few pieces of furniture, nursing bottle, telephone, puppets, crayons, drawing paper, water colors, finger paints, and some transportation toys such as cars and trucks. These materials would be sufficient for play therapy and could fit a space as small as a suitcase.

If a special room is to be put aside for play, it should have the following features. The playroom should be kept simple. Other than basic furniture, the only things which should be there are toys. The floor and walls should be washable and easily cleaned. The room should have acoustical ceiling tile and wall materials which will absorb and reduce sound. It would be helpful to protect the windows with screening. The room should be bright and attractive, well lighted, well ventilated, and play materials should be visible and available. There should be a sink with running hot and cold water, a sand box, and a wooden bench for use as a table or work area. Materials should be kept on shelves which are easily accessible. Regardless of the mess made in previous play sessions, the room should be put in order so that it is always neutral and free from the suggestive indicators regarding which play materials were used by a previous individual or group using the playroom.

It would greatly enhance the child's sense of freedom if the child were provided with a smock, an old shirt, or some sort of coverall to protect clothing. The child will then have the freedom to be messy.

ESTABLISHING LIMITS

Rationale for Limits

In his discussion of play therapy, Ginott (1961:103-105) offers five reasons for establishing limits:

1. Limits direct catharsis into symbolic channels.
2. Limits enable the helper to maintain attitudes of acceptance, empathy, and regard for the child and not be distracted from those attitudes.
3. Limits assure the physical safety of the child.
4. Limits strengthen ego controls.
5. Limits are set for reasons of law, ethics, and social acceptability.

Landreth, Strother, and Barlow (1986) indicate that limits consistently anchor the play experience to the world of reality, give the child a sense of responsibility in the relationship, and safeguard the helping process from possible misconceptions, confusion, guilt feelings, and insecurity.

The use of durable and inexpensive media which is easily cleaned in a playroom will obviate the need for limits relating to materials (with a few exceptions). It is evident that some limits bearing on the relationship are required if the child is to learn how to deal with the real world and if the purposes of the play experience are to be met. There appears to be general agreement (Dorfman, 1951; Ginott, 1961; Axline, 1969; Moustakas, 1973; Mcmahon, 1992; O'Connor & Menges, 1997; Carroll, 1998) that the following limits serve to improve the psychosocial quality and effectiveness of play experiences.

Time Limit–A time limit is determined and held to. The helper tells the child the time limit and toward the end the helper reminds the child that there are only a few minutes left. When the child learns that time limits are part of everyone's reality, the child will begin to make profitable use of the time available for play.

Taking Toys from the Playroom–Toys should remain in the playroom. Broken toys should also remain in the playroom, otherwise some toys would be broken for the purpose of taking them home. If a child wants to show a toy to a parent, then the child may ask the parent or teacher to the playroom to see it. Children should be allowed to take home paintings and clay work that they themselves create.

Breakage of Toys/Destruction to Room–Children's destructive urges and feelings should be recognized, reflected, and respected, but limits on action should be invoked and implemented. It is more of a help to the child to let the child face the limits that human relationships require than to let the child give rein to destructive *actions*. There is little self-enhancing value in permitting a child to break playroom equipment or toys. The child's negative actions should be channeled toward materials in the playroom designated for the purpose.

Physical Assault–There is no benefit in letting a child physically assault another child or the helper. It is generally agreed that this is a limit which should not be modified under any circumstances. It is more helpful for the child to channel aggressive feelings through symbolic actions against play materials which are there for that purpose. Permitting a child to attack another person can cause harm not only to that person but to the child who needs to learn that mutual respect requires some control of feelings and that the unbridled expression of anger through physical assault is no solution for the child's problems.

Limits should not be mentioned before the need for them arises. If limits are kept to a minimum and are introduced only when the need emerges, then the play experience progresses more naturally. There appears to be little advantage in beginning the play experience by prescribing limitations on actions that may never occur. Children's everyday experiences usually prepare them for some prohibitions upon their actions and it is better to wait until the need for limits comes up before identifying them.

PARENTS AND PLAY: FILIAL THERAPY

As a consultant to parents, the play therapist can help parents to use play to facilitate the psychosocial development of the child. The value of play as a vehicle for fostering the psychosocial development of the child cannot be underestimated. The play therapist and parents can work together to use the extraordinary power of play to enhance the psychosocial maturity of children (Moustakas, 1973, 1997).

Landreth and his colleagues (Bavin-Hoffman, Jennings, & Landreth, 1996; Bratton & Landreth, 1995; Chau & Landreth, 1997; Cleveland & Landreth, 1997; Glazer-Waldman, Hilda, Zimmerman, Landreth, & Norton, 1992; Harris & Landreth, 1997; Kraft & Landreth, 1998; Landreth & Lobaugh, 1998; Landreth, 1991), recognizing the crucial importance of the parent-child relationship to the healthy development and mental health of children, have extended and more fully developed *filial therapy* in which parents are educated in the overall principles and methodology of client-centered play therapy. The heart and soul of the filial therapeutic program is regularly scheduled parent-child play therapy sessions at home in which the parent is the therapeutic agent of change. Through a ten-session training program parents learn how to create a nonjudgmental, understanding, empathic, and accepting environment for thirty-minute play times in which their children feel safe enough to explore other parts of themselves as persons and learn new ways of relating to their parents. The parent does not initiate or direct play activities. The child, within appropriate boundaries, is free to direct one's self to be creative, to be silly, to be somber, to be serious, and to enjoy just being without any fear of parental rejection or judgment.

The goals of the parent-child play sessions are: (1) to help the child shed distorted perceptions or misperceptions of the parent; (2) to enable the child to openly communicate thoughts, feelings, and behaviors which have been unexpressed; and (3) to help the child, through the incorporation of newly perceived parental attitudes, develop greater feelings of self-respect, self-worth, and confidence. In the filial therapy training program parents learn how to reflect feelings, to set limits, to unconditionally accept the child, and to let the child take the lead. They also learn not to criticize, not to ask leading questions, and not to preach. Parents who have participated in filial therapy training programs have demonstrated significant changes in acceptance of their children, respect for their children's feelings, and recognition of their children's need for autonomy. Self-esteem of both parents and children and closeness between parents and children have increased.

PARENTS AND PLAY THERAPY: THE TOY LENDING PROGRAM

Another approach parents can use in facilitating their children's development is the toy lending program. The toy lending program is based on two basic ideas: that play activities should be self-rewarding so that a child participates because of the enjoyment the child receives, not because the child is coerced or coaxed; and that psychosocial development cannot take place without free expression. The goal of a toy lending program is to create psychosocially helpful play environments in the home and to encourage play between parents and children as a medium for getting to know each other and learning about each other's psychosocial needs. In play at home, the child should also be free to give vent to feelings of anger and frustration and be able to talk to the parent(s) about the experiences and circumstances which cause these feelings.

Initiating a toy lending program is not difficult. The components are simple: a meeting place, a group of interested parents, a presentation on the psychosocial purposes of play, demonstrations on how play elicits feelings, and identification of the play materials which evoke feelings, role playing opportunities to engage in play, and the formation of a support group atmosphere in which parents can be encouraged in their play efforts to contribute to the psychosocial development of their children.

In conclusion, the psychosocial benefits of play cannot be underestimated. Play is the child's natural language for expressing a wide range of feelings. When the counselor attempts to assist a child to express feelings only through verbal interactions, the experience can be frustrating for the child who typically does not possess the language to express those feelings. But when the counselor establishes a play relationship with the child, the child is able to express feelings which are more accurate, honest, natural, and spontaneous. The feelings which previously could not be expressed now emerge because of the stimulus provided by play materials.

USING PLAY MEDIA TO FACILITATE A CHILD'S SELF-AWARENESS

LUCY WEEKS

Rationale for the Use of Play

The child's response to life, in the form of continual striving, growing, and changing as the child observes and experiences the world and the people in the child's life, can be supported and nourished by the child's self-awareness as a valued human being. If the child knows love and acceptance from others, the child will more readily accept the self. If the child is continually unsure of the self as a person of worth, much of the child's energy for growth is spent in defending the self against the hurt of not being completely acceptable. Through play the child expresses the self and feelings; the child experiments and tries out behavior; the child comes to know the self more fully and vicariously experiences what the child would like to become.

A child's play in the presence of, or with, an adult frequently represents the child's self-concept and how the child perceives an environment, and the child often implicitly assumes that the adult is able to understand both. The more acceptance, warmth, and understanding the child receives from an adult, the more the child is able to reveal the self. As the child sees the self through childhood's natural medium of play, the child comes to a greater self-awareness and self-understanding.

A Child's Problem and Attitudes

I would like to describe one elementary school child as I have seen him through the medium of play and with the aid of audiotapes and my notes, to trace a developing self-awareness as he struggles to understand and express himself. All names and references are changed and with this agreement I have the generous permission of the child's parents to use the material collected for professional writings and understandings. The boy himself was happy to use the tape recorder, and often would play back, for his own listening, the tape of the previous session.

I came to know Gid initially as a boy who was constantly in difficulties with his teachers and his playmates. In the fourth grade, in public school and in church school, he was alternately disruptive and inattentive, rude or in tears, and at times destructive. His elementary school teacher was concerned at what seemed evidence of deep anger when he gouged and mutilated his desk. Efforts to play with others usually ended in tears followed by solitary activity. The same behavior was observed in church school and he caused exasperation in all who were in contact with him. A difficult and unhappy classroom pattern seemed to have been firmly established and was continuing when I first came into contact with Gid. He was brought to me, trembling and scared, by an exasperated teacher. I asked him to sit down and talk things over and tried to assure him that I was not there to punish, but that perhaps we could find some way to help him. He said: Well—well—those—they—the others won't let me simmer down.

Counselor: They won't let you simmer down.

Gid: No—they—they—they—they're always after me.

I suggested he might like to meet with me once a week for a while, to which he agreed eagerly. Later, at a conference with his mother to make arrangements, he was very silent and agreed to meet with me with a very matter-of-fact, "Yeah, I'd like to." He remained across the room and aloof and I confirmed the appointment with Gid and ended the interview by avoiding his mother's tendency to discuss Gid in his presence.

Place: Playroom and Materials

The playroom is a large basement with a blackboard, piano, building blocks, books, and puzzles. There is a sandbox full of toys—trucks, shovels, etc. Nearby is a doll house with furniture and dolls of all sizes and kinds. Near the sandbox is a table and bench where I leave out clay, colored Play-Doh®, and finger paints and paper. There is an adjoining lavatory with toilet and wash bowl, and paper towels. The two doors to the room are closed when the room is used, but there are glass panes through which an adult can see.

Counselor Attitudes and Atmosphere for Play

Other than his acting-out behavior in the classroom, Gid seemed to be a very self-controlled child. At times he was impassive and detached. I felt that a child-centered play climate could provide Gid with a completely accepting, permissive, and relaxed atmosphere where he could play out his feelings and perhaps come to discover himself more easily and more fully than he had yet been able to do. He needed to find an adult who could respect him entirely, uncritically, with all his tension and confusion.

The time was set for one hour each week. At times we went on a little longer, but an hour and a half was the maximum. The room itself and the closed doors limited the play area quite clearly. If Gid decided to leave early, this ended the session for the day. With Axline's (1969) discussion of limits in mind, I was prepared to channel aggressive play, or to stop destructiveness, if necessary. The occasion never arose.

STAGES IN SELF-AWARENESS

Testing Out the Situation

In our first session in the playroom, I told Gid the hour was his to do as he pleased, that he could use any of the toys or equipment he found there. He stood still and surveyed the room, then wandered from one thing to another, picking up, inspecting, and then dropping a toy. His constant glances in my direction indicated his doubt as to how much freedom I would allow. His whole body gradually relaxed, no words were exchanged until he found the tape recorder which delighted him. I showed him how to use it and then suggested that we tape our sessions together and that at any time he could turn it back and listen to himself or that he could turn it off. He proceeded to try it out, and handled it in a competent manner. I sensed in him a pride in his ability. He discovered the piano and played a few notes, looked over his shoulder several times, and played a few more notes before inspecting more of the toys.

Gid: Who uses this room anyway, the nursery?

Co: Yes, on Sundays it's for the little people.

Gid: Ha, sandbox, doll houses, dolls–house–doll house–dolls–I don't play with dolls.

Co: Lots to play with, but you don't play with dolls.

Gid: I want to hear my voice again.

Co: You want to hear it.

Gid: Yeah.

Tension and Catharsis

Earlier in the session Gid had run the tape back and played it again without hesitation. This time he seemed confused and looked at me. I showed him how again.

At this point I felt that permissiveness and support were better than the assumption that he could do it and perhaps the pressure to succeed which might have been implied.

He had been testing the situation, checking out the use of the room, and watching me for reactions. Gid's rejection of the doll house, his repeating (almost stammering) the words of rejection, seemed to say he was not ready to look at a family situation. It was a brief look at himself and his subsequent confusion at the tape recorder indicated that the doll house had produced some tension. He returned to talking about family when he compared my age and his father's. He then tried to speak of his grandfather, who had died recently, but could not complete what he wanted to say.

Gid: When were you born, Mrs. W.? What year?
Co: You are wondering how old I am?
Gid: My father, he is 47 and you're older.

He went to the piano, played a simple tune, using both hands, banged one hand on the keys, then stopped. A long silence. . . then, "You know what, Mrs. W.?

Co: What, Gid?
Gid: My—my—my-gran—my—no, my father—

He turned to the piano again and banged the keys as hard as he could with both hands. Then he said again, "My father, he's 47." Then he turned to the piano again and banged the low notes one by one moving up the keyboard a little way, then back to the low notes harder and faster. Was the question of death his real concern here in speaking of age?

Gid then repeated the same piano banging very hard and loud. He once looked at me as if expecting to be stopped. Then he began again, went to the tape recorder and replayed the tape, listening intently. He repeated this behavior four times. Then:

Gid: OK, I'm going to get a drink.

There was a change in the tension and tempo of his movements. He went to the bathroom, carefully adjusting the door so that it was not quite closed. This pattern was typical of Gid's playroom behavior for several months. Tension seemed to build up in him; he found release in some intense activity such as pounding clay, banging the piano, or hammering wooden blocks, with little or no verbalization even when feelings and actions were reflected to him. Then he would suddenly depart to the bathroom and return to use paints or the sand table. I later began to wonder if this amounted to catharsis followed by flight from the disturbing thoughts and feelings inside him. It was certainly catharsis, and each time I waited for signs of self-awareness, meanwhile letting him set the pace.

At another point, Gid indicated something of his inner feelings by drawing on the blackboard. He had been very silent and very restless, picking up and dropping one thing after another. At the blackboard, he fiddled with chalk, asked if we had colored chalk, then drew up a chair, stood on it and moved one piece of chalk from top to bottom of the board in great peaks and valleys.

Gid: You know what this is, Mrs. W.? Mountains and glaciers—gl–glaciers, glaciers. And nobody on them, nobody around—no *one* person. Not–not–not–Do you like ice cream, Mrs. W.? You know the best ice cream cone there is? It's at Andy's. I'd like a big cone each Friday. Can we get one?

And so we arranged to get ice cream at the end of each session. Gid seemed to be picturing something for me—either loneliness, or a desire for solitude, and he moved away from it so quickly I accepted it without words. Later I questioned my lack of response to his blackboard drawing. Would a reflection have helped him become more aware of what he was picturing?

During the first months, another clue to Gid's feelings came regularly on arrival at his house at the end of the afternoon. He would sit a moment in the car and survey the yard, the number of bicycles in the driveway, etc.

Gid: Do I have to go home now?
Co: You'd like to stay.
Gid: I like it there by myself, but you'll get some colored chalk next time?
Co: Mm. I'll see if I can get some good colors.
Gid: OK–that brother of mine is home.

He got out of the car slowly. Often he would say, "I wonder who is home?"

Blaming Others

In the subsequent weeks, Gid referred to his own behavior in school and blamed others. He could speak of himself, but could not acknowledge responsibility.

Gid: You know what, Mrs. W.? I couldn't think of anything to write until I stood out in the hall for a while. The teacher made me.
Co: At school.
Gid: Yeah. I stood there and thought of a story I could write, but the others had theirs all done when I got back in the room.
Co: It was hard to write when you were in the room with everyone else.
Gid: It was hard to think.
Co: But you could think when you were by yourself.
Gid: Yeah. They make me do things.
Co: The other kids make you do things.
Gid: Well, I get all excited, all simmered up.

And later: comments on self—

Gid: I forgot what I got a D in, maybe it was writing. I got an A in math.

Co: A D is discouraging, but you like math.

Gid: Yeah. It's good; I can do it. You know I like rocks—I'll tell you about them. (He gave me a long description of various rock samples he had at home.)

Co: It feels good to know about some things like math and rocks.

Gid: You know—I–I–I like to forget some things.

Co: You like to forget; you feel better.

Gid: Mmm—some—sometimes. (A long silence while he carefully screwed lids on paint jars.) Then: I could eat some ice cream now.

At times like this I feel strongly the need to accept *his* pacing as he grows more aware of himself.

Fantasy

Gid often mentions distant places and large sums of money in his conversations. As he was painting he said:

Gid: Purple. (He began to hum to himself.) Purple and black, or dark green, that's what it makes. (Still humming.) I'll make a map of the U.S.—try anyway—they never let me—they make me laugh. Florida—ha-ha-*thing*, ha-ping-thing-ping. Know what? Oh, that's wrong. (He went to wash his hands, returned to the table. He reached for the clay.) I'm going—going to—to—I'm going to Germany to college.

Co: To Germany.

Gid: Did you ever go far away, Mrs. W.?

Co: To far away places.

Gid: Yes, all on your own, just away. You know how much money baseball players make? A million—no, a trillion dollars.

Co: A lot of money. (He dropped the clay abruptly and went to the blackboard, picked up chalk and then dropped it back in the tray. He was restless.)

Self and Reality

About two months later he was talking about going to New York City, "on his own—all by himself." But a week later he said:

Gid: You know last time I said I wanted to go to New York by myself. Well—I like baseball and I like to sort of dream—dream about going away but I'd really want my family. I guess I just think things but—well—I know—I really know—well—.

Co: You know that you're dreaming and you know what's real, too.
Gid: Yeah, yeah. There's dreams and there's real things.

In early sessions, Gid seemed to use play materials as a means for catharsis. He was often restless, endlessly picking up, then dropping, whatever he came upon as he drifted around the room, silent until he suddenly settled to piano, play or paint, and finally, one day, the sand table. At two different times he pulled out the doll house, then shoved it back against the wall vigorously. He never seemed to notice two puppets lying on the shelf, one white and one black skinned.

I began to see real changes in Gid after one particularly rough day at the playroom. He had arrived extremely tense and silent. This appointment was the result of a very incoherent telephone call from Gid the day before. Less than a week had elapsed since I had last seen him and I was aware of family stresses in the background. In the playroom Gid was throwing paint on papers and the floor, with no words at all. Suddenly he stopped and looked at what he had done, and then with tears running down his face, he squatted down and started to pry up the clay.

Co: You feel very angry, and then very sad.

Gid just nodded his head and put his head down and sobbed. I put my arm around him and in a few minutes he was quiet. I handed him a tissue and he said tearfully, "Can we get some ice cream?"

Carefully Gid began to put things in order, papers and clay in the box and tops on paint jars.

Gid: I'll turn out the lights and you close the door.

He seemed to be closing the door on those moments. He avoided the playroom the next Friday and asked to stay in my office. It was soon after that I realized he was playing with more purpose.

During his third month of play therapy, he entered the playroom one day and went straight to the puppets, picked up the white one, and began talking, at first in a whisper.

Gid: See that—he is goop—he is a dumbhead, always in trouble—a mess.
Co: Always in trouble—a mess.
Gid: We could bury him in the sand so he couldn't get up. But he'd do it—he would—he—he'd kick his way out—and he, he'd—maybe he'd hurt someone, too.
Co: He'd get out, he would, but it might hurt.
Gid: Here—now—ah—oh—oh.

Gid dug a hole, put the puppet in very gently, and swiftly covered him up. He piled trucks and shovels on top of the pile of sand, and then just stood looking at the pile. Suddenly he spoke in a very tender voice.

Gid: He's got sand up his nose–he–he can't breathe. Come on–we'll help him out. He'll be OK. Come on, you help me.

So I helped him uncover the puppet. He held it up high and looked at it.

Gid: You, you've got friends. You didn't need to kick–you might have broke your leg.

Co: Friends can help. He didn't break a leg.

Gid: Well–yeah–sand's like–like–well–it's easy if it's a lot. I could eat a huge ice cream cone.

Gid continued to play with the puppet for several sessions, talking to it, alternately giving it a rough time and treating it with warmth and tenderness.

Erickson (1964) has said that "to 'play it out' is the most natural self-healing measure childhood affords." To Gid, the puppet was himself, and through it I listened, and reflected as he played out some of his own hurt, anger, and doubts. He made the puppet call Sam names and kick him (Sam is Gid's older brother) and finally:

Gid: (with puppet, using high voice) Plonk–dead he got it–a bat, no, a ball right in the face Ah–ah–oh–oh–no, not quite–he'll go to the hospital–they'll fix him–he–he'll *think*–I guess–we'll–we-ee'll see.

And yet three weeks later he returned to a direct reference to his brother and how they called each other names.

Gid: He calls me 'weekend,' get it? And I call him the 'bonk."

Co: And how do you feel when he does?

Gid: Oh, I go after him and make him say–he's a dope (laughing).

Co: And does Sam feel hurt?

Gid: Sometimes. But when he tells me, I never do it. Sometimes it's fun having a brother around. Sometimes it's lousy.

But now Gid could accept his feelings about his brother.

Reflection about Self

After eleven months of weekly sessions, Gid could talk directly about himself. Now he preferred to stay upstairs in my office and talk. He would fling himself in the armchair and swing his legs across the arm.

Gid: You know what, Mrs. W.? I've sort of got used to things I–we–I got Mrs. R.'s dying out of my system (a neighbor) and Midget's dying (his puppy)–and my grandfather. I don't know if we'll go to Seattle –But it's OK somehow.

Co: You sort of find it easier to take what comes, even if Seattle leaves you feeling uncertain.

Gid: It isn't Seattle. That might be OK—except I'd have to leave Billy and Jack (friends). Maybe—well—I-uh—I don't have to forget things—you know.

Co: You feel more comfortable—more—

Gid: Yeah. I'm feeling—huh? Funny, that's good—I'm *feeling*—that's it. Oh, boy—you know, I'm gonna make that team—and I got good marks—an-an—well—I guess I'm gonna go on wanting ice cream, though (chuckling).

The following week, Gid said:

Mrs. W., I used to think about what you were like and now I think about what I'm like.

After that I saw Gid less frequently. He telephoned if he wanted to talk, and his last phone call was a jubilant one to tell me he'd made the baseball team. His parents and teachers reported that he improved in his grades and behavior. He gained in self-confidence, stability, and self-understanding.

CONCLUSION

Any elementary school or community agency could profitably use a "play center." A small room would serve quite adequately if provided with clay, paints, and puppets. Small doll figures would aid the child in expressing concerns with the child's world. The immaturity of the child may limit verbalization, but the child's ability to speak through clay can demonstrate to the child and to the counselor the child's feelings and perceptions. As Gid began to express himself, he used puppets, clay, and the truck in the sand with purpose and meaning, but as he became more sensitive to himself and his environment, he used materials less, and became more verbal.

Erickson (1964) speaks of play as the infantile way of mastering experience by meditating, experimenting, and planning. These are three steps which the child counselor would desire to facilitate in a child. The stages of play first observed and classified by Lowenfeld (1935) are still accurate. I believe they were illustrated by Gid's use of play materials and his subsequent ability to speak more realistically and insightfully about himself. In early play sessions, Gid showed great tension and restlessness. He tested out the counselor's acceptance at first, then found release from tension through *bodily activity*. He talked very little, and when he did, it was to a great extent about interests other than self and family. When he mentioned his own behavior, it was to blame others, a refusal of responsibility for his actions, and he would move away very rapidly from any subject that made him uncomfortable. A counselor needs great patience at these times and a conviction that the child can and will grow in awareness and toward a more positive concept of self—at the child's own pace. The counselor's trust in the child's own pacing will give the child the freedom to grow when the child is ready.

Gid soon began to use play media with more purpose. He found a means to express what he had experienced (*repetition of experience*), and what he dreamed (*demonstration of fantasy*). He expressed himself, often with great feeling, and seemed to move to a greater realization of himself and his environment. His next steps were toward a more realistic assessment of himself and a greater acceptance of his family and peers (*realization of environment*).

Erickson (1964) also speaks of the ego's capacity to find a self-cure in play, but he also says this about the child's play. "Such peace gained by play must, however, be sustained by new insight on the part of the parents."

While insight and cooperation on the part of the parents are highly desirable, I believe Gid has made significant gains in spite of continuing parental turmoil in the background, and the burden of his mother's fluctuating emotional distress.

Within the elementary school the counselor may profitably serve as consultant to teachers and parents, but my experience with Gid confirms Rogers' (1951) belief that the child's capacity for self-help and growth can occur without planned change in the child's environment.

REFERENCES

Allen, F. H. (1942). *Psychotherapy with children.* New York: Norton

Amster, F. (1943). Differential uses of play in treatment of young children. *American Journal of Orthopsychiatry, 13*, 62-68.

Axline, V. (1964). *Dibs: In search of self.* Boston, MA: Houghton Mifflin.

Axline, V. (1969). *Play therapy.* New York: Ballantine Books.

Bavin-Hoffman, R., Jennings, G,. & Landreth, G. (1996). Filial therapy: Parental perceptions of the process. *International Journal of Play Therapy, 5*, 1, 45-58.

Beiser, H. R. (1955). Therapeutic play techniques: Play equipment for diagnosis and therapy. *American Journal of Orthopsychiatry, 25*, 761-770.

Bleck, R. T., & Bleck, B. L. (1982). The disruptive child's play group. *Elementary School Counseling and Guidance, 17*, 137-141.

Bratton, S., & Landreth, G. (1995). Filial therapy with single parents: Effects on parental acceptance, empathy and stress. *International Journal of Play Therapy, 4*, 1, 61-80.

Caney, S. (1972). *Toy books* New York: Workman.

Caplan, R. & Caplan, T. (1973). *The power of play.* New York: Anchor Books.

Carroll, J. (1998) *Introduction to therapeutic play.* Malden,MA: Blackwell Science.

Chau, I. Y. F., & Landreth, G. (1997). Filial therapy with Chinese parents: Effects on parental empathic interactions, parental acceptance of child and parental stress. *International Journal of Play Therapy, 6,* 2, 75-92.

Cleveland, J., & Landreth, G. (1997). Children's perceptions of filial therapy. *TCA–Journal, 25,* 1, 19-29.

Dorfman, E. (1951). Play therapy. In C. R. Rogers, *Client-centered therapy* (Chapter 6). Boston: Houghton Mifflin.

Ellis, M. J. (1973). *Why people play.* Englewood Cliffs, NJ: Prentice-Hall.

Erickson, E. H. (1964). Toys and reasons. In M. R. Haworth (Ed), *Child psychotherapy: Practice and theory.* New York: Basic Books.

Ginott, H. G. (1961). *Group psychotherapy with children.* New York: McGraw-Hill.

Glazer-Wildman, H. R., Zimmerman, J. E., Landreth, G., & Norton, D. (1992). Filial therapy: An intervention for parents of children with chronic illness. *International Journal of Play Therapy, 1,* 1, 31-42.

Harris, Z. L., & Landreth, G. (1997). Filial therapy with incarcerated mothers: A five week model. *International Journal of Play Therapy, 6,* 2, 53-73.

Kraft, A., & Landreth, G. (1998). *Parents as therapeutic partners: Listening to your child's play.* Northvale, NJ: Jason Aronson.

Krall, V. (1989). *A play therapy primer: Therapeutic approaches to children with emotional problems.* New York: Human Sciences Press.

Landreth, G. (1993). Child centered play therapy. *Elementary School Guidance and Counseling, 28,* 1, 17-29.

Landreth, G. (1991). *Play therapy: The art of the relationship.* Muncie, IN: Accelerated Development, Inc.

Landreth, G., & Lobaugh, A. F. (1998). Filial therapy with incarcerated fathers: Effects on parental acceptance of child, parental stress, and child adjustment. *Journal of Counseling and Development, 76,* 2, 157-165.

Landreth, G., Strother, J.., & Barlow, K. (1986). A reaction to objections to play therapy. *School Counselor, 33,* 164-166.

Landreth, G., & Verhalen, M. (1982). Who is this person they call a counselor? *School Counselor, 29,* 359-361.

Levy, D. M.. (1939). Release therapy. *American Journal of Orthopsychiatry, 9,* 113-136.

Levy, J. (1978). *Play behavior.* New York: John Wiley.

Lowenfeld, M. (1935). *Play in childhood.* London: Gollancz.

McMahon, L. (1992) *The handbook of play therapy.* New York: Routledge.

Meeks, A. R. (1968). *Guidance in elementary education.* New York: Ronald Press.

Moustakas, C. C. (1959). *Play therapy with children.* New York: Harper.

Moustakas, C. C. (1973). *Children in play therapy.* New York: McGraw-Hill.

Moustakas, C. C. (1997). *Relationship play therapy.* Northvale, NJ: Jason Aronson.

Nelson, R. C. (1968). Play media and the elementary school counselor. In D. C. Dinkmeyer (Ed), *Guidance and counseling in the elementary school* (267-270). New York: Holt, Rinehart and Winston.

O'Connor, K. & Menges, L.M.B. (eds)(1997) *Play therapy: theory and practice: a comparative presentation.* New York: John Wiley and Sons.

O'Dessie, O. J. (1997). *Play therapy: A comprehensive guide.* Northvale, NJ: Jason Aronson.

Orlick, R. (1983). Enhancing love and life mostly through play and games. *Humanistic Education, 21,* 153-164.

Piaget, J. (1951). *Play, dreams and imitation in children.* New York: Norton.

Pulaski, M. A. (1971). *Understanding Piaget.* New York: Harper and Row

Rogers, C. R. (1951). *Client-centered therapy..* Boston, MA: Houghton Mifflin.

Rubin, P. B., & Tregay, J. (1989). *Play with them: Theraplay groups in the classroom:* Springfield, IL: Charles C Thomas.

Schiffer, M. (1969). The therapeutic play group. New York: Grune and Stratton.

Chapter 10

EVALUATING COUNSELING AND COUNSELORS

EVALUATING COUNSELING

The counseling profession cannot move forward on the basis of gratuitous statements regarding the outcomes and effectiveness of counseling. What can be gratuitously asserted can be gratuitously denied, and incidental and haphazard approaches to evaluation contribute very little to our understanding of counseling or to its improvement. McLeod (1994:1) points out that,"There is considerable evidence, mainly from surveys of counselors and psychotherapists in the USA (Cohen et al., 1986; Morrow-Bradley & Elliot, 1986), that practitioners of psychological therapies do not read research articles, and do not consider research to be particularly relevant to their work." We believe what is needed to overcome this resistance to counseling research is well-designed action research studies conducted at the local level to demonstrate the effectiveness of counseling in the total helping process (Frey, Raming, & Frey, 1978; Oetting, 1977; Wilson, 1985).

Diverse and complex problems confront the counselor who wishes to measure counseling outcomes and process. An understanding of these problems is necessary if counselors are to carry out meaningful studies of counseling theory and practice (Lewis, 1970). The existence of these problems does not mean that the counselor cannot conduct meaningful and valuable research. However, an effective counselor who is rendering significant assistance to clients will not always have the time to conduct an elaborate research study regarding the counselor's effectiveness. The more effective the counselor, the greater will be the demand for his or her services. The counselor's primary obligation is to provide counseling assistance to clients.

In most settings, the counselor would need the help of a research consultant to design studies that would meet the criteria suggested in the literature of counseling psychology as a definition of valid research. Like the practicing physician, lawyer, or dentist, the practicing counselor will leave elaborate and sophisticated research to full-time researchers. However, this does not mean the professional counselor cannot become involved in designing and carrying out simple action research and evaluative studies that would have value at the local level and implications for improving counseling practice. Simplicity of design and execution are not necessarily exclusive of validity and meaning. Simple, clear, and well thought-out studies can provide valuable data to the counselor to help in gauging and improving the effectiveness of the counselor's work (Ohlsen, 1983). We believe that good practice generates good theory and that research grounded in practice improves the quality and outcomes of counseling. Counseling action research promotes systematic and rigorous thinking which benefits counseling practice (Hadley & Mitchell 1995) and embodies the scientist-practitioner approach (Hoshmand & Polkinghorne, 1992) reflecting the person-centered tradition of inquiry consistently practiced by Rogers throughout his career.

Evaluation Objectives

The objectives of evaluation revolve around two pivotal questions. Are we helping clients? How can we improve counselor and counseling effectiveness to be of greater assistance to clients? These are not only the concerns of counselors but also of the community at large. It is well for counselors to bear in mind that community members are not unreasonable in their desire for evidence that demonstrates the value of counseling. Altogether too many counselors feel it is impossible to evaluate counseling and have avoided planning any procedures to verify its worth (Shertzer & Stone, 1980). Counselors, through the use of audio and video tape recording, case studies, and opinion surveys, can gather the kinds of information needed to answer their questions and the questions rightfully raised by a community. Although such evaluation techniques have their limitations, this does not mean that they are of little value. On the contrary, they provide reasonable evidence, which can be used to improve counseling and to inform the public and professionals of the benefits of a counseling service (Tolbert, 1972; Pietrofesa, Hoffman, & Splete, 1984).

What are the purposes and objectives of evaluation? We view the following objectives as being appropriate for evaluating person-centered counseling:

1. To increase the growth of those being evaluated
2. To foster client progress
3. To help the counselor gain new insights into counseling

4. To improve the counseling process
5. To provide a basis for improving a total human services program
6. To clarify and validate hypotheses underlying counseling activities
7. To provide data upon which a sound program of public information and public relations can be built
8. To increase the psychological security of professional staff by having them appraise the results of their efforts
9. To provide evidence of the value of counseling
10. To facilitate smoother institutional and interinstitutional relationships
11. To persuade administrators of the value of counseling services so that additional services can be provided, when needed
12. To help programs gain acceptance
13. To determine the effectiveness of counseling as a process of assisting clients to achieve both social and personal goals
14. To help effect larger institutional contributions to social progress
15. To determine which approach to counseling will produce a desired result, under what conditions, and with which clients

Establishing Criteria

Measuring the outcomes of counseling is basically a question of measuring human behavior, for, if counseling has been successful, positive behavioral changes have taken place. But objectively measuring behavioral changes involves first selecting objective and salient evaluative criteria. What are the criteria we use to establish that a change in behavior has occurred through counseling?

We view the following as appropriate criteria for evaluating the effectiveness of person-centered counseling, as it pertains to client behavior:

1. Reduction in number of personal problems
2. Increase in the voluntary use of the counseling service
3. Reduction in number of norm-violating behaviors
4. Development of personal goals
5. Reduction in court appearances
6. Increase in participation in community activities
7. Improved integration between self and work
8. Increase in insight and self-understanding
9. Increase in self-acceptance and self-respect
10. Increase in self-sufficiency
11. Increase in acceptance of and respect for others
12. Assumption of responsibility
13. Improved behavior, generally
14. Reduction in personal stress and tension

The criteria for judging successful outcomes are related to our subjectivity regarding what we think is appropriate. Rogers (1951:1179-180) has given an illustration of the complexity involved in selecting objective evaluative criteria:

> While there is ample clinical evidence that behavior frequently changes during or after therapy, it is difficult to prove that this change resulted from therapy or to show that it represents improvement. Improvement, for one client, may mean a new willingness to differ with his wife, while for another it may mean fewer quarrels with his spouse. For one client improvement may be indicated by the fact that he now gets an A in courses where he formerly received C or D, but another client may show his improvement by a lessened compulsiveness, by taking a B or a C in courses where he formerly received nothing but A. One man may show that he has profited from therapy by a smoother and more adequate adjustment to his job, another by achieving the courage to leave his job for a new field. Clinically, each of these behaviors may seem to be clearly an indication of improved adjustment, but there is no doubt that such judgments are subjective and hence open to question.

The criterion problem is perhaps the single most vital issue affecting the process of evaluation (Shertzer & Stone, 1980). Generally speaking, the application of most criteria that have been identified in the literature of counseling research has not yielded data to validate that counseling is helpful. This is because criteria have not been derived from the individual client and the client's unique situation. Each client has different needs and goals, and what may be needed in evaluating the effectiveness of counseling is sufficiently subjective criteria that can also encompass the diversity and complexity of human behavior. The uniqueness of each individual and the distinctiveness of each counseling relationship suggest that the case study or individual longitudinal approach may represent the best approach for measuring the outcomes and values of counseling (Goldman, 1977; Smith, 1981). For example, Client A's growth may best be measured in terms of increased self-sufficiency; client B may be self-sufficient and this client's growth may best be measured in terms of an increase in insight, and so on. The application of three or four common criteria in evaluating the effectiveness of counseling with clients A, B, and C would most likely reveal minimal success. However, the utilization of particular and different criteria, defined in accordance with the singular growth needs of each client and the client's idiosyncratic concerns, would most likely indicate optimal success—assuming, of course, that counseling has been effective.

For example, one way to evaluate progress and growth in counseling would be to trace the shifts from the "me" to "I" modes of functioning as suggested by Zimring (1988). Zimring observes that the "me" is the recipient self which is passive in its lack of initiating and the "I" is the active and initiating self which is characterized by mastery and agency. Three contents are important for the shift from the "me" to the "I": values, feelings, and intentions. The shift from the "me" to the "I" frequently involves values and valuing with the "me" concerned with values determined by others and the "I" more involved with personal values.

Zimring (1988:169) has conceptualized comparative criteria for differentiating the "me" and "I" modes of functioning in Table 1. His work suggests observable documentable criteria which can be employed in a variety of ways to measure growth in counseling particularly in the attainment of mastery and decision making by the client.

Table 1. Comparison of the "Me" and "I" Modes of Functioning.

ME	*I*
1. Socially defined self	1. Personally defined self
2. Behavior guided by incorporated values	2. Goals set by own plans and standards
3. Morality defined by society's values.	3. Personal values and morality
4. Agenda for what has to be done is set by others	4. Agenda set by self
5. Enables problem solution according to social standards	5. New creative solutions
6. Repository of social knowledge and expectations	6. Contains self-knowledge
7. Provides social viewpoint in line with assimilated social values	7. Reacts creatively to 'me' attitudes and interactions
8. Passive recipient or reactive self	8. Proactive
9. Concerned with past and future	9. Experiencing the present
10. Focus on others	10. Focus on self
11. Lives in roles	11. Acts from present personal values

Complementing Zimring's concept of "me" and "I" modes of functioning is Hendricks's (1986) idea of levels of experiencing which offers a therapeutic criterion for determining growth and change. She describes three different levels of experiencing (1986:147-150):

Low experiencing level is characterized by:
1. Use of past tense
2. Reporting of external events
3. Events or emotions are described as flat and self-evident.

Middle experiencing level is characterized by:
1. Mainly a descriptive narrative of events
2. Personally felt meanings are referred to, but briefly, without initial elaboration.

High experiencing level is characterized by:
1. An inner exploration of personally felt meanings is the main focus.
2. Present tense is being used.
3. There are pauses as one waits to let words or images come from the felt sense.
4. One uses language metaphorically: "The feeling is like. . . ."
5. One uses language to point to the implicit: "it," "that," "some thing"–what is sensed but not yet known.

According to Hendricks high experiencing has an inherent positive change directionality. As a client discriminates and deals with levels of implicit experience there is internal directionality and movement which can be documented through tape recordings.

Evaluative Methods

Evaluative methods and approaches vary in degree of validity in determining the connection between personal growth and counseling. Following are some of the approaches and tools that can be utilized for purposes of evaluating counseling effectiveness:
1. The experimental approach which includes the "after only" design, the "before and after" design, and the "before and after with control group" design.
2. The tabulation approach–the number of clients, the number of counseling sessions, and the nature and kinds of problems discussed.
3. The follow-up approach.
4. The expert opinion, the "information please" method–a subjective evaluation by experts
5. The client opinion ("what-do-you-think?" method) characterized by opinionnaire surveys.
6. The external criteria, the "do-you-do-this?" method, in which the first step is to set up certain standards against which the program to be evaluated is compared.
7. The descriptive approach in which practices are analyzed and described.
8. The case-study approach characterized by a longitudinal in-depth view of each client.

Among the tools that have been discussed in the counseling journals are audio and videotape recordings, health records, sociometric devices, logs and diaries, standardized tests, checklists, rating scales, inventories, questionnaires, anecdotal records, stenographic reports, case studies, and tally sheets.

A variety of evaluative approaches and tools are at the disposal of the counselor. Some counselors may not be prepared to do an adequate job of evaluation with a number of the methods and instruments previously mentioned. Others, who do have the necessary background, may not have the time or the energy to use some of the methodologies described. It is suggested that three approaches can be reasonably used by the practicing counselor without taking an unreasonable amount of time and energy away from counseling and consultation and without demanding a high level of preparation in evaluation and measurement procedures.

Case Study Method

The case study method is a practical approach for measuring the outcomes of counseling. The case study method represents a many-sided approach to understanding and measuring the unique behavior of a particular person (Goldman, 1974; Smith, 1981). Qualitative data for the case study can be obtained through audio and videotape recordings of counseling sessions, observations of client behavior, and client self-reports.

Audio and video recordings provide the most appropriate and useful means for evaluating the quality of counseling. The foremost research concern of the professional counselor is the *quality*, not the quantity, of counseling relationships. From tapes, the counselor will harvest a richness of data yielded by no other psychometric source. Personal growth on the part of the client can be discerned by the contrast between the client's recorded behavior at the beginning of counseling and the client's recorded behavior in the terminal stage.

Of course, the case study method will require more than the use of tape recordings since behavioral outcomes require some kind of measurement following termination of the counseling relationship. It would also be helpful to have an independent observer appraise the data collected in order to objectively verify the effectiveness of counseling. The case study method provides versatility and flexibility, and a number of other methods and tools can be used to complement this approach.

Although the case study is a valuable method for determining the effectiveness of counseling, Goldman (1977:367) points out why it has not been used in recent years:

> The case study used to be regarded as a method of research but appears to have been little used for research purposes in recent years or even decades, perhaps because of the exclusive emphasis placed on quantified methods and group data. Now one sees case vignettes used, if at all, only to illustrate the kinds of changes that occurred during a study. But even that kind of use is rarely found; it is almost as if numbers are the only acceptable kind of research data, all else being "subjective" and therefore contaminating the purely scientific study of the phenomenon. How ironic, that a field whose invention and growth were in large measure intended to humanize institutions has set up criteria for research that value most highly the nonliving number.

Survey Method

Through the use of questionnaires, clients and others can evaluate the effectiveness of counseling. Although some specific outcomes could be measured with this approach, the survey method would seem to be more appropriate for evaluating the global outcomes of counseling. It represents a practical way to elicit the data needed to confirm or disconfirm an hypothesis. Isolating specific questions for consideration tends to objectify, intensify, and standardize the observations that respondents make. Questionnaires and other survey methods have been subject to severe criticism, but many of their common weaknesses can be avoided if this method is carefully structured and administered. Business, industry, and political parties make frequent use of the opinionnaire approach with a high degree of effectiveness using the results to make some very important decisions. Although it has its limitations, the survey method yields the kind of data in which community members are interested. It is a means of collecting reasonable information (Hackett, 1981).

Tabulation Method

The tabulation method provides a quantitative descriptive analysis of counseling and gives information from which inferences about the quality of counseling can be drawn. Professional counselors can keep track statistically of the counseling program's trends by maintaining daily tally sheets and statistics to determine quickly and easily the types of problems clients are bringing into counseling, and whether clients are becoming voluntarily involved or whether counseling is initiated from other sources. Additional statistics could include the number of individual and group counseling sessions, the number of consultations, the number of clients using the counseling service, and the mean number of counseling sessions per client (Boy & Pine, 1963).

Experimental Method

Controlled experimentation is one of the most scientific and rigorous procedures for evaluating a counseling program and measuring the outcomes of counseling (Pietrofesa, Hoffman, & Splete, 1984). In the experimental method, two or more groups of subjects are matched on all but one variable; one group is provided with a specific experience (the experimental group) and the other is not (the control group). Comparisons between the groups are made to determine whether any statistically significant differences occur after the experimental group has undergone the particular treatment.

Controlled experiments in counseling usually center on matching a group of counseled persons with a group of noncounseled persons, or matching a group of clients counseled by one approach, a group of clients counseled by another approach, and a third group of persons not counseled.

The problems of experimental design are randomization of sampling, equating groups, controlling relevant variables, and defining the nature of the treatment variable and operating within that definition. Such problems can be overcome, but they require sophistication and skills usually not possessed by the professional counselor. What is needed in organizations, institutions, and agencies in which counseling is practiced is a research person who is knowledgeable about the counseling process and who has the high-level skills, competencies, and know-how to conduct experimental studies. A person of this caliber could function primarily as a researcher and perhaps serve several human services groups. This person could design the experiments, analyze the data, and give an objective appraisal of the services. Until such a person is available, it is doubtful that counselors can employ the experimental method in a reasonable and realistic way in most work settings.

Even in the hands of an exceptionally skilled researcher, the experimental method of evaluating a counseling program still contains two major problems. First, the application of the experimental design requires that treatment and control conditions be held constant throughout the length of the experiment (Shertzer & Stone, 1980). This means that all clients must receive the same amount of the treatment to which they are assigned, so that clients receiving one type of treatment are not contaminated by the other (Pietrofesa, Hoffman, & Splete, 1984). If data about differences between treatments are to be meaningful, treatments cannot be modified while the experiment is in progress. In accepting the rigorous conditions of the experimental method, one is asked to fit the treatment to the design, rather than vice versa. Therefore, the use of the experimental method conflicts with the fundamental principle that evaluation should encourage the continual improvement and modification of a counseling program. Counselors cannot be expected to limit their counseling service to accommodate the constraints of a design just to guarantee internally valid data. As counselors learn about the strengths and weaknesses of their counseling, they may have to change and sometimes radically alter a counseling program in order to do justice to their clients.

A second major weakness of the experimental method is that it yields data about the effectiveness of two or more treatments after the fact. Therefore, it is useful as a judgmental device but has little value as a decision-making tool. After-the-fact data are not provided at appropriate times to enable the counselor to determine what a counseling service should be accomplishing or whether it should be altered in process. Often, by the time experimental data have come in, it is too late to make decisions about plans and procedures whose nature often determines the difference between the success or failure of a service to begin with.

Obstacles and Problems in Evaluation

Obstacles one might encounter when evaluating counseling programs fall into three problem areas: problems in connection with the selection of evaluation devices, problems in connection with the interpretation and use of data secured through the employment of evaluative devices and problems in connection with the organization and administration of the program. There are obstacles inherent in the counseling function that are indicative of lack of a research "breakthrough." These obstacles are:

1. The specific objectives of counseling are stated in generalities rather than in specific behavioral outcomes.
2. Counseling terminology requires strict adherence to precise definitions. These are lacking.
3. Many variables outside of counseling may influence the behavior believed to result from counseling.
4. There is confusion over process evaluation and product/outcome evaluation. Too often the latter is neglected.
5. Counselors enter into research hesitantly.

The problems of evaluation group themselves as follows:

1. Lack of a clear, acceptable statement of objectives in terms of observable client characteristics and behavior.
2. Failure to relate counseling objectives to institutional objectives.
3. The use of immediate and easily available criteria accompanied by failure to validate the immediate criteria against long-term goals.
4. The tendency to regard certain goals as equally desirable for all clients, thereby ignoring individual differences.
5. Confusion of means with ends or of process with outcomes.
6. Excessive use of subjective reactions.
7. Little or no attention to determining a satisfactory experimental design.

The person-centered counselor is confronted with the problem of clarifying and defining terminology so that certain meaningful hypotheses, ideas, and concepts can be scientifically tested and verified. More than thirty years ago Landsman (1966:570) stated that the following concepts "cry out for clarification" and this is still true today:

1. Being, becoming, non-being and nothingness, being-in-the-world, being there
2. Anguish, agony, anxiety, and angst

3. Loneliness and encounter
4. Despair and dread
5. Commitment
6. Being-able-to-be, being-allowed-to-be, having-to-be-in-this-world .

Landsman points out that "of all these terms," only one appears in Verplanck's *Glossary of Some Terms Used in the Objective Science of Behavior.* However, he does cite studies by Jourard (1963), Blazer (1963), Privette (1964), and Puttick (1964) as representing rigorous experiments which included operational definitions that met the standards of behavioral science.

The obstacles that have been presented are not insurmountable. The professional researcher who has the time and the facilities can produce well designed experimental studies and long-term longitudinal and developmental studies. Often such studies require a team of researchers, paraprofessionals, and computer facilities. The practicing counselor who is expected to render a counseling service daily and who does not have the facilities and time can still gather meaningful data to validate the efficacy of counseling. What prevents most counselors from accomplishing evaluation studies is the obstacle of internal attitudes toward research and evaluation (Wilson, 1985). Counselors have been so inundated with publications pleading for high-level research studies that they have developed the feeling that there is virtually little they can do to validly evaluate their counseling and its outcomes. As we pointed out earlier, this need not be the case.

If we regard evaluation as the process by which we determine the degree to which client and program objectives have been achieved, we can safely measure the attainment of these objectives through the use of statistics gathered in the local program, by studying recordings of counseling sessions, and by the skillful employment of questionnaires. Although the statistics gathered may not be elaborate or sophisticated and the qualitative data may be subjective, they will provide an adequate and fair measure of the substance and the effects of counseling.

C. H. Patterson (1962:570) has recommended the following time-honored procedures for evaluative studies:

1. Select and describe the objectives or outcomes that the program or service should achieve. Define client and program goals in terms of measurable outcomes.
2. Define the criteria that are acceptable as indicators of the achievement or lack of achievement of these objectives.
3. Select or devise instruments to measure the defined criteria.
4. Design the experiment in terms of the samples and their selection, the experimental or statistical controls, the administration or identification of the treatment or independent variable, and the application of the criterion measures.

5. Perform a statistical analysis of the data to determine the effectiveness of the treatments in terms of the outcome criteria .

Patterson's recommendations would seem to be more applicable to the experimental approach, but they also constitute general principles that can be modified by the practicing counselor who wishes to use the survey, case study, or tabulation methods of evaluation.

Conditions for Evaluation

The following appear to be the minimal and necessary person-centered conditions for the development of accountability and evaluation programs that will improve counseling skills and facilitate improved behavior for clients.

1. A plan of accountability and evaluation that is developed by counselors, supervisors, and clients working together, and has evolved from a free and open discussion of the philosophical, theoretical, and empirical considerations that influence their work.
2. A clearly stated philosophy and rationale for accountability and evaluation developed by counselors, supervisors, and clients.
3. An on-going process of accountability and evaluation characterized by continuous feedback and established monitoring points so that the counselor and appropriate supervisory personnel have specific time referents for gauging and discussing the progress of the counselor and the behavior of the counselor's clients.
4. A clear statement of performance standards and criteria that is understandable and acceptable to counselors, supervisors, and clients.
5. A plan of accountability and evaluation that accommodates judgments and observations from both the internal (counselor) and external (supervisor) frames of reference.
6. A plan of accountability and evaluation that includes an annual review of processes, performance criteria and standards, roles, and responsibilities.
7. A plan of accountability and evaluation that takes into consideration local conditions, needs, and resources.
8. Clearly defined but flexible methodological procedures for collecting data to test performance criteria used in evaluating and supervising counselors; for instance:
    (a) Counselor and supervisor analyze and critique audio and/or videotapes of the counselor's counseling skills.
    (b) Counselors and colleagues analyze and critique audio- and/or videotapes of each other's counseling.
    (c) Counselor conducts research into his or her effectiveness as a counselor and shares the results for critique with supervisor and colleagues.

(d) Periodically, the counselor prepares a self-evaluation and the supervisor writes an evaluation of the counselor. Together they share the results and discuss areas of agreement and disagreement.

Counselors statistically keep track of their work by maintaining daily tally sheets which enable them to know quickly and easily the types of problems, issues, and concerns that clients are bringing into counseling; whether these clients are volunteering for counseling or counseling is initiated from other sources; the number of consultations; and the number of different clients using the counseling service.

9. A plan of accountability and evaluation that can be defined and modified on the basis of periodic feedback from all who are affected.
10. An annual orientation by supervisory personnel and counselors to inform the public how counselors are evaluated and to share the results of program evaluation.
11. A plan of accountability and evaluation in which all participants share responsibility. For each goal the parties involved would decide not only what is to be accomplished but also what they are to be responsible for.
12. A plan of accountability and evaluation based on needs assessments, philosophical considerations, and goal formulations emanating from collaborative efforts.

A sensible plan of accountability and evaluation calls for the establishment of new relationships and the reshaping of traditional roles. Many more individuals will be involved. When the community and the counseling agency move into real partnerships, the issues of accountability and evaluation will not be viewed within a framework of superior/subordinate relationships. Shared responsibility is the key to successful and sensitive accountability and evaluation.

EVALUATING THE COUNSELOR

A counselor who is judged to be competent achieves this status as the result of how people who work with the counselor generally feel about him or her. This situation is not unusual in that the public generally tends to judge the physician and dentist in the same manner. No one outside the field of medicine really knows much about the medical skills of the physician; they tend to judge the physician's competency according to how *they feel* about the physician. If their feelings tend toward the positive, the physician is accepted as being competent. Even in a national presidential election, the typical voter casts a vote for one candidate instead of another out of a feeling that gravitates the vote toward a particular candidate. Very few people vote as a result of a logical and scientific evaluation of the candidates.

Competency Criteria

The professionalization of counseling requires the development of certain competency criteria whereby the counselor can be evaluated with a higher degree of sophistication than at present (Carr, 1977). In fact, the development of such criteria is still the missing link in the professionalization of counseling. More adequate state certification and licensing standards are beginning to emerge for the counselor; a code of ethics exists that serves as the standard for professional behavior; national concepts of the counselor's proper role have emerged; and national standards for the preparation of professional counselors have become more clarified. These accomplishments have been steps forward in the professionalization of counseling, but another task remains to be accomplished: the development of criteria whereby the on-the-job competency of the counselor can be determined.

There are some counselors who might object to the development of such criteria, preferring instead to exist in the current nebulous state in which the evaluation of their competency is essentially left to chance. Sometimes there is more safety in having no criteria, because then no one really knows what to expect. But, unless the profession of counseling begins to identify some criteria denoting counselor competency and to evaluate itself against such criteria, the full professionalization of counseling will never be achieved.

Who is to judge the competency of the counselor? Those who align themselves with the internal-frame-of-reference concept would argue that the counselor is the best source of information regarding competency. Those who align themselves with the external-frame-of-reference concept would argue that the counselor's competency, if it is to be known in any true sense, must be determined by sources external to the counselor since a self-evaluation may be distorted and self-serving. The logical solution is to evaluate the competency of the counselor from both the internal and external frames of reference. That is, the counselor must be a participant in determining professional competency, but at the same time, the counselor must allow evaluations by those colleagues who are in a position to adequately judge the counselor's competency. A counselor may possess a personal perception of competence that enables the counselor to function easily and well, but this perception may be limited because his or her frame of reference is only personal. When engaging in personal perceptions, the counselor is able to see much, but often this perception is obscured because he or she has no frame of reference external to the self. Therefore, counselors can learn much about how others view their competency by participating in a cooperative evaluative process whereby both the counselor's self and exterior-to-self concepts of competency are blended into a composite picture.

Who will evaluate the counselor's competency from an external frame of reference? It appears that the colleagues who would be in the best position to render such an external evaluation would be the director of the institution or organization that employs the counselor, provided that this person possesses a sufficient degree of professional sophistication about counseling to be adequately involved in such an evaluative process. Acquiring evaluations beyond such a director would be left entirely to the counselor. If the counselor felt that it might be profitable to also secure the evaluations of other supervisors and colleagues, these evaluations could be incorporated into a wider external-to-self picture.

The counselor's self-evaluation and external-to-self evaluations can then be synthesized in a meeting between the counselor and those who are performing the external-to-self evaluations. In an open and free discussion, the areas of strength and weakness could be identified, and both the counselor and external evaluators can become involved in firming up the strengths and identifying the weaknesses. In fact, the counselor could vastly improve a professional role if, when a weakness is identified, discussion could center upon whether this weakness is part of the personhood or competency of the counselor or is due to administrative patterns or procedures that obstruct the counselor's performance duties. For example, if the counselor is externally evaluated to have weak rapport with clients, is this condition due to the counselor's attitude or is it due to the fact that the counselor is so involved in administrative functions that clients see the counselor more as an authority figure than as a counselor? The pursuit of this question will shed much light upon the counselor's role and its effect upon an evaluation.

At first glance, defining the criteria for evaluating a counselor appears to be a difficult problem; but the lack of specific definitions for some criteria may lend itself to the initiation, at a local level, of meaningful discussions of what constitutes, for example, an effective counselor. Such discussion among administrators, staff members, and counselors will lead to the development of a common language and understanding regarding the complex dimensions of counseling. When such dialogues occur in local organizations, they would be the first step in the development of measurable and understandable criteria. When the problem of evaluating practicing counselors is tackled at the grass roots level and local criteria are developed, then, slowly but surely, through the collection, analysis, and synthesis of locally conceived evaluative instruments, usable competency criteria will emerge. Such criteria would be applicable in a variety of community and agency settings, and would mirror the commonalities of effective counseling regardless of different theoretical orientations.

Criteria are intended to reflect what members of the profession agree are common bases of practice among effective counselors. The criteria should be flexible enough to accommodate different theoretical positions. Thus, the behavior modification counselor or the person-centered counselor, for example, can be evaluated and can also engage in self-evaluation although they possess different theoretical and process models of counseling.

Counselor Involvement

The use of an evaluative instrument as part of the total evaluation process (with particular emphasis on counselor self-evaluation) may motivate counselors not only to examine their practice but also to look inwardly at themselves as persons. If counselors in a particular organization develop an evaluative instrument with their supervisor, and have an opportunity as individuals and as a group to modify and refine it so that there is general agreement regarding criteria, the counselors have a useful form of self-evaluation. For some, it would not be an especially easy task to look at themselves and at their practice according to external criteria agreed upon by the group. Many counselors have not been disposed to view themselves and what they are doing because they have operated in settings that have:

1. Developed arbitrary evaluative criteria and imposed these criteria on counselors without due regard or recognition of the counselor's involvement in evaluation, thus creating negative attitudes about any kind of evaluation.
2. Employed criteria used to evaluate other staff members as "suitable" criteria for evaluating counselors without recognizing and accommodating the essential differences between other staff functions and counseling, thus creating resistance to evaluation.
3. Utilized a haphazard and "willy-nilly" approach to evaluation, thus not inviting the confidence and the professional respect of counselors.
4. Established adequate criteria but have not implemented the evaluation process in a way consistent with the principles of democratic supervision.

Following is a sample instrument (Figure 1) for evaluating counselor competency. It represents a fundamental first step in developing an evaluative instrument that can be used locally, as well as nationally. The instrument can be easily quantified and the data derived from its use can furnish a picture of the counselor's on- the-job competency. Such a picture is necessary if counseling is to become more professionalized.

Evaluative instruments may have national implications as the counseling profession moves toward determining competency criteria and the degree to which counselors meet these criteria. When used in harmony with counselor involvement and the evaluative procedures suggested in this chapter, it has much potential for improving the counselor's competency in a variety of professional settings.

Figure 1. An Instrument for Evaluating the Counselor.

Circle one number for each item

Strong				*Weak*	*Personal Characteristics*
1	2	3	4	5	Is alert and enthusiastic
1	2	3	4	5	Is professionally ethical
1	2	3	4	5	Is professionally involved
1	2	3	4	5	Is self-motivated
1	2	3	4	5	Is emotionally balanced
1	2	3	4	5	Relates easily to others
1	2	3	4	5	Is genuine

Relations with Clients

1	2	3	4	5	Is sensitive to clients
1	2	3	4	5	Motivates clients to seek counseling
1	2	3	4	5	Has rapport with clients
1	2	3	4	5	Is a facilitating agent
1	2	3	4	5	Respects the dignity and worth of the individual
1	2	3	4	5	Has a facilitative image in the community
1	2	3	4	5	Has ability to handle a wide range of client problems

Relations with Referents

1	2	3	4	5	Is sensitive to referents
1	2	3	4	5	Is cooperative with referents
1	2	3	4	5	Attends to referrals
1	2	3	4	5	Is available to referents
1	2	3	4	5	Has a professional image among referents
1	2	3	4	5	Provides referents with an opportunity to be heard
1	2	3	4	5	Is conscientious in following through with referents

Relations with Staff

1	2	3	4	5	Is sensitive to the roles of other staff
1	2	3	4	5	Communicates easily with staff
1	2	3	4	5	Is a facilitating agent with staff
1	2	3	4	5	Is aware of the demands made on staff
1	2	3	4	5	Is receptive to staff
1	2	3	4	5	Has good rapport with staff
1	2	3	4	5	Attends to staff referrals

Relations with Administration

1	2	3	4	5	Is sensitive to the role of the administrator
1	2	3	4	5	Has a professional rationale for counseling
1	2	3	4	5	Meets with the administrator regarding program development
1	2	3	4	5	Communicates easily and effectively
1	2	3	4	5	Functions effectively as a resource consultant
1	2	3	4	5	Attends to administrative referrals
1	2	3	4	5	Functions in a well-organized manner

Professional Attitudes and Activities

1	2	3	4	5	Is sensitive to research findings
1	2	3	4	5	Contributes to the counseling profession
1	2	3	4	5	Periodically evaluates own counseling skills

Personal Characteristics

1	2	3	4	5	Is aware of both the art and science of counseling
1	2	3	4	5	If professionally enthusiastic
1	2	3	4	5	Has a professional balance between theory and practice
1	2	3	4	5	Is aware of the counselor's professional role

General Rating

1	2	3	4	5

Strong _____ Weak

(Check relative position on the line)

Emerging Trends in Counseling and Psychotherapy Research

The challenges and complexities of doing counseling research can appear to be daunting, but we hope this chapter provides a platform for a hopeful stance in addressing the questions of counseling theory and practice which always loom in our work. We are encouraged by the work of practitioners and theorists in counseling and view the contribution of McLeod (1994) as posting roadsigns for us in the journey to achieve a compassionate understanding of the counseling processs and its outcomes in improving the human condition. McLeod (1994:189-191) suggests six hopeful trends in counseling and psychotherapy research:

1. **Greater awareness of the relationship between research and practice.**
2. **Permission to be reflexive** with an increased awareness of the need to explore the meaning of research for both researcher and participant.
3. **Openness to new methods of inquiry** transcending the traditional mode of therapy research which overly relied on the use of quasi-experimental research designs.
4. **Research oriented to discovery rather than verification** emphazing more heuristic or discovery forms of research concerned about what is possible as opposed to what is known and believed.
5. **Appreciation of the power relationship between researcher and researched** generating questions about "who is research for?" and a deeper understanding of issues around empowerment and social responsibility in research.
6. **Displacement of the overly-psychological concept of the person** suggesting that counseling and psychotherapy should not be based on psychology but should encompass the contributions of philosophy, sociology, anthropology, theology, the arts, and literature to deepen our understanding of human behavior and consequently counseling theory and practice.

REFERENCES

Blazer, J. A. (1963). An experimental evaluation of transcendence of environment. *Journal of Humanistic Psychology, 3*, 49-53.

Boy, A. V., & Pine, G. J. (1963). *Client-centered counseling in the secondary school.* Boston: Houghton Mifflin.

Carr, R. (1977). The counselor or the counseling program as the target of evaluation? *The Personnel and Guidance Journal, 56*, 112-118.

Frey, D. H., Raming, H. E., & Frey, F. M. (1978). The qualitative description, interpretation, and evaluation of counseling. *The Personnel and Guidance Journal, 56*, 621-625.

Goldman, L. (1977). Toward more meaningful research. *The Personnel and Guidance Journal, 55*, 363-368.

Hadley, R. G., & Mitchell, L. K. (1995). *Counseling research and program evaluation.* Pacific Grove, CA: Brooks/Cole.

Hackett, G. (1981). Survey research methods. *The Personnel and Guidance Journal, 59*, 599-604.

Hendricks, M. H. (1986). Experiencing level as a therapeutic variable. *Person-Centered Review, 1*, 2, 141-162.

Hoshmand. L. T., & Polingkhorne, D. E. (1992). Redefining the science-practice relationship and professional training. *American Psychologist, 47*, 55-66.

Jourard, S. (1963). *The transparent self.* Princeton, NJ: Van Nostrand.

Landsman, T. (1966). Existentialism in counseling: The scientific view. *The Personnel and Guidance Journal, 43*.

Lewis, E. C. (1970). *The psychology of counseling.* New York: Holt, Rinehart, and Winston, 202.

McLeod, J. (1994). *Doing counseling research.* London: Sage.

Oetting, E. R. (1979). The counseling psychologist as program evaluator. *The Counseling Psychologist, 7,* 89-91.

Ohlsen, M. M. (1983). Evaluation of the counselor's services. In M. M. Ohlsen (Ed.). *Introduction to counseling.* Itasca, IL: F. E. Peacock, 357-371.

Patterson, C. H. (1962). *Counseling and guidance in schools.* New York: Harper.

Pietrofesa, J. J., Hoffman, A., & Splete, H. H. (1984). *Counseling: An introduction* (2nd ed.). Boston: Houghton Mifflin.

Privette, G. (1964). *Factors associated with functioning which transcend modal behavior.* Unpublished doctoral dissertation, University of Florida.

Puttick, W. H. (1964). *A factor analytic study of positive modes of experiencing and behaving in a teacher college population.* Unpublished doctoral dissertation. University of Florida.

Rogers, C. R. (1951–renewed 1979). *Client-centered therapy.* Boston: Houghton Mifflin.

Shertzer, B., & Stone, S. C. (1980). *Fundamentals of counseling* (3rd ed.). Boston: Houghton Mifflin, 414- 441.

Smith, M. L. (1981). Naturalistic research. *The Personnel and Guidance Journal. 5,* 9, 585-589.

Tolbert, E. L. (1972). *Introduction to counseling* (2nd ed.). New York: McGraw-Hill, 364.

Wilson, N. S. (1985). School counselors and research: Obstacles and opportunities. *The School Counselor, 33,* 111- 119.

Zimring, F. M. (1988) Attaining mastery: The shift from the "me" to the "*I.*" *Person-Centered Review, 3,* 2, 165-175.

Chapter 11

PERSON-CENTERED COUNSELOR EDUCATION

Although ideas exist regarding the process of preparing a person to become a counselor, there has been little evidence that these ideas have been translated into a theory of counselor preparation. This is essentially because ideas do not often lend themselves to being converted into the strict requirements of a theory. A theory must be more than an idea or hunch regarding the best way to do something. Patterson (1992:225), in speaking about the supervision of counselor education students, underlines the importance of theory in counselor education when he says:

> The supervisor should work from an explicit theoretical base, both in the supervision process and in the process of therapy. Theory provides congruence for the student in both processes. It also provides structure for the student's expectations of supervision and therapy. There should be a knowledge base that precedes supervision, so that teaching theory is not the major time focus in supervision.

We would argue that a theory must be more than a gratuitous assertion or cybernetically-based flow chart. Theory must be lived throughout a counselor education program, particularly a person-centered counselor education program (Boy & Pine, 1984).

Blocher and Wolleat (1972:39-40) recognize the absence of theories of counselor education when they state:

> There have been few attempts to formulate theories of counselor education or to develop models for counseling training which could systematically guide content, methods, or evaluation.
>
> . . . A theory of counseling provides direction for the counselor in his interaction with clients, whereas a counselor education theory guides the interaction of a counselor educator with his students.

Few attempts have been made to develop a theory of counselor education because the criteria, which outline the requirements that must be met in order to have a theory, are difficult standards.

There are criteria, however, that must be met if one desires to judge whether an idea meets the requirements of being a theory. These criteria of a theory have been identified by Stefflre and Grant (1972) and have been used primarily to judge whether a theory of counseling meets certain standards. The essence and intentionality of these criteria can be applied to judging a theory of counselor education and can be converted as follows: (1) assumptions regarding the nature of the person, (2) beliefs regarding learning theory and changes in behavior, (3) a commitment to certain goals of education, (4) a definition of the role of the educator, and (5) research evidence supporting the theory. These criteria of a theory have also been generally identified and supported in the writings of Dimick and Huff (1970), Patterson (1973), and Hansen, Stevic, and Warner (1986).

In the following restatements of the Stefflre and Grant (1972) criteria of a theory, and the accompanying references indicating the evidence that supports the fact that each criteria has been met, person-centered teaching emerges as a bona fide theory of instruction that can be applied to counselor education:

1. Assumptions regarding the nature of the person (Coulson & Rogers, 1968; Rogers, 1951: 481-533; 1969: 221-297).
2. Beliefs regarding learning theory and changes in behavior (Pine & Boy, 1977,: 75-139; Rogers, 1951:482-533).
3. A commitment to certain goals of learning (Boy & Pine, 1971, 107-118; Rogers, 1951, 399-414; 1969, 103-145, 157-166, 279-297).
4. A definition of the role of the educator (Lyon, 1971, 183-230; Pine & Boy, 1977, 3-33; Rogers, 1951, 399-414; 1969, 29-97; 1970, 468-483).
5. Research evidence supporting the theory (Blocksma & Porter, 1947; Faw, 1949; Gross, 1948; Lyon, 1971, 263-289; 1977; Rogers, 1969, 327-342; Schwebal & Asch, 1948).

A PERSON-CENTERED VIEW

Mearns (1997: Introduction x) asserts that person-centered counseling requires more preparation and a greater intensity of preparation than other mainstream counseling approaches because of the daunting challenge of personal development which is required in the education of a person-centered counselor. And, along similar lines, Natiello (1987:203) observes that living out a person-centered theory presents challenges for person-centered counselor education:

In my interactions with helping professionals who call themselves "Rogerian" and in my experience in a training program for helping professionals, I have become quite aware that the theory of the person-centered approach is grasped quite readily. but the translation of theory into practice tends to be problematic, diverse, or oversimplified.

However, in confronting the challenge set forth by Mearns and Natiello, we believe that the the cohesiveness of the person-centered viewpoint gives it a decided advantage. It can be applied as person-centered teaching and supervision in counselor education and it can be applied by enrollees and graduates of a counselor education program as person-centered counseling. When it is applied in the educational, counseling, and supervisory processes, it takes on the characteristics of being comprehensive and empathic, resonating to where the counselor education student is at in terms of his or her needs. Person-centered theory resists the encapsulation inherent in the *au courant* emphasis on developmental psychology and stages in the supervision of counselors-in-training (Bernard, 1992; Davenport, 1992). Patterson, in responding to a question put forth by Freeman (1992:223), "Have you perceived that counselors go through a developmental sequence and that you have to adapt supervision to different levels in different ways?" makes the case for a person-centered approach in counseling supervision:

> Students start at different levels, and, ideally, they end up at a proficiency level. I never think where is this student "at" in the process, in terms of stages. It just is alien to my method of supervision and thinking. I provide the supervisory relationship. That same relationship facilitates the work of the individual supervisee without addressing level. I am responding to that supervisee at that moment. There is no need for the supervisor to think about adjusting his or her response according to levels. The process is a continuous one, with the student becoming more proficient over time.

Person-centered theory is essentially a counseling theory but early adherents saw it as being logically convertible and applicable to the process of education *and* supervision. Soon after the appearance of Rogers' first major contribution, *Counseling and Psychotherapy* (1942), there emerged an awareness that the viewpoint was also applicable to teaching (Blocksma & Porter, 1947; Faw, 1949; Gross, 1948; Schwebel & Asch, 1948). Rogers (1951) confirmed this interest in his book, *Client-Centered Therapy*, by devoting Chapter 9 to "Student-Centered Teaching." This applicability to teaching was further extended and confirmed by Rogers (1969) in his book, *Freedom to Learn*, and is evident in more recent contributions (Rogers, 1977, 1980, 1983). The convertibility and applicability of the person-centered counseling view has also, of course, been recognized in organizational behavior, families, parenting, groups, marriage and its alternatives, leadership, pastoring, and general interpersonal relationships. Rogers (1951:384) has traditionally recognized the applicability of the concepts of person-centered counseling to the teaching and learning process: "If the creation of an atmosphere of acceptance, understanding, and respect is the most effective basis for facilitating the learning which is called therapy, then might it not be the basis for the learning which is called education?".

What will be the behavior of the counselor educator who has internalized the attitudes of person-centered teaching? Rogers (1951:427) has described that behavior as follows:

> He creates a classroom climate which respects the integrity of the student, which accepts all aims, opinions, and attitudes as being legitimate expressions of the student's internal frame of reference at that time. He accepts the feelings and emotionalized attitudes which surround any educational or group experience. He accepts himself as being a member of a learning group, rather than an authority. He makes learning resources available, confident that if they meet the needs of the group they will be used. He relies upon the capacity of the individual to sort out truth from untruth, upon the basis of continuing experience. He recognizes that his course, if successful, is a beginning in learning, not the end of learning. He relies upon the capacity of the student to assess his progress in terms of the purposes which he has at this time. He has confidence in the fact that, in this atmosphere which he has helped to create, a type of learning takes place which is personally meaningful and which feeds the total self-development of the individual as well as improves his acquaintance with a given field of knowledge.

Rogers (1951:389-391) identified certain characteristics of person-centered teaching as principles and hypotheses:
1. We cannot teach another person directly; we can only facilitate his learning.
2. A person learns significantly only those things which he perceives as being involved in the maintenance of, or enhancement of, the structure of self.
3. Experience which, if assimilated, would involve a change in the organization of self tends to be resisted through denial or distortion of symbolization.
4. The structure and organization of self appears to become more rigid under threat; to relax its boundaries when completely free from threat. Experience which is perceived as inconsistent with the self can only be assimilated if the current organization of self is relaxed and expanded to include it.

5. The educational situation which most effectively promotes significant learning is one in which threat to the self of the learner is reduced to a minimum and differential perception of the field of experience is facilitated.

Counselor education is a process in which the student counselor exists in an atmosphere where authenticity can emerge (Rogers, 1962:420). The creation of such an atmosphere is directly in the hands of the counselor educator, who must be free of the facades generally characteristic of the endeavor we call education:

> We would also endeavor to plan the educational program for these individuals so that they would come increasingly to experience empathy and liking others, and that they would find it increasingly easier to be themselves, to be real. By feeling understood and accepted in their training experience, by being in contact with genuineness and absence of facade in their instructors, they would grow into more and more competent counselors.

For the counselor educator who feels that the concept of person-centered teaching has merit theoretically but is not operative because of the limitations imposed by a particular institution, Rogers (1951:395) offers the following: ". . . every group has some limitations, if only the fact that they meet for a limited rather than an unlimited number of hours per week. It is not the fact that there are limitations, but the attitude, the permissiveness, the freedom which exists within those limitations, which is important".

In an attempt to identify what happened to the student as a result of the student's experience with person-centered teaching, Gordon (1955:100) reviewed 11 historic studies and found that:

> Students seem to learn as much or more factual information; they participate more; they enjoy the experience; and they acquire certain other important learnings, such as clinical insight, greater personal adjustment, socially integrative behavior, skills of working cooperatively with others, and the freedom to communicate their deeper feelings and attitudes.

Gordon (1955:154) also identified certain attitudes which, when housed in a teacher, will inhibit a learning group's thrust toward self-generated and personally relevant knowledge: ". . . our own insecurities, our lack of faith in people, our tendencies to use others for our own ends, our need for prestige and status, our lack of tolerance of ambiguity, our fear of hostility expressed toward us, and the inconsistencies that often appear in our systems of values.

In describing the interpersonal relationship that facilitates learning, Rogers (1970:81) states that it is characterized by realness, prizing, acceptance, trust, and empathic understanding. These characteristics are identical to those Rogers has described as being characteristic of effective counseling and psychotherapy. The person-centered message, for both counseling and teaching, is basically the same. A counselor or teacher who possesses these characteristics will create a counseling or learning environment that facilitates the development of the client or student. Once again, the counselor or teacher must model these human and facilitative qualities in order for them to emerge in a client or student.

> There is a widespread belief that teaching and counseling are vastly different functions, probably brought about by unhappy personal experiences and the comparison of good counseling with bad teaching. I find the best of modern teaching is remarkably like good counseling and the best of modern teaching is very like good person-centered teaching and surely, a counselor training program, which hopes to produce effective counselors, ought itself be a model of the philosophy and practices it preaches.

In commenting upon empathic understanding, Rogers (1975:7) states that: "An empathic way of being can be learned from empathic persons".

Rogers (1977: 7-22) sees the educational process as occurring along a continuum. One end of the continuum represents a teacher-centered approach to teaching while the other represents a person-centered approach.

Following is a summary of what Rogers considers to be characteristic of a teacher-centered approach to teaching:

1. The teacher is the possessor of knowledge, the student the expected recipient.
2. The lecture, or some means of verbal instruction, is the major means of getting knowledge to the recipient. The examination measures the extent to which the student has received it.
3. The teacher is the possessor of power, the student is the one who obeys.
4. Rule by authority is the accepted policy.
5. Trust is at a minimum.
6. The students are best governed by being kept in an intermittent or constant state of fear.
7. Democracy and its values are ignored and scorned in practice.
8. There is no place for the whole person in the educational system, only for his or her intellect.

Following is a summary of what Rogers considers to be characteristic of a person-centered approach to teaching:

1. The facilitative teacher shares with students the responsibility for the learning process.
2. The student develops his or her own program of learning, alone or in cooperation with others.

3. A facilitative learning climate is provided.

4. The focus is primarily on fostering the continuing process of learning.

5. The discipline necessary to reach the student's goal is a self-discipline.

6. The evaluation of the extent and significance of the student's learning is made primarily by the student.

7. In this growth-promoting climate, the learning tends to be deeper, proceeds at a more rapid rate, and is more pervasive in the life and behavior of the student than traditional learning.

We (Pine & Boy 1977:115-121) have identified certain principles of learning that undergird the process of person-centered teaching. These principles are summarized as follows:

1. Learning is the process of changing behaviors in positive directions.

2. Learning is an experience that occurs inside the learner and is activated by the learner.

3. Learning is the discovery of the personal meaning and relevance of ideas.

4. Learning is a consequence of experience.

5. Learning is a cooperative and collaborative process.

6. Learning is an evolutionary process.

7. Learning is sometimes a painful process.

8. One of the richest sources for learning is the learner himself or herself.

9. The process of learning is affective as well as cognitive.

10. Learning is enjoyable.

11. Learning is an experience that expresses values.

12. The learner is a free and responsible agent.

13. The process of problem solving and learning are highly unique and individual.

14. Teaching is learning.

In commenting on the last of the preceding principles, Arbuckle (1975:170) states that: ". . . the goal of the program will be student and staff learning rather than staff teaching".

Arbuckle reinforces the idea that both students and staff are involved in the learning process in a person-centered counselor education program. In more traditional programs, the emphasis is strictly on staff teaching and student learning; a decidedly superior-subordinate approach that is directly opposite the process that characterizes person-centered teaching.

We (Pine & Boy 1977: 122-127) also have identified conditions that facilitate learning in the process of person-centered teaching. These conditions indicate that learning is facilitated in an atmosphere:

1. Which encourages students to be active.

2. That facilitates the student's discovery of the personal meaning of ideas.

3. That emphasizes the uniquely personal and subjective nature of learning.

4. In which difference is good and desirable.
5. That constantly recognizes the right to make mistakes.
6. That tolerates ambiguity.
7. In which evaluation is a cooperative process with emphasis on self-evaluation.
8. Which encourages openness to self rather than a concealment of self.
9. In which students are encouraged to trust in themselves as well as external sources.
10. In which students feel they are respected.
11. In which students feel they are accepted.
12. Which permits confrontation.
13. In which the teacher creates conditions by which the teaching function is lost.

Following is what Rogers (1969: 109-202) considered a rationale that should undergird a graduate program in counseling. Rogers sees this rationale as applicable to any program of graduate education, not just in the field of counseling.

1. The student has the potentiality and desire to learn.
2. The program is rooted in reality.
3. The program provides opportunities for meaningful learning.
4. The program provides a psychological climate suitable for self-directed and significant learning.
5. The teacher encounters the student as a person and reacts himself or herself as a person.
6. The program relies on the student's self-criticism and self-evaluation.
7. The program develops the whole person, ". . . not simply someone who is informed from the neck up but someone who exists in a significant relationship to others and to himself".
8. The program permits the person to become a fully professional person— a scientist, a practitioner, a facilitator of learning, ". . . not at some future date, after he has received his degree, but during every day and year of his graduate work" .

Rogers (1969:192) suggests three criteria for admission into a graduate program in counseling: intelligence, empathic ability, and a degree of spontaneous curiosity and originality. Regarding the first criterion, intelligence, Rogers defines it as a: ". . . high degree of ability in problem solving. My reason for this criterion is simply that, in general, intelligence 'pays off.' Of two professional individuals completely equal in every other respect, the brighter one of the two is probably more likely to make a lasting contribution".

Felker (1973:147) noted the same thing when he said: ". . . intellectual ability, and counseling effectiveness are not antithetical".

White (1978) conducted a study among 596 counselor educators in which their theoretical orientations to counseling were identified. In rank order, the four counseling theories that had the most adherents were eclectic, person-centered, humanistic, and behavioral. White, however, provides no information indicating that those counselor educators who are oriented toward person- centered counseling translate that orientation into person-centered teaching. We observe that if a counselor educator is oriented toward person-centered counseling, then such an orientation would naturally find its expression through person-centered teaching, if the orientation is intellectually and affectively real.

In one sense, all counselor educators are person-centered because they all appear to focus upon student counselors and their needs. What is distinctive about person-centered teaching is that the *process*, as well as the objective, is person-centered. Being person-centered is an *attitude* rather than a technique.

Coombs (1988) expresses concern that preoccupation with methods and behavior has extended into counselor education programs. Most programs assume that persons become counselors by learning about counseling and practicing its methods and generally emphasize content *and learning how to counsel.* For Coombs the task of *counselor* education must *be* seen as a problem in personal becoming rather than the traditional "how to" concept. He believes that the implementation of the concept of personal counseling suggests counselor education programs need to shift from an emphasis on methods and techniques to focusing on the counselor belief systems that determine them.

In writing about the development of counseling skills, Mearns (1997:116) suggests that skills are developed from the "inside out" rather than from the "outside in": "The 'inside out' conception of skill development is a central and distinguishing feature of the person centered approach. "

According to this viewpoint, then, the primary purpose of the counselor education program is to help the student to "dissassemble the various blocks to his congruent relating" and to help the student release the sensitivity, prior knowledge, and experience which the student has gathered through a lifetime of interactions with others. Through such a process students can learn how to (Mearns, 1997: 116-117).

1. Release empathic sensitivity.
2. Respond in a range of ways to assist the client's focusing.
3. Release a widening portfolio of ways of communicating warmth.
4. Release congruent responsiveness.
5. Comunicate clearly and openly.
6. Express confusion where it exists.
7. Challenge the client in ways that encourage the client's congruent response.
8. Maintain empathy across a range of difficult clients.
9. Experience a consistent congruent nonjudgmental attitude across a range of clients.

10. Establish psychological contact with different parts of the client's self.
11. Enter the client's world with willingness, confidence, and non-invasive respect.
12. Achieve stillness to meet the client.

We have not included all the skill areas which Mearns (1997) has identified in his "Inside-Outside Skills Curriculum", but it is clear from the preceeding skill areas that preparing to become a person-centered counselor is a challeging, complex, and sophisticated process. As important as the acquisition of counseling skills is, the inside-outside perspective reminds us that the most critical and practical thing we can learn in counseling is insight as to what is happening as we do it. In counselor and therapist education it is often said, "Technique is what you use until the therapist arrives" (Palmer, 1998:5).

In comparing counselor education to other professional preparation programs, Coombs (1986:74) identifies another dimension of challenge and complexity:

> The medical profession does not speak of its training programs as "Learning to Doctor," nor does the legal profession refer to its programs as "Learning to Law." Instead, they speak of becoming physicians or lawyers. Just so, the education of counselors must be seen not as learning to counsel but as an intensely personal process of becoming a counselor. This represents a basic shift in thinking from a behavioristic philosophy emphasizing teaching, controlling, directing, and "making" counselors to a position focusing upon personal growth and student discovery of personal meaning. The implications of that concept require changes in thinking and practice for many aspects of professional education programs.

One implication for counselor education programs is that students must be expected to take major responsibility for their own learning. In several programs Coombs and his colleagues sought to accomplish this goal in a number of ways (1986:77).
   (a) Faculty consensus that student commitment and involvement were basic policy with high priority for action.
   (b) Involvement of students in all faculty committees and meetings with full rights of participation and voting. This was usually accomplished by election of student representatives responsible for attending meetings, representing their constituents, and reporting back to the student body.
   (c) Active search by faculty and staff for barriers to communication followed by appropriate steps for their elimination or resolution. Students can and will add much to the functioning and quality of pro-

grams, if they honestly feel they have vital roles in the determination of their own destiny.

(d) Encouragement of faculty-student interaction socially as well as professionally.

(e) Continuous involvement of students in planning the next steps for their own growth.

Such processes engage students in all aspects of the preparation program, engender continuous relationships between faculty and students and among students with each other, and models a person-centered way of being throughout the program.

The Effects of Person-Centered Teaching

Counselor educators who create a meaningful teaching-learning relationship will find that intellectual and affective growth occurs among students as a result of their positive reactions to the communicating atmosphere in which they exist (Pine & Boy, 1977, pp. 14-16). As a result of their involvement with a skilled, competent, and psychologically whole counselor educator:

1. ***Students assume responsibility.*** Students become involved in the pursuit of knowledge and assume the responsibility for their intellectual growth because of the teacher's attitude in the relationship. Since the teacher has freed them to learn, they learn.

2. ***Students are accepted.*** Students feel that they are respected as persons who have a worthy contribution for both today and tomorrow. The positiveness of the teacher's attitude enables students to feel an acceptance that encourages them to relate comfortably to the teacher. It is this attitude that enables students to sense a comfort in the relationship, which facilitates their development.

3. ***Students are motivated.*** As a result of their experience with a teacher's enthusiasm for knowledge, students develop a desire to delve into the elements of knowledge. They sense a value in knowledge and acquire a desire to learn those things that are pertinent.

4. ***Students are actively involved in the process of growth.*** Intellectual maturity occurs for students because the teacher's educational process is focused upon students and their needs. In such a relationship the teacher is not the dominant figure, since the educational process is designed to produce an active, participatory involvement on the part of the student.

5. ***Students interact on a human level.*** Because of their association with a communicating teacher, students do not assume a superficial role but react to learning at an affective level. Anyone who has deeply learned

anything has learned it because there was an accompanying emotionality in the process. What was being learned was deeply significant; the learner felt its importance in a visceral manner.

6. ***Students exist in a safe atmosphere.*** Students must feel free from threat or coercion if they are to be secure enough to respond to the learning process. No one has ever been coerced into learning or changing behavior. Such changes have occurred because one has felt safe enough to inquire into knowledge or into oneself. When the teacher provides an emotionally safe atmosphere, students are able to find progressive significance in the association.

7. ***Students are understood.*** The psychologically integrated teacher is vitally concerned with the learners' frame of reference. The teacher's awareness of students finds its expression in an understanding attitude that enables students to be hesitant or confident, aware or insensitive, courageous or fearful. An understanding of how students feel about the various dimensions of existence is part of the attitude of an effective teacher. When students feel understood, they are able to move in an unfaltering manner in the learning process.

8. ***Students are self-disciplined.*** They find the resources within themselves to be their own masters because they have existed in learning relationships that facilitated their awareness of the importance of managing themselves. Teachers bring this into awareness by providing an atmosphere in which students learn to rely upon themselves for control rather than upon an external source. Teachers furnish students with the opportunity of self-management by providing an atmosphere in which students engage themselves in the more difficult task of looking to themselves rather than to authority figures for answers.

9. ***Students communicate with ease.*** When students associate with an effective teacher, they are able to communicate comfortably and honestly. They feel no need to be defensive in a relationship in which they know that they can be themselves. Such comfort enables them to respond to learning with much more accuracy, since their verbalizations and questions are not couched in language designed to protect rather than to reveal. They are able to discuss issues of relevance rather than what they feel the teacher wants to hear.

10. ***Students achieve insight.*** As a result of their association with a psychologically whole teacher, students are able to discover the fundamentals of learning or of themselves. They are able to bring meaning into their experiences because the relationship provided them with an opportunity to weigh and sift, and eventually come to grips with the deeper components of learning or of the self. They are involved in a communicative process that gradually enables them to shed more light upon things to be learned and assimilated. Such an opening of one's

self to experiences occurs because the teacher provides an atmosphere in which students' insights are far more relevant and significant than if the students were merely provided with the teacher's concept of appropriate insight.

11. ***Students are aware of facilitative attitudes.*** Because of the qualitative nature of their association with a teacher, students do not have to be told directly what attitudes are facilitative and nonfacilitative. As human beings, they are aware of which attitudes help or hinder their functioning as persons. They become sensitive to self-facilitating attitudes because they have had an opportunity to ponder those attitudes that either enhance them or cause them turmoil. They are not only more aware of self-facilitating attitudes, but they see themselves in relationship to others and shape these attitudes so that they are able to function effectively in human relationships. They look beyond themselves rather than enclosing themselves. The feelings of others in response to their attitudes are more openly sensed and internalized.

12. ***Students are valuing.*** Students become involved in the development, processing, and synthesizing of values, ordering them in a hierarchy that is beneficial to their functioning and to others. Because of their association with a psychologically whole teacher, they reject the values that hamper their development and move toward those that enable them to find more meaning from learning and life. This sifting and processing of values occurs because students exist in an open relationship in which they confront these values and are, in turn, confronted by them. It is only when students reject certain nonsustaining values that they move toward deeper personal values. Effective teaching enables each student to become involved in the processing of values.

13. ***Students respond to genuineness.*** They sense the genuine quality of the teacher and react by becoming more genuine themselves. Students can easily sense a lack of genuineness. If the teacher has an unconditional, positive regard for students, this attitude finds its expression in a genuineness that the student internalizes. When students respond to the genuine quality of the teacher, they involve themselves in learning as a reaction to that quality. They trust the relationship and find that they are able to accelerate their progress. Such genuineness must exist if students are to have inner feelings of assurance in the relationship.

Student counselors respond primarily to the teacher as a person, and optimal intellectual learning and personal development occur through the relationship of the student with psychologically mature counselor educators.

The challenge for counselor educators is twofold: to seek and create the opportunities that will stretch and expand themselves as persons;

and to create conditions whereby students also can grow and become more fully functioning persons and effective counselors. The latter task will be accomplished more easily and effectively as the counselor educator moves toward becoming a psychologically mature person.

A Generic Perspective

A generic perspective of counselor education is based upon the view that there are global philosophic and psychological concepts which can be applied to a full range of different clients. What makes persons the same is their humanness; and because of this shared humanness, a counseling process which is sensitive to that humanness is generic in character, can be learned by student counselors, can serve as the conceptual foundation for the counselor education program, and can be applied.

In their humanness, clients are substantively and primarily alike (Rogers, 1980). They differ only in their incidental or secondary characteristics (age, gender, intelligence, socioeconomic status, ethnic group, race, or problem) (Vontress, 1979). They all have human responses to interpersonal relationships which enhance or diminish them as persons. When they are diminished, their psychological stability is negatively affected regardless of the configuration of their incidental or secondary characteristics (Patterson, 1986).

As Vontress (1979:121) notes: "Counseling organizations and associations should devote time and resources to helping counselors understand and accept the fact that all humans are basically alike".

The human response to being physically abused is the same regardless of whether the abused person is a child or octogenarian. Since the human response is the same for both, the counseling process used to help both persons is substantively the same. It may differ only in its incidental or secondary elements (the words used by the counselor may differ with each); since the counseling process is basically the same, a generic counselor education program can focus on that process and its applicability to different client populations (Arbuckle, 1975).

In a generic concept of counselor preparation, a basic and necessary viewpoint is that a counselor's work setting determines whether the counselor is called a school counselor or a mental health counselor, *not the counseling process itself; the counseling process is basically the same whether it is applied in a school or mental health center.* This, of course, assumes that the school counselor engages in therapeutic counseling rather than functioning as a guidance counselor (one who helps students select courses, gain admission to college, and identify a post high school job). When a generic counselor education program identifies the counselor's role as therapeutic, it makes no distinction among the settings in which that role can be applied. When a counselor education program defines the school counselor's role as strictly cognitive (guidance) and the mental health counselor's role as strictly affective (therapeutic), there is justification for having separate programs of counselor education.

Caulfield and Perosa (1983:179-180), in a project recommending the development of counselor education programs which are generic, based their viewpoint on the following:

1. School and community mental health counselors are more alike than different and share many skills necessary for the competent delivery of services.
2. Counseling skills are generalizable across a variety of settings, including schools, community agencies, industry, and the health professions (Southern & Hannaford, 1981).
3. Schools are community agencies that utilize both psychological principles and educational concepts. Likewise, community agencies make use of educational skills along with psychological techniques. Both school and agency counselors must use the same basic knowledge of human behavior. These basic theories are not situational and do not change dependent on the agency in which one works. Experience in both settings will enrich rather than weaken the preparation of counselors.
4. Counselors in both settings need to develop cooperative methodologies and open lines of communication to facilitate the growth of clients needing services in both environments.
5. Counselors prepared to function in both settings will have enhanced employment potential and will be prepared to give maximum services to the community and public.

Caulfield and Perosa (1983:184) reached the following conclusion:

Because graduates of counseling programs face a constantly changing job market, counselor educators must systematically revise existing curricula to meet employment realities. At the same time, program integrity and quality need to be ensured. While the traditional routes emphasize the differences between agency and school counseling, the innovative approach tends to stress their similarities. It is hoped that counselor educators now will have a wider set of options to debate and evaluate as they engage in future program redesign.

CONCLUSION

Counselor education's challenge is to develop programs which serve the counseling needs of clients. As programs develop, however, the counseling needs of clients can sometimes be pushed into the background. Programs instead begin to respond to special interest groups, funding agencies, or accrediting organizations. When the responses become self-serving, then the legitimate needs of both clients and counselor education programs can become lost in a sea of pervasive influences. Being person-centered means being person-centered all of the time. A person- centered counselor education program cannot avoid this commitment and responsibility. Like person-centered counseling, person-centered counselor education must often endure misconceptions, but it is always worth the effort. It provides the opportunity for students to experience person-centered values and, in turn, to pass these values on to clients. As our world changes, these values are enduring.

REFERENCES

Arbuckle, D. S. (1975). An existential-humanistic program of counselor education. *Counselor Education and Supervision, 14,* 168-174.

Bernard, J. M. (1992). The challenge of psychotherapy based supervision: Making the pieces fit. *Counselor Education and Supervision, 31,* 232-237.

Blocher, D. H., & Wolleat, P. L. (1972). Some reactions to Zifferblatt and a report of a practical attempt at the development and evaluation of a counselor education model. *The Counseling Psychologist, 3,* 35-55.

Blocksma, D. D., & Porter, E. H., Jr. (1947). A short-term training program in client-centered counseling. *Journal of Consulting Psychology, 11,* 55-60.

Boy, A. V., & Pine, G. J. (1971). *Expanding the self: Personal growth for teachers.* Dubuque, IA: Wm. C. Brown, 107-118.

Boy, A. V., & Pine, G J. (1984). Student-centered counselor education. California *Association for Counseling and Development Journal, 5,* 21-27.

Caulfield, T. J., & Perosa, L. J. (1983). Counselor education—Quo vadis. *Counselor Education and Supervision, 2,* 178-184.

Coombs, A. (1986). Person-centered assumptions for counselor education. *Person-Centered Review, 1,* 1, 72-82.

Coulson, W. R., & Rogers, C. R. (Eds.) (1968). *Man and the science of man.* Columbus, OH: Charles E. Merrill.

Davenport, D. S. (1992). Ethical and legal problems with client-centered supervision. *Counselor Education and Supervision, 31,* 227-231.

Dimick, K. M., & Huff, V. E. (1970). *Child counseling.* Dubuque, IA: Wm. C. Brown, 59.

Faw, V. E. (1949) A psychotherapeutic method of teaching psychology. *The American Psychologist, 4,* 104-109.

Felker, S. (1973). Intellectual ability and counseling effectiveness: Another view. *Counselor Education and Supervision, 13,* 146-150.

Freeman, S. C. (1992). C. H. Patterson on client-centered supervision: an interview. *Counselor Education and Supervision, 31,* 219-226.

Freeman, S. C. (1993). Reiterations on client-centered supervision. *Counselor Education and Supervision. 32,* 213-215.

Gordon, T. (1955). *Group-centered leadership.* Boston: Houghton Mifflin, 154.

Gross, L. (1948). An experimental study of the validity of the nondirective method of teaching. *Journal of Psychology, 26,* 243-248.

Hansen, J. C., Stevic, R. R., & Warner, R. W. (1986). *Counseling: Theory and Process* (4th ed.). Boston: Allyn and Bacon.

Lyon, H. C., Jr. (1971). *Learning to feel—Feeling to learn.* Columbus, OH: Charles E. Merrill, 183-230, 263-289.

Mearns, D. (1997). *Person-centered counselling training.* London: Sage.

Natiello, P. (1987). The person-centered approach: From theory to practice. *Person-Centered Review, 2,* 2, 203-216.

Palmer, P. (1998). *The courage to teach.* San Francisco: Jossey-Bass.

Patterson, C H. (1973). *Theories of counseling and psychotherapy.* New York: Harper and Row, xv-xvi.

Patterson, C. H. (1986). *Theories of counseling and psychotherapy* (4th ed.). New York: Harper and Row.

Pine, G. J., & Boy, A V. (1977). *Learner-centered teaching: A humanistic view.* Denver: Love.

Rogers, C. R. (1942). *Counseling and psychotherapy.* Boston: Houghton Mifflin.

Rogers, C. R. (1951-renewed 1979). *Client-centered therapy.* Boston: Houghton Mifflin. Chapter 9, Student-centered teaching, 399-414; Chapter 11, A Theory of personality and behavior, 481-533.

Rogers, C. R. (1962). The interpersonal relationship: The core of guidance. *Harvard Educational Review, 32,* 416- 533.

Rogers, C. R. (1969). *Freedom to learn.* Columbus, OH: Charles E. Merrill, 29-97, 103-145, 109-202, 157-166, 221-297, 327-342.

Rogers, C. R. (1970). The interpersonal relationship in the facilitation of learning. In J. R. Hart & T. M. Tomlinson (Eds.). *New directions in client-centered therapy.* Boston: Houghton Mifflin, 468-483.

Rogers, C. R. (1975). Empathic: An unappreciated way of being. *The Counseling Psychologist, 5,* 2-10.

Rogers, C. R. (1977). The politics of education. *Journal of Humanistic Education, 1,* 7-22.

Rogers, C. R. (1980). *A way of being.* Boston: Houghton Mifflin.

Rogers, C. R. (1983). *Freedom to learn in the 1980s.* Columbus, OH: Charles E. Merrill.

Schwebel, M., & Asch, M. J. (1948). Research possibilities in nondirective teaching. *Journal of Educational Psychology, 39,* 359-369.

Southern, S., & Hannaford, C. (1981). Health counseling: An emergent specialization. *Counselor Education and Supervision, 21,* 7-15.

Steff/re, B., & Grant, W. (Eds.). (1972). *Theories of counseling.* New York: McGraw-Hill, 4-7.

Vontress, C. E. (1979). Cross cultural counseling: An existential approach. *The Personnel and Guidance Journal, 58,* 117-122.

White, L. (1978). Theoretical orientations of counselor educators. *College Student Personnel, 19,* 132-135.

Chapter 12

BEYOND COUNSELING: FOUR CONTRIBUTORS TO PSYCHOLOGICAL STABILITY

Anyone in touch with the vibrancy of life realizes that there are many persons who deal with it in an easy and relaxed manner. We're aware of them in restaurants, at the ocean, at religious services, at zoos, in taverns, at parties, in our neighborhood, and in our homes; we're aware of them selling merchandise, building a highway, riding to work, walking in the park. They are psychologically stable people—people who have learned to absorb the self-enriching fullness of life. They don't have incapacitating personal, social, or economic problems. They know who they are, why they exist, and where they are going. They generally feel good about life, and they radiate a positive attitude that others can easily feel and absorb. They love their families, find personal satisfaction in their work, and enjoy the simple pleasures of life. Life is not perfect for them, but they deal with it, cope with it, confront it, manage it, and flow with it. They do what they should, at the time they should do it, by using their human intuition—an intuition based on a profound self-awareness and sense of their presence in the world; their self-concepts are highly positive (Sheehy, 1986).

As professional counselors, we have engaged in individual and group-counseling with a cross section of troubled clients. In our capacity as reasonably observant persons, existing outside the context of professional counseling relationships, we have seen people who have never been professionally counseled living honest, open, and relatively untroubled lives. These people never need counselors, psychologists, or psychiatrists. They have learned, without professional assistance, how to bring full and satisfying meaning to their lives. They have developed themselves so that they embrace life—they have penetrated the meaning and purpose of their behavior. Certainly, they have personal problems, but they deal with them and solve them—they are not so overpowered by them that they become psychologically incapacitated to the point of needing professional assistance.

The existence of these persons captured our personal and professional interest and prompted us to devote this chapter to an understanding of the gravitas of their behavior. In essence, we desired to develop a profile of the psychologically stable and happy person; a person who possesses an enriched, expanded, and enhancing perception of the self. As we began looking into why some persons who were not receiving professional assistance were handling life better than those who were receiving assistance, we made some false starts and took many appealing paths that led us nowhere. Certainly, the happy people we knew were not personifications of the personality theories espoused in textbooks. Many of the freewheeling people we knew were too busy with life to have time for the hallowed truths regarding human nature as revealed in the psychological literature. They were too busy going to ball games, watching TV, earning a living, camping, making love, talking, listening, meditating, dancing, and laughing. They were too deeply engaged in penetrating the substance of life to care about the august insights of the scholars. They didn't need anyone to explain what life was all about because they knew. They knew because of their sensitive contact with life.

These happy people came from a wide socioeconomic range and included construction workers, barbers, secretaries, plumbers, printers, teachers, nurses, physicians, engineers, and bartenders. But why were they able to lead such a psychologically stable life? After all, as professional counselors, we believed in the importance of the therapeutic relationship as a catalyst for self-development—as a process that would enable people to discover the positive potential of the self and translate it into a more psychologically stable self-concept.

THERAPEUTIC HUMAN EXPERIENCES

The clients who were able to improve and live a more psychologically stable life used the counseling process as one mode of self-development. For them, counseling was a therapeutic human experience that made them feel psychologically stronger. But what about the vast majority of humanity who had never had any contact with members of the psychotherapeutic professions? Why were they doing well while others needed professional assistance? What was the experience in their lives that was the equivalent of counseling and psychotherapy? A professional helping relationship is characterized by liberality, honesty, acceptance, understanding, positive regard, concreteness, and empathy. Were they getting help from persons without professional credentials in counseling and psychotherapy? Of course they were! They were getting human therapeutic help from each other. Existing in the lives of these psychologically stable persons were individuals and groups who cared for them and who expressed that caring by being available to them when they needed to talk, to cry, to be happy, to emote, or to siphon off anger.

A person needs human therapeutic experiences as a basic and necessary component of psychological stability. Those who have no one with whom they can communicate seek out the therapeutic assistance provided by a professional. Those who have someone to whom they can turn receive therapeutic assistance because they experience a caring attitude. Husbands and wives can receive such therapeutic assistance from each other, just as it can come from deeply human relationships between employer and employee, brother and sister, black and white persons, neighbor and neighbor, between co-workers, and between friends. The psychologically stable person reaches out to others by giving and receiving love. This reciprocal caring for each other is a therapeutic human experience for both the one who is giving and the one who is receiving (Bergin, 1980).

In the history of civilization, one component of psychological stability has always been provided through interpersonal caring that has been passed from generation to generation and from culture to culture. When people care enough for each other to extend their caring to each other, we possess a survival quality that not only is the foundation of counseling and psychotherapy, but is the basis for a variety of caring relationships between and among nations.

THERAPEUTIC WORK EXPERIENCES

If the self is to be psychologically stable, it must not only engage in therapeutic human relationships, it must also be involved in therapeutic work experiences. That is, the person who lives a psychologically stable life finds meaning in the work that is performed to earn a living. The person realizes that the financial rewards of work are important, but he or she also realizes that the personal meaning of work is even more important. A plumber who feels that plumbing is a contribution to public health and sanitation finds that work is a therapeutic experience because it is a fulfillment of a basic urge to contribute to the well-being and development of humanity. The plumber may not be fully conscious of the importance of a work contribution, but it is part of the motivation that enables the plumber to gain therapeutic satisfaction when a plumbing problem is solved. The printer who is sensitive to the historical importance of print feels fulfilled when a work order is finished, the outcome is examined, and the finished product is packaged for a customer. The musician who composes or performs derives a great deal of personal therapy from the knowledge that music contributes to the relaxation and enjoyment of others.

Work can be therapeutic and it is another dimension of the person who lives a psychologically stable life. The people who handle life without the need for counseling and psychotherapy not only have caring human relationships in their lives, they also derive therapeutic satisfaction from their jobs. The child who feels parental love and respect and who is fascinated by the work of learning possesses two positive components that contribute to psychological well-being.

The National Career Development Association's special interest group "Work and Spiritual Values" states that work, at its roots, is a spiritual matter (1990:3):

In a World of High Flux:
      personal centeredness may be lost
      family connections severed
      geographical roots torn up
      community fractured

Work in This World of High Flux May Be:
      unconnected to wider special purpose
      unconnected to deep individual fulfillment
      unconnected to commitments and meanings

In Such High Flux Spiritual Problems May Develop Because Human Beings Need:
      to be personally centered
      to have family connections
      to have geographical roots
      to be part of a community

Persons Need Their Time and Energy Commitments (Work)
      to be connected to wider social purpose
      to feel deep individual fulfillment
      to have commitments
      to experience meaning in what they do

Work Can Be a Vital Part
      of personal centeredness
      of family connections
      of geographical roots
      of community

If These Needs Are Not Tended To, a Spiritual Crisis Emerges. Work, At Its Roots, is a Spiritual Matter.

Ashley Montagu (1950) indicated that the personally relevant life is characterized by the presence of love. Donald Super (1957) noted that a person, through work, can achieve psychological balance or imbalance; that those who work simply to earn money to pay the bills are psychologically unfulfilled. One who engages in work that is fulfillment of the self will derive psychotherapeutic benefits from that work.

We seemed to be headed in a clear direction. Those who can deal and cope with life and are not in need of professional psychotherapeutic assistance are those who have human and work experiences that contribute to their psychological stability. But there was more to these people—something that went beyond their ability to gain satisfaction from therapeutic human work and work experiences. Being psychologically stable surely demanded something more. But what?

THERAPEUTIC SPIRITUAL EXPERIENCES

Uncovering the third dimension of the psychologically stable person was more difficult because the academic world was often so coldly empirical that it failed to consider the spiritual nature of the person. After all, the reverend Freud had called humanity's spiritual tendency a neurotic need to identify with an idealized Authority Figure because of an unfulfilled need for parental love during childhood (Zilborg, 1963). Karl Marx described religion as the opium of the people. George Bernard Shaw had sprinkled his writings with satire and diatribes aimed at anyone who might consider a Being beyond the self (Weintraub, 1969). Shakespeare had carried the recurrent and subtle theme that a person's belief in something beyond the self was often an impairment (Craig, 1931). The recent "God is Dead" movement was a startling reminder that religious people had historically stood aside and watched human deterioration—they were too busy constructing dogmas, administrative patterns, and edifices to be concerned with the needs of human beings. They were so entranced with raising their eyes toward heaven that they were blind to the human misery beneath their noses.

Academia had conditioned us to be skeptical about the place of spirituality in the life of the psychologically stable person. But as we began to desensitize ourselves from these prejudices against organized religion and looked at the other possible dimensions of persons who were psychologically stable, we began to realize that these people were indeed spiritual—not, perhaps, by being members of an organized church (although some were church members), but they were spiritual in their personal life style and in their attitude toward others. They possessed a sense of their position in the evolution and civilization of humanity. They wondered about the deeper issues of life and the meaning of existence in much the same way that the Jews evolved toward monotheism in a polytheistic world which, for countless centuries, had worshipped mountains, oceans, animals, the sun, and the moon.

The psychologically stable person is spiritual in that such a person thinks about and has compassion for the human condition. This person goes beyond the self to consider the plight of humanity and one's obligation to do something about that plight. Such an individual may reject organized theistic religions but is spiritually aware of a caring for other people. This person may consider absurd the idea of a life hereafter, but he or she does contemplate death and hopes that somehow the meaning of one's life will continue in the memory of others. The psychologically stable person desires that one's contribution to life be remembered after death. This person considers something beyond the self but doesn't call that something God, but may call it Mother Nature, the Great Outdoors, Lady Luck, Good Fortune, or a Good Horoscope; there is an attempt to penetrate the meaning and substance of existence and the future. The person may prefer to be called an agnostic, an atheist, or a humanist, but he or she often possesses a more honest spirituality than do many who piously kneel before God. The psychologically stable person lives a life that includes time to ponder the spiritual dimensions of existence and whether one's personal life is a contribution to the development and the enhancement of others. Frankl (1948) says that within each of us is the concept of an unconscious god which prompts us to care about the well- being of others. The psychologically stable person is theistically or secularly spiritual. A person is spiritual when he or she thinks about the well-being of others and wants to contribute to that well-being.

The psychologically stable person does not believe in God as someone with a white robe, a shepherd's staff, and a long white beard, but believes in something beyond the self. There is a spiritual relevancy to this person's existence; a desire to have one's earthly tenure mean something, and this desire, this spiritual inclination, becomes translated into an essential ingredient of the psychologically stable life. This person is aware that one's life is an important contribution to the well-being of others.

In describing the person of the future who will contribute to the survival of humanness in our society, Rogers (1980) indicates that such a person will be characterized by:

> A yearning for the spiritual. These persons of tomorrow are seekers. They wish to find a meaning and purpose in life that is greater than the individual. Some are led into cults but more are examining all the ways by which humankind has found values and forces that extend beyond the individual. They wish to live a life of inner peace. Their heroes are spiritual persons–Mahatma Gandhi,

Martin Luther King, Teilhard de Chardin. Sometimes, in altered states of consciousness, they experience the unity and harmony of the universe..

We felt that we were getting somewhere. Three basic elements had been identified, elements which contributed to psychological stability, elements that sustained the persons who led personally meaningful lives and who were not in need of professional psychotherapeutic assistance. Yes, such persons engaged in therapeutic human, work, and spiritual experiences, but was there another dimension that contributed to the person's psychological stability?

THERAPEUTIC RECREATIONAL EXPERIENCES

The identification of the fourth element of psychological stability occurred on a professional trip to Tucson, Arizona. The trip lasted for just over three days, but it was an expanding experience because it possessed not only therapeutic human, work, and spiritual experiences, but it possessed a fourth experience. We had never considered it as the fourth element in the life of a psychologically stable person. This fourth element emerged at LaFluente, a Mexican restaurant that featured a rollicking Mariachi band. The food was magnificent—it contributed to the evening. The Mariachi band played joyous music that produced feelings of elation and euphoria.

But what category of therapeutic experience was this? It was the missing dimension which, because of its simplicity, we had previously overlooked; it was the fourth contributor to psychological stability: the recreational experience. In our search for another category of therapeutic experiences, we had become too complex in our thinking. We had neglected to fully appreciate the therapeutic value of recreation because of its obviousness; while attempting to penetrate the meaning of the forest, we had overlooked the trees at our elbows.

The therapeutic value of recreation is generally not treated by psychological theory builders, but anyone who has observed the psychologically stable person realizes the importance of recreation in the life of that person. Recreation means to re-create, to re-create the self so that it can become renewed and participate in life with greater vigor. Recreation contributes to psychological stability by enabling the participant to engage in an activity that can produce psychological relaxation and, sometimes, even a needed amount of tension. Winston Churchill found relaxation in painting—through it, he found expression that enabled him to re-create himself. Henry David Thoreau found the peace and harmony of nature at Walden Pond. Mark

Twain was enraptured and psychologically uplifted by the beauty of Hawaii when, as a young man, he was attempting to find his place in the literary sun. John F. Kennedy was psychologically uplifted while sailing a sloop or participating in a game of touch football. Dr. Sol Roy Rosenthal, professor of preventive medicine at the University of Illinois College of Medicine, accumulated evidence indicating that people who engage in risk-action recreational activities, such as mountain climbing, sky diving, automobile racing, or fox hunting, experience unusual psychological exhilaration as a result of their participation (Furlong, 1969).

As a therapeutic experience, recreation has not received enough serious attention in the literature of psychology. It didn't possess the depth to attract the serious consideration of the scholar. Recreation has been thought to be something frivolous that is more for the masses than for those inhabitants of the polite and washed world of scholarship. Although Aristotle and Plato acknowledged the value of recreation as a contributor to the full life, the modern scholar tends to think little of recreation. Perhaps Robert Maynard Hutchins, who became President of the University of Chicago at the age of 27, set the tone for contemporary scholars when he indicated that whenever he thought of exercise, he instead took a nap so that the inclination would pass.

It is interesting to note that scholars who might not publicly acknowledge the therapeutic value of recreation do take vacations, lie in the sun and listen to Beethoven, attend cocktail parties, go fishing and hunting, swim, play squash, shoot billiards, play polo, or recompose themselves by ordering from the top of the menu in the finest of restaurants. Perhaps they do not acknowledge the therapeutic value of football's Super Bowl, drinking beer at the local tavern, stickball, television, or gambling, because if they admit an interest, they will somehow lose their identity with a community of scholars.

Although there may be a lack of extensive scholarly interest in the therapeutic value of recreation, anyone who lives a psychologically stable life realizes how recreation contributes to that stability. By itself, a therapeutic recreational experience cannot produce psychological stability, but when linked to and integrated with therapeutic human, work, and spiritual experiences, recreation becomes the fourth dimension necessary for the attainment of psychological stability.

ATTAINING PSYCHOLOGICAL STABILITY

A person who superficially engages in each of these four therapeutic experiences in an attempt to acquire instant psychological stability will not achieve the desired goal. Such a person goes through the motions, but is not viscerally committed or engaged. This type of person will scurry about looking for another with whom he or she can engage in verbal diarrhea; occasionally stay at work for an extra twenty minutes; say a quick "help me" prayer on the subway; or make sure to get tickets for everybody's favorite play. In order for the self to move toward psychological stability, there must be an ever-increasing and deeper level of qualitative involvement in each of the four categories of therapeutic experiences. The more the person invests in improving the quality of these therapeutic experiences, the more the self becomes psychologically stable.

The person, however, never achieves full psychological stability, because today's feelings of psychological stability will not be viable next week inasmuch as personal psychological perfection will always be beyond our grasp; it will always be something that we only temporarily and partially possess. We will never attain perfection because we will always desire to expand and go beyond the perfection we now possess; we will never become, but will always be involved in the process of becoming. This seems to be the nature of human nature.

The mission is not to become psychologically perfect since this is impossible. The best that we can do is to commit ourselves to improve while living with the awareness that perfect psychological stability is impossible to obtain. For the person who works at improving one's psychological stability, the only time that one should come close to perfection is at the moment before death; at that moment, the person should be all that one can ever hope to become.

The psychotherapeutic professions can point out the existence of human depersonalization and alienation in our society, and we fully acknowledge the fact of their existence. What we do question is the attitude rampant among some members of the psychotherapeutic professions, an attitude implying that the only way a person can achieve psychological stability is within the offices of counselors, psychologists, and psychiatrists. To us, this is a narrow view, especially because there is certainly help being given by persons who are not members of the psychotherapeutic professions.

If we historically consider what has propelled the person from prehistoric times to the present, we will find psychological stability as a primary contributor; and history will document that it emerged because the person engaged in balanced and integrated human, work, spiritual and recreational therapeutic experiences.

If, in turn, one contemplates the future of humanity, one will realize that the psychologically stable person is necessary for the preservation of civilization, and to achieve that stability the person must have access and exposure to human, work, spiritual, and recreational therapeutic experiences.

A person might mistakenly select one or two of these therapeutic experiences that appear to provide for greater psychological stability than the others; but if a person does this and neglects the other therapeutic experiences, he or she will not attain the psychological stability that endures over a lifetime. Such stability eventually erodes because it does not possess the depth which emerges from a balanced exposure to the four catalytic therapeutic experiences.

SOME CONCLUSIONS

1. Psychological stability occurs because of a balanced, integrated, and continuous involvement in therapeutic human, work, spiritual, and recreational experiences. A balanced involvement in the four therapeutic experiences means that one must have contact with one's emotions in order to ascertain the degree of psychological stability that exists in one's life. A person must translate this sensitivity into conscious awareness so that the person knows when the stability does or does not exist. When there is stability, the self feels strong and reinforces this stability. When there is lack of stability, one must be aware of what is causing this lack and become involved in a particular therapeutic experience that has the potential for creating the desired stability.

An integrated involvement in the four therapeutic experiences is much like the integration that exists among the four seasons. Spring, summer, fall, and winter are distinct each from the others, and yet there is a blending among them. Each season has its own particular refreshing characteristics, but each mingles with the following season to form an integrated whole.

A continuous involvement in each of the four therapeutic experiences indicates that attaining psychological stability is a process rather than an event. Psychological stability cannot occur when a person devotes this hour or this day to a particular therapeutic experience in the hope that there will be a magical result. Continuous involvement means that the development of psychological stability never ceases; it occurs continually in the apparently mundane and innocuous experiences of daily living. As a process, it is always moving toward an improved level of development.

2. The extent to which one becomes psychologically stable is proportionately related to the degree of qualitative involvement in each of the four therapeutic experiences available. Having a balanced, integrated, and continuous involvement in the four therapeutic experiences is the beginning point for developing psychological stability. The depth of involvement in each of the therapeutic experiences influences the degree of psychological stability attained. Merely to flit from one therapeutic experience to another will leave the person unfilled since such superficial contacts are much like admiring the packaging of a gift without appreciating the gift itself.

Working toward psychological stability requires an immersion in each of the four therapeutic experiences in an effort to discover its heretofore unknown depths. The self becomes involved in a search for the hidden value of each therapeutic experience, but there must be a deep desire to seek, a desire to plumb the depths of each therapeutic experience in order to penetrate and absorb its potential.

A qualitative involvement in each of the four therapeutic experiences will lead the self deeper into personal awareness—a sensitivity to the inner core of a person's existence which influences overt behavior. But qualitative involvement demands not only the desire, but also an investment of time—how much time is relative to the individual—but the investment must be made if psychological stability is to be attained. Although we live in a world of instant everything, the development of pyschological stability cannot occur with the same quickness. It occurs only when one takes the time to search out the stabilizing elements of each of the therapeutic experiences; and the search is exciting because of the knowledge that today's qualitative involvement can be deepened tomorrow, thus continually affecting the degree to which psychological stability can be achieved.

3. One cannot achieve psychological stability by engaging in only one, two, or three of the four therapeutic experiences available. Each of the four therapeutic experiences is part of the whole. Unto itself, each of the four therapeutic experiences has only a limited value; but when joined with the others, it is enriched because it becomes integrated with and contributes to the formation of the whole.

When the self limits itself to an involvement in either human, vocational, spiritual, or recreational experiences, or a combination of two or three of these experiences, it decreases the degree to which it can be psychologically stabilized. The self becomes more psychologically stable when it absorbs the inherent value within each of the four therapeutic experiences.

Whenever one senses psychological instability, it is usually due to the absence of one or more of the therapeutic experiences in one's life. The person who has experienced human, work, and spiritual experiences may sense this void because of the absence of the recreative powers of recreational experiences. Another person who has profited from therapeutic recreational, work, and spiritual experiences may still sense a void because the person has not engaged in psychologically enriching human experiences. On it goes—psychological voids exist because of the absence of one or more of the four therapeutic experiences in a person's life.

The self expands, life becomes more full and personally relevant, when one consciously seeks out a complementary involvement in each of the four therapeutic experiences.

4. Among the four therapeutic experiences, a person devotes more psychic energy to the one that produces more psychological stability than do the others. To divide the time available for the four therapeutic experiences into quartiles would hamper the expansion of the self. Not all of the four therapeutic experiences have an equal value in the life of an individual, but all should be experienced if the self is to achieve psychological stability. But the four therapeutic experiences cannot be allocated equivalent periods of time with the expectation that equal involvement will insure psychological stability.

Among the four therapeutic experiences, one usually has more strength than the others for contributing to our psychological stability. When one discovers which of the four therapeutic experiences has more of an effect than the others, one expends more psychic energy when engaging in that therapeutic experience than when engaging in the others. This particular therapeutic experience, when known, holds more promise for contributing to our psychological stability than others, and more time is allotted for experiencing it than is provided for the others. Once again, balancing one's involvement in the four therapeutic experiences does not mean devoting an equivalent amount of time to each; it does mean devoting more time to the one that affects our psychological stability more than the others, but without neglecting the other three therapeutic experiences that also contribute to our psychological stability.

5. Involvement in therapeutic human experiences is the catalyst that enables the self to discover the contributions of work, spiritual, and recreational experiences to psychological stability. The psychologically stable person typically experiences more personal relevancy in therapeutic human relationships. These provide the foundations whereby the self feels comfortable enough to project itself toward therapeutic work, spiritual, and recreational experiences.

To feel comfortable with people, to deeply care about the dimensions of their existence, to extend oneself toward others in honesty, openness, and empathy, indicates a willingness to risk the self. A feeling of psychological stability enables the self to project itself toward therapeutic work, spiritual and recreational experiences. Because it has experienced viable human relationships, the self is more free to penetrate the therapeutic values of work, spiritual, and recreational experiences. The self is free because it does not feel threatened or diminished in human relationships. Such freedom in human relationships must first be sensed and internalized if the self is to gain by its involvement in the other therapeutic experiences.

Inner freedom enables a person to be more true, real, and genuine as one engages in therapeutic work, spiritual, and recreational experiences. When the self has been involved in enriching human relationships, it possesses the freedom to seek out the therapeutic values contained in work, spiritual, and recreational experiences.

6. *The self that has been psychologically strengthened by a qualitative engagement in the four therapeutic experiences will transcend itself and consciously and humanly extend itself toward other persons.* The self that has psychologically stabilized itself through an involvement in therapeutic human, work, spiritual, and recreational experiences has a tendency to go beyond itself; since the self feels confident, it moves toward other persons. A person returns to others when free to do so; when one feels psychologically stable, one completes a therapeutic cycle by returning to a caring attitude toward others. When a person is psychologically stable, he or she is no longer suspicious or distrustful of others. Since the person feels comfortable with the inner self, the person in turn feels comfortable in relationships with others, comfortable enough so that other persons take on dignity and worth that were previously overshadowed—not because they did not possess inherent dignity and worth, but because the self was so inhibited that it was not able to appreciate or love and respect others.

The cyclical nature of the four therapeutic experiences is, indeed, a phenomenon. Human therapeutic experiences serve as catalysts that propel the self toward enriching work, spiritual, and recreational experiences; and when the self becomes sufficiently strengthened through this quartet of therapeutic experiences, it consciously and humanly shapes itself, moves itself, and extends itself toward enriching the existence of others.

7. *The psychologically stable person attempts to replace the tolerance of persons with an empathic sense of unconditional positive regard for others.* The psychologically stable person refuses to "put up" with others or tolerate them. To tolerate the existence of another person is inimical with the psychologically stable person since to tolerate means, "I'll put up with you no matter how much I dislike you." The psychologically stable person realizes that the true test of its stability is the ability to have reverence for the differences among persons. It is relatively easy to have a kinship with people who are like ourselves, but this kinship can produce a neuroticism that has separated and will continue to separate humanity. The psychologically stable person accepts differences, sees beauty in differences and realizes that the self can be further expanded when it evolves toward an unconditional positive regard for the differences among persons. The psychologically stable person is committed to appreciating these differences. These differences are seen as less important than the humanity possessed by all persons.

In an effort to protect the self from pervasive influences, some have concentrated on accentuating the differences among people and reinforcing separateness. From a foundation of unconditional positive regard, the psychologically stable person sees these differences as artificial and superficial barriers among persons, and attempts to understand them. But the psychologically stable person doesn't concentrate on the differences; he or she looks for common human elements among people and realizes that, in their humanness, people are alike.

8. The psychologically stable self values its stability but has no inclination to move other persons in the same direction; it respects psychological pluralism because it is evidence of the existence of personal freedom. The psychologically stable person seeks not to tamper with, manipulate, or convert others. Since the psychologically stable person values personal freedom, there is no attempt to impose personal values on others. The psychologically stable person realizes that human respect can only be achieved when the individual is free to hold personal values. One attempts to impose values on another only when one feels that one's values are superior to those held by the other person, but the psychologically stable person doesn't feel the need for such a psychological crutch. The psychologically stable person has discovered certain values, but there is also the realization that these values are personally relevant because they were freely chosen. In contacts with other persons, the psychologically stable person doesn't attempt to impose personal values on others. Instead, an atmosphere of communication is created in which the other person is able to discover personal values. When a person discovers personal values, these values will deeply motivate his or her behavior. When one merely transplants the values of another into one's own life, these transplanted values eventually erode because they were not self-determined.

9. The psychologically stable self has a reverence for the people of the past who have contributed to civilization, is more relevant in its present state of being, and possesses a psychic temperature that insists that a viable legacy be passed on to future generations. The psychologically stable person feels a part of humanity in the here-and-now but is also appreciative of the unknown persons of the past who have contributed to the development of whatever degree of humanness exists in the world today. The psychologically stable person has a sense of a personal posterity, a sense that one must contribute to increasing the level of humanness today so that unborn generations will inherit a more human and caring world.

The psychologically stable person realizes that his or her life is important only insofar as it is a contribution to the enrichment of the human condition. The psychologically stable person doesn't want to exist at a superficial and uninvolved level. There is a desire to experience the thunder and the rainbows of life. Why? Certainly for personal reasons, but also for others—the others of today with whom to share a meal, a conversation, a laugh—and the unknown others of tomorrow whose world will be better or worse because of whatever we contribute.

10. Participation in the four therapeutic experiences is a psychologically stabilizing process for all age groups regardless of nationality, race, culture, socioeconomic status, political affiliations, sexual preference or religious inclinations. The process of improving one's psychological stability is available to anyone. It is not the preserve of a privileged few on whom Lady Luck decides to smile. A Yugoslavian, a Mongolian, an Italian, a Brazilian, a Russian, an American—each can improve psychological stability by a qualitative involvement in each of the four therapeutic experiences. Be the person Black, Oriental, or Caucasian; financially wealthy or impoverished; seven years old or seventy-seven years old; liberal or conservative; Republican or Democrat; Socialist or Communist; atheist, agnostic, or theistur therapeutic experiences. Be the person Black, Oriental, or Caucasian; financially wealthy or impoverished; seven years old or seventy-seven years old; liberal or conservative; Republican or Democrat; Socialist or Communist; heterosexual, homosexual or bisexual; atheist, agnostic, or theist—all can achieve psychological stability in proportion to the value one places on engaging in each of the four therapeutic experiences.

Psychologically stable persons exist in any country or culture, and an investigation of their life styles will reveal that they have qualitatively participated in a combination of therapeutic human, work, spiritual, and recreational experiences. In all countries and cultures, persons can experience personally relevant human experiences, can seek out the intrinsic values in work being performed, can be spiritually linked to others, and can enjoy recreational experiences. The only barriers are self-conceived barriers that one can easily construct. The beauty of the four therapeutic experiences is that they are easily available to all persons, but one must sense their psychological value and must seek out opportunities to experience them.

11. The psychologically stable self senses an internationally emerging convergence of humanity in various areas of thought; it possesses a deep sensitivity to the psychosocial, philosophical, technological, and biological evolution of humanity and the importance of one's place in that evolution. The development of sophisticated communications media, especially satellite television programs that have hemispheric or international audiences, has produced a sense of unity among formerly divergent peoples, a sense that they are essentially alike. They cry, feel, debate, emote, love, and fear—together—internationally. People, on an international scale, are beginning to see and sense a commonality in their concern for survival; they see themselves when they experience the art, dances, culture, and technology of other nations; they sense that among persons, birth and marriage are universally joyous occasions and that death produces sorrow in all of humanity; they realize that intelligence, hope, worship, collectivism, and violence are universal characteristics of people, and they respect all of these characteristics except violence.

The international convergence of humanity is a new and refreshing experience for civilization. For the first time in history, the person is truly beginning to sense a link between the self and the international community of persons. In the darker periods of our past, some relied on the neurotic need to be devious, to be suspicious and skeptical of those who were different. It is becoming increasingly more difficult to convince the people that they must make war in order to survive, because international satellite television is beginning to draw people closer to people. As this occurs, it will become more difficult for persons to want to kill others, because this emerging international community of persons is influencing the development of positive regard and respect for each other.

12. It is impossible to achieve perfect psychological stability; a person will always be involved in the process of becoming more adequate but will never achieve full personal adequacy because one's reach will always exceed one's grasp. A qualitative involvement in each of the four therapeutic experiences will not result in the attainment of perfect psychological stability. Such perfection is impossible because the nature of a human being is evolutionary; a person progresses, from one stage to the next, but never reaches an apex, since today's sense of psychological stability, no matter how perfect it appears to be, will not and should not be satisfying tomorrow. The goal tomorrow, then, is not only to bring the self to its former level of stability but to move the self to the next higher level. Such a developmental process never ceases, since it is a process rather than an act. As a process, it is continuous, and perfect psychological stability is never attained. It is the struggle to improve, to mature, grow, and develop to one's temporary limits, and to realize that these limits *are* temporary—that there is an even higher level that can be achieved in proportion to the quality of one's involvement in therapeutic human, work, spiritual, and recreational experiences. But we cannot achieve perfect psychological stability.

CONCLUSION

The ideas presented in this chapter can become a reality through the formation of a human development center. Such a center can be sponsored by any community group with a strong commitment to improving the human condition: local government, churches or synagogues, family services agencies, schools and colleges, mental health agencies, or substance abuse organizations; or all of these groups can contribute staff and resources in the initiation, development, and operation of such a center. At the present time, human services agencies work in isolation from each other. Their services are often duplicated and unsynchronized with each other. They often appear to be working at cross purposes.

A human development center would be the first step in integrating and coordinating human services. It would enable therapeutic human, work, spiritual, and recreational services to be offered under one roof. It would enable each of these experiences to make its balanced contribution to the development of psychological stability among the citizens of a community.

REFERENCES

Bergin, A. (1980). Psychotherapy and religious values. *Journal of Consulting and Clinical Psychology, 43,* 95-105.

Craig, H. (1931). *Shakespeare: A historical and critical study with annotated texts of twenty-one plays.* Glenview, IL: Scott Foresman.

Frankl, V. (1948). *The unconscious god.* New York: Simon and Schuster.

Furlong, W. (1969). Danger as a way of joy. *Sports Illustrated, 30,* 52-53.

Montagu, A. (1950). *On being human.* New York: Hawthorn books.

Rogers, C. R. (1980). *A way of being.* Boston: Houghton Mifflin.

Sheehy, G. (1986). *Spirit of survival* New York: William Morrow.

Super, D. E. (1957). *The psychology of careers.* New York: Harper and Row.

Weintraub, S. (1969). *Shaw: An autobiography.* New York: Weybright and Talley.

Zilborg, G. (1964). *Freud and religion.* Westminster, MD: Paulist/Newman, 31.

AUTHOR INDEX

249

SUBJECT INDEX

A

Actualization, 4, 14, 86–88, 91–100 (*see also* Self-actualization)
Actualizing tendency, 13–14
Affective vocabulary, 47–48, 56–61
Affirmation and unconditional positive regard, 13, 68, 86–100, 120–21, 126–28, 154
Affordances, 18, 75, 76–77 (*see also* Phase Two processes)
Assimilation, 11–12
Attitudinal core conditions, 13–14, 126–28
  beliefs and values, 86–100
  counselor conditions for reflection of feelings, 44–49, 71–72, 73
  nonverbal empathy, 46–47, 119
Attitude modeling, 11

B

Behavior
  conceptual framework for understanding motivation, 68–69
  feelings, influence on, 32–61
  modification in natural sequence, 76–77
  self-actualization, 4, 5, 14, 86–88, 91–100
Being there, 117
Belief systems
  client values, 91
  counselor values, 83–100

C

Case studies
  Carl Rogers and Beate Hofmeister: interview, 130–41
  play therapy, 183–92
Children and play therapy, 163–92 (*see also* Play therapy)
  unique features of play, 163–65
Clarification/exploratory questions, 22–24, 51 (*see also* Communications)
Clearing the air, 35 (*see also* Feelings)
Client-centered group counseling, 145–47

communication modes, 155–56
confrontation, 156–59
  guidelines for constructive experience, 159
counselor, facilitator, person, 150–55
  characteristics, 151
  goals, 154
democratic nature, 147–49
nonfacilitative attitudes and approaches, 152
stages, focus, agenda, 149–50
unethical behaviors, 153
Client-centered necessity re modality integrations, 7
Client-centered therapy, 7–8, 68–69, 73, 86–100
  (*see also* Person-centered counseling)
  achievement goals, 69
  client direction in Phase Two, 19–21, 77–79, 90
  client focus v. problem focus, 73, 90, 121–22
  client values and morality, 86, 91
  comprehensive counseling, 70–71
  counselor beliefs and value system, 83–100
    attitudinal values, 86–100
  counselor role, 69–70, 73–74
  heretical camps, 7
  orthodox camps, 7
  reflective process, 31–61
  response pattern, 74, 77
  therapeutic methodology choice by client, 18, 77–79, 90
  transition from Phase One, 16–19, 55–56
    client characteristics, 18–19, 55–56
Client feelings
  conditions for counselor reflection of feelings, 44–49
  counselor reflection process, 4, 14–15, 31–61, 76–79
Client fragility, 8

254

Play materials
  aggressive toys, 177
  blocks, 177
  clay, 177
  doll family/house, 176
  finger paints, 177
  puppets, 178
  sand, 177
  selection criteria, 175–76
  toy animals, 177
  water, 177
Play therapy, case study, 183–92
Play therapy, 163–92 (*see also* Play therapy
  approaches)
  application of person-centered principles,
    163–92
  categories by stages
    practice games, 165
    symbolic games, 165
    games with rules, 165–66
  characteristics of play therapy, 167–68
  play materials, structured/unstructured,
    167, 192
    play media and expression of feelings,
      167, 192
    problem solution, release of tension/emo-
      tion, 167, 192
  cognitive development, 165–66
    sensory-motor experience; symbolic
      thought emergence, 165
  expression through activity, 167, 192
  play, learning, and expression, 163–65
  psychosocial value, 166–67, 182
  safe projection, 168
Play therapy, history and approaches,
  168–75
  counselor as playmate, 174
  existential approach, 170–72
    child-centered approach, 171–72
    relationship therapy, 170–71
    core attitudinal conditions, 170–71
  filial therapy, 180–82
  group play therapy, 172–73
  individual play therapy principles, 173–75
    limitations and rationale, 179–80
  play materials, 175–78
    selection criteria, 175–76
  playroom, 178–79
  psychoanalytic approach, 169

release therapy, 169
Playroom, 178–80
  limitations and rationale, 179–80
Positive regard and unconditional acceptance, 13, 68, 86, 120–21, 126–28, 154
Psychoanalytic approach to play therapy,
  169
Psychologic stability, 232–48
  summary, 241–48
  therapeutic human experiences, 233–34
  therapeutic recreational experiences,
    238–39
  therapeutic spiritual experiences, 236–38
  therapeutic work experiences, 234–36
  work and spiritual values, 235

Q
Questions, clarification/exploratory process,
  22–24

R
Reflection of feelings, 4, 14–15, 31–61
  advantages in counseling process, 43
  body reflections, 54
  facial reflections, 54
  reiterative reflections, 54
  situational reflections, 54
  word-for-word reflections, 54
Reflective process, 31–61 (*see also* Feelings)
  additives, incorporating, 55
  affective vocabulary categories and terms,
    56–61
  concrete reflections, 54
  conditions for counselor reflection of feel-
    ings, 44–49
  core attitudinal conditions, 13–14, 86–100,
    126–28
  process of reflection of feelings, 49–54
  roots of, 41–43
Relationship-centered counseling, overview,
  3–25
  belief and values system, 86–100
Relationship-centered counseling, principles
  of, 9–10, 24–25
  beliefs and values, 86–100
  counselor creed, 22
  counselor role, 103–12
  parallel response, emotional or intellectual
    77